MOULDS OF
UNDERSTANDING

MOULDS OF UNDERSTANDING

A Pattern of Natural Philosophy

JOSEPH NEEDHAM
F.R.S. F.B.A.

Edited and Introduced by
GARY WERSKEY

London   George Allen & Unwin Ltd
Ruskin House   Museum Street

First published in 1976

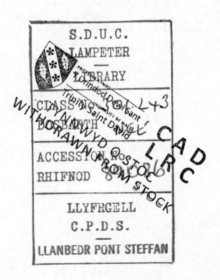
Printed in Great Britain
in 11 point Baskerville type
by Willmer Brothers Limited, Birkenhead

for
SHIH HSÜEH-YEN

Acknowledgements

The idea for this book originated at the publishers, George Allen & Unwin, and the project took shape through the combined efforts of the firm's staff, Dr Needham and myself. Brian Hurwitz was a most helpful 'lay' reader and 'representative young scientist'. Muriel Moyle has enhanced yet another of Needham's works with her excellent index. Above all, I should like to thank Joseph Needham himself, for he played an essential role in defining the aims and overseeing the execution of the entire volume.

Essays Two and Four originally appeared in Needham's *The Great Amphibium* (London: Student Christian Movement Press, 1931). Essay Three formed part of Needham's *The Sceptical Biologist* (London: Chatto and Windus, 1929). These essays are reprinted here with the kind permission of their original publishers. The remaining essays were first published in Britain by George Allen & Unwin: Essays Five, Six, Eight and Nine in *Time: The Refreshing River* (London, 1943); and Essays One and Seven in *History Is On Our Side* (London, 1946). Essays Ten and Eleven have never appeared in book form before.

One last point is that, in Essays One and Nine, three dated, non-essential and relatively brief passages have been excised from the original versions. These cuts are marked thus: [.....] Otherwise the essays are reprinted unchanged here, with a few additional explanatory footnotes supplied by the editor. These are indicated by square brackets in the footnotes at the end of each essay.

G.W.

Contents

THEMISTIUS. Thefe Opinions seem to me to be very reafonable. Have you counfell'd your Friende to give his Effays to the printers?

ELEUTHERIUS. I have. He hath befides this, fome more Generall titles to the Stile of Sceptick, which, I confefs, interefted me as much as the former. Although he doth not, I thinke, exprefsly fay fo, 'tis clear that he looks doubtfully on all thofe Men who counfel, as upon all those Ideas which involve, Abandonment or Loss of one of the broad Mouldes of Action or of Thought into which men of all Times have pour'd their Effort. He is not so fuperficial as to fuppofe, for inftance, that what men feek in Natural Philofophy is the fame as that which they feek in Religion, but he views, it feems, with the greateft Averfion, fuch Philofophers as would have none of the latter, as well as such Divines as have little love for the former. I feare Terentius is a sad Sceptick; he will not joyn himfelf whole-heartedly to any Campe, and will not allow even to Metaphyfics herselfe, the right to fay to men "By me all your questions fhall be anfwer'd, and all your defires be fatisfied."

From the 'Prefatory Dialogue' to
Joseph Needham's *The Sceptical Biologist*
(London, 1929), pp. 6–7.

Introduction

Understanding Needham

by
GARY WERSKEY

I

These political and philosophical essays by Joseph Needham, the world's leading authority on the history of science and technology in Chinese culture, have been selected with the interests of two groups of readers in mind. First, there are the many devotees of Dr Needham's unparalleled investigation entitled *Science and Civilisation in China*.[1] They will already be aware that behind this three-decade-old and continuing study lies a social vision of great breadth and complexity. This world-view, however, was most systematically expressed in writings that pre-dated the China project, and these have for some time been virtually unobtainable. With their re-publication in *Moulds of Understanding* it is hoped that they will assist the efforts of scholars, students and laymen alike to evaluate the background of Needham's tireless researches into the Chinese past.

Yet this collection also addresses itself to a second audience, one which is preoccupied with the alienation and repression specific to a science-based capitalist society. Needless to say, this way of life has inspired in recent years a wide variety of responses, especially on the part of a significant number of men and women who have come of age since the early sixties. Some of them are now living in 'alternative' communities. This is said to represent an extreme form of protest against the twin tyrannies of the dehumanised technocratic job and the depersonalised private life.[2] Others have sought social change in a more traditional manner through the medium of revolutionary political practice by and on behalf of the working class. Interestingly enough, though these two groups believe themselves to be pursuing diverging ends with distinctive means, they share two related points in common. They are equally opposed to the practical and theoretical dominance of science in Euro-American societies. Such a domination is, in their view, leading not only to the denigration of non-scientific modes of knowledge, but to the development of technologies and ideologies designed to consolidate and extend the power of governmental and industrial technocrats. In contrast to such dangerous trends in their own Western culture, many young radicals— whether of an overtly political or religious bent—have drawn inspiration from the past and present experience of Asian societies. Buddhism, Taoism and Zen, not to mention the Divine Light and Hare Krishna sects, have attracted an unprecedented number of followers in the West, partly because the mystical ethos of these faiths has appeared to be so profoundly at odds with the arrogant, non-reverential attitude towards Nature (including humanity itself) that is the trademark of modern science and technology in the service of capitalism. Mao's China has served as another beacon light from the East; in this case, as an example of how science can be advanced not just for, but by, the people (as opposed to a privileged scientific élite).

Such respect for the people of Asia and their cultures, until recently so rare on the part of Westerners, has long been a hallmark of Joseph Needham's life and work. And this is not the only instance in which his social thought is in tune with the orientation of today's political and religious activists. For Needham is a christian who believes that the essence of religion resides in a mystical, alogical appreciation of the 'numinous', i.e. the sense of the holy.[3] That kind of mysticism, he feels, lies at the core of all the great religions. As such, it must necessarily be regarded as one of several equally valid 'moulds' which give shape to human experience. Hence Needham's fear—first expressed over forty years ago—that scientific domination might increase to the point where the validity of religious experiences would be (wrongly) called into question. Even more alarming to Needham was the possibility that a society under the sway of attitudes appropriate only to the laboratory might become ruthlessly intolerant of individuals who failed to conform to their rulers' expectations. Nevertheless, the dangers of such 'scientism' have never prevented him from upholding the validity and importance of scientific work as such. Indeed as a well-known biochemist and a pre-war advocate of his own sort of Marxism, Needham believed the day would come when all truly human activities could prosper and be integrated through the collectivist ethics and technical achievements of a world co-operative commonwealth. A christian-Marxist-scientist-historian-sinophile : is it any wonder that he has since described himself as an 'honorary Taoist' trying to make 'a contribution to political religion and scientific faith' ?[4]

There are of course many differences between Needham's world-view and those of our latter-day radicals. It should already be clear, for example, that he is attempting to put together what they are endeavouring to pull apart. In other words, Needham is an avowed 'syncretist', or resolver of opposites. Moreover, his primary tool for integrating diverse tendencies is the much disputed doctrine of emergent evolution, which argues that the emergence of higher levels of social organisation is an evolutionary inevitability. For the moment, however, what strikes one as extraordinary about the older essays in this collection is how often they adopt a 'contemporary' stance on issues which are now of central importance to a broad spectrum of social rebels. In order to understand such foresight it will therefore be necessary to situate Needham's thought in its historical context. That section will then be followed by a brief critical analysis of his social philosophy and an even briefer, more personal reflection about the man who forged this work out of his own foundry of experience.

II

Even when very young, Needham felt himself to be 'a person who absolutely could not do without a "world-view".'[5] Born in 1900, he was very much the only child of Dr Joseph Needham, a religiously-minded Harley Street physician, and Alicia Adelaide Montgomery, a composer of romantic songs. Thus religion, science, philosophy and art were already juxtaposed as the dominant modes of thought in Needham's boyhood. Their influence was deepened through his unlimited access to the family's rather good collection of books. It was furthered, Needham has since recalled,[6] through weekly visits:

'to the Temple Church in London, where at that time [c. 1910] Bishop E. W. Barnes was Master. The result was that ... I used to listen Sunday after Sunday to discourses on the pre-Socratic philosophers and mediaeval scholasticism and all kinds of things which would not ordinarily come into sermons; but ... Barnes was himself a mathematician and a Fellow of the Royal Society, and one of the most stimulating preachers—or perhaps one might better say lecturers—that anyone could have.'

Barnes's modernism was subsequently echoed in the bible classes of F. W. Sanderson, Headmaster of Oundle, where Needham was at school during the First World War. As it happened, Sanderson was a close friend of H. G. Wells, whose romances of science and socialism constituted Needham's first introduction to politics or practical ethics. Yet this early interest in political affairs hardly went beyond a defence of socialist principles against the Victorian conservatism of his father. Indeed even down to the end of his undergraduate career at Cambridge, Needham could still be characterised as a shy, learned and religious student poised on the brink of a medical career. The other-worldly cast of his life was reflected in his two-year-long novitiate as a lay brother in the Oratory of the Good Shepherd.

A number of events conspired in the early and mid-1920s to bring about a re-definition of Needham's scientific, religious and political commitments. His admission in 1921 as a post-graduate student in Sir Frederick Gowland Hopkins' biochemical laboratory introduced him to far more than a scintillating intellectual environment; it brought him into contact with the freest and most democratic community of scientists then operating in Cambridge. 'All of Hoppy's geese', it was said, 'turned into swans,' and Needham was no exception to this rule.[7] Not only was he able to begin his own synoptic study of chemical embryology, but in 1924 his proposal of marriage to a promising young biochemist named Dorothy Moyle was accepted as well. The following year saw the Needhams journey to the marine biological station of Roscoff in Brittany, where they encountered Louis Rapkine, a Polish-born colleague of working-class extraction. Such was the nature of the class divisions in British society at the time that this was Needham's first sustained encounter with someone who had first-hand experience of proletarian life. Rapkine was also a Marxist and hence able to introduce some kind of order into his bourgeois English friend's somewhat vague ideas about socialism. As Needham's notions of science and politics began to change, so too did his conception of religion. It was around this time that the Needhams, now back in Cambridge, began to visit the parish church at Thaxted in Essex. There they encountered that remarkable blend of superb music, beautifully enacted liturgy, close congregational comradeship and militant left-wing socialism associated with the Rev. Fr Conrad Noel. But while Needham's religion was growing less theological and his science was becoming more philosophical, he did not always succeed in putting his socialist ideals into practice. In fact during the General Strike of 1926 he worked on the old Great Eastern railway as an engine-driver,[8] though he led a walk-out of the volunteers when the company attempted to use the 'national emergency' as an excuse for victimising the railwaymen.

It was not until the General Election of 1931 that Needham became active in the university and town branches of the Labour Party. Inspired first by the economic dislocations and mass unemployment of the depression, and later by Hitler's rise to power, he extended his political involvement in several ways. He joined forces with J. D. Bernal and other left-wing researchers to launch the Cambridge Scientists' Anti-War Group and to rejuvenate the Association of Scientific Workers both locally and nationally. This was part of a wider revival of political consciousness among scientists, many of whom came to feel that capitalism could no longer make use of their knowledge and expertise.[9] The Needhams sat for years on the Cambridge Trades Council as the A.Sc.W.'s official delegates, and in 1935 he became Branch Chairman of the Socialist League, a Labour Party ginger-group then headed by Sir Stafford Cripps. From the outset of the Spanish Civil War Needham also involved himself in a whole series of activities, fund-raising for Basque refugees, medical aid for the Republicans, voluntary industrial assistance, etc. Another important dimension of Needham's political life was his activity in speeches and articles for various other popular-front causes.

Like most socialist intellectuals in the 1930s he drew heavily upon the theory and (supposed) practice of Soviet Marxism. Indeed his introduction to the doctrine of dialectical materialism can be dated with some precision. At the beginning of July, 1931, a Russian delegation to the Second International Congress of the History of Science and Technology arrived in London.[10] Within a week of their arrival Needham was already finding himself much impressed, not just with Russia's evidently massive investment in scientific research, but also with three aspects of Soviet philosophy. One was the ability of the dialectic to sort out to his satisfaction a complex controversy between two schools of philo-sophical biologists.[11] Another was the application of Marx's materialist conception of history to the problem of explaining why modern science originated just when and where it did. The final point, which indeed Needham did not fully develop until after reading Engels' *Dialectics of Nature*, was that in Russia the dialectic was itself seen to be a constitutive part of Nature, i.e. it was a *natural* process that guaranteed the emergence of ever more complex levels of social organisation up to and including com-munism. Each of these elements of post-revolutionary Marxism was quickly assimilated into Needham's evolving and expanding world-view.

On the other hand, it would have been difficult even at the time to have described the outlook fashioned by Needham as any kind of Marxist orthodoxy. For his pre-existing commitments both to a non-reductionist (see ref. 9) evolutionary biology and to a revolutionary form of christian mysticism pre-dated the thirties and persisted beyond them. Among other things, this meant that the acceptance of a dialectic in nature rested more on its relationship to scientific than to political practice. There is also the suggestion in some of Needham's work that dialectical laws represent little more than a philosophical codification of practices already familiar to working scientists. However, although Needham used this 'scientistic' version of the dialectic as a frame-work for much of his later writing, he was unique among left-wing scientists at the time in his refusal to allow it to over-ride other forms of human understanding.[12] As the essays which follow bear out, he was also keenly aware of the dangers of scientific domination, from which followed his hope that the numinous and alogical claims of religion would be able to co-exist in some form with those of scientific socialism. At the same time, Needham was prepared to tell his co-religionists that unless they began to take a more active hand in bringing about the Kingdom of God on Earth, their churches would not be likely to survive the coming holocausts of capitalist crises and social revolutions.[13] It is ironic, to say the least, that Needham's efforts to achieve co-operation between the various spheres of social activity had to be undertaken in such a divisive fashion.

A final twist to the development of Needham's social thought came in 1936 when three Chinese biochemists arrived in Cambridge to start work in Hopkins' laboratory. There was Shen Shih-Chang, Wang Ying-Lai and—most influential—Lu Gwei-Djen. To their great surprise Needham, by then Sir William Dunn Reader in Biochemistry, began to immerse himself in the study of their language and culture. Why this happened and what it led to have been adequately described elsewhere.[14] Nearly four decades later he remains unexcelled in the West as a champion of China's present as well as her past social and scientific achievements. Indeed through his work on the multi-volume series *Science and Civilisation in China,* Needham has at last been able to find a span of space and time large enough for him to refine, elaborate and confirm to his own satisfaction the essentials of his natural philosophy.

III

We are now in a position to bring together and assess the three principal strands of Needham's world-view. The first of these is that 'all the great forms of human experience are fundamentally valid, even though they may sometimes, indeed often, seem to be in flat contradiction with each other'. The second involves 'the recognition of emergent evolution, . . . in which one [can] trace a continuity between cosmic, inorganic, biological, human and social evolution'.[15] The third focuses upon the relationship between the moulds of understanding—'into which men of all Times have pour'd their Effort'[16]—and the cosmic process which underlies them. These themes are the respective subjects of Parts II–IV.

In Part II, which contains some of Needham's earliest essays, the author examines the various and competing claims of aesthetics, history, philosophy, religion and science as modes of thought and action. The last two forms receive the most sustained treatment. Essay Two expresses alarm at the extent to which the world of 1930 is already dominated by science. The advance of science-based technologies is encouraging naive optimism about the future, as well as a growing predilection for a ruthless, mechanistic and amoral treatment of both Man and Nature. Religion, as Needham argues in Essay Three, is retreating. Furthermore, theologians must cease claiming a privileged

position, in relation to scientists, to speak about natural philosophy; or an equal epistemological status based on an assertion of
the ultimate subjectivity of all knowledge. Otherwise they will fail
to preserve the distinctive features of religious experience. For
Needham these are a preoccupation with the ethical, qualitative
aspects of human life and with the mysterious, even alogical core
of the surrounding universe. He therefore maintains (in Essay
Four) that science and religion are both valid and universal,
though distinct, moulds for understanding ourselves and our
world. Unfortunately, says Needham, there are considerable
psychological barriers placed in the way of that minority of
'balanced souls' who might wish to cross and re-cross the boundaries between scientific and religious experience, and such difficulties are bound to intensify in the increasingly science-
dominated societies of the time.

Part III attempts to define and elaborate the cosmic process
through which mankind is evolving towards ever higher levels of
social organisation. If that strikes the reader as 'a re-valuation of
the idea of progress', he or she will be well prepared for Essay
Five, 'Integrative Levels'. Here Needham puts forward, in the
manner of a latter-day Herbert Spencer, a great evolutionary
chain ranging back to the origins of the earth and downwards to
sub-atomic particles. His basic contention is that over time matter-
energy has undergone a series of irreversible transformations
resulting in a succession of larger and more complex 'envelopes' of
space, or 'levels'. The latest level to emerge during the evolutionary process has been that of the great capitalist nation-states.
They, however, will inevitably be superseded by a higher organisational stage, namely a world-wide socialist commonwealth. In
the achievement of this evolutionary leap forward Needham
indeed acknowledges the possibility of localised setbacks in the
short run. Yet, as the title of one of his earlier works confidently
asserted to his fellow socialists, Needham has faith that 'history is
on our side'. Essay Six sets this optimistic message against the
philosophical pessimism of the second law of thermodynamics,
which predicts the heat-death of the universe through the degradation of solar energy. To Needham this process is an inevitable
concomitant of rising levels of physical, biological and social
organisation. He also intimates that with the realisation of international socialism science may be able to develop new techniques
for conserving and utilising more efficiently available reserves of

energy. At the moment (1941—Essay Seven), however, scientific workers operating under the wasteful auspices of monopoly capitalism are unable to increase man's independence and control over the environment. In other words capitalists are holding back the guarantors of further evolutionary progress; hence the days of the former are (rightly) numbered.

By the beginning of Part IV Needham's socialist ethics are already well to the fore. Indeed it is through his own idiosyncratic Marxism that he is able to link up the forms of human experience not only with each other but also with the cosmic process itself. Essay Eight criticises his earlier essays for their failings in those directions. They were oriented to a passive contemplation of the world, because, as Needham admits, they were concerned with the ahistorical condition of men and women as individuals. But once he was able to perceive the human species as a social collectivity, Needham's thought could shift to an active confrontation with the necessity for changing the world. Now he is able to appreciate communism for what it is—the consequence of all previous evolution; the moral theology appropriate to our times. Until its development on a global basis, Needham continues in Essay Nine, the great moulds of understanding—science, religion, philosophy, etc.—will grow increasingly distorted, and not only in the fascist-ruled capitalist societies.

Of all these modes of thought and action, the scientific is the most crucial from the standpoint of continuing evolutionary progress. Hence it is the most endangered. That is why Needham has no hesitation in urging his fellow scientists to support 'the people' in their struggle to bring about scientific socialism. At the same time he warns against the possibility of the new régime succumbing to a 'hashish of science', which might have an even greater potential for rationalising repression than the much abused 'opium of religion'. Nevertheless, he contends, the problem of evil will remain; so, too, will the attempts to experience the numinous, the holy. In fact, only by cultivating all the various forms of human achievement will the socialist state of the future be able to avoid a 'Brave New World' in which the price of social progress has been the negation of individual freedom and well-being.[17] Moreover, Needham is confident that such a cataclysm can be avoided if working-class leadership is attuned to the humanistic message behind the writings of Marx, Engels and Lenin.

The two remaining (and considerably more recent) articles in
this volume summarise the broad outlines of Needham's philosophy in the light of his researches into ancient and modern
Chinese culture. Their general message is relatively simple. The
people of Asia have at different times in their history been the
chief architects of evolutionary advancement, not least in the area
of man's scientific mastery over Nature. Yet Europeans, their
pride swollen by comparatively recent achievements in science,
have neglected the extent to which their intellectual hegemony
has rested upon techniques and ideas devised by supposedly
inferior races. Ironically, there is now in the West a profound
mood of disillusionment with the unthinking extension of scientific domination over other forms of human experience, not to
mention the non-human environment. As a token of inter-racial
solidarity and a first step towards the resolution of such internal
social conflicts, Needham enjoins us to draw upon the accumu-
lated wisdom of China and its people. In particular he reminds us
of the secular, this-worldly cast of Chinese ethics, one of the main
features of which has been the integration and harmonisation of
the great forms of human understanding. Needham concludes on
the hopeful note that China's resumption of her position as a
world leader at the cutting edge of social evolution may well
encourage us to seek socialist remedies for our 'scientific' ills.

Here then is a world-view characterised by an ontological com-
mitment to emergent evolutionism and an ethical standpoint
associated with the mainstream of socialist thought. According to
Needham, both his ethics and his ontology are compatible with—
indeed they can be said to derive from—the Marxist doctrine of
dialectical materialism. He is of course aware that his evolutionary ethics seem to some to represent an unblushing example of
the 'naturalistic fallacy', in which a whole series of 'oughts' are,
according to professional philosophers, illogically deduced from
what 'is'.[18] He is also sensitive to the charge that positing the
'inevitability' of socialism may sound like an encouragement to
political quietism. Yet Needham feels that anyone who shares the
faith that informs his natural philosophy would be unlikely to let
the suffering attendant upon the protracted existence of capitalist
societies simply run its course. As for the philosophers' complaints,
he could well reply that the connection he is drawing between
evolution and ethics is not quite so normative as they might have

thought. For what Needham is saying about the direction of
evolutionary change is that it hardly supports anti-Marxists who
see in socialism a violation both of human nature and of the
course of natural history. On the contrary; the transformation of
class society is the next logical stage of social development. And it
should be undertaken in order to bring to fruition 'the simple,
natural, healthy, human desires of the mass of mankind, for love,
for children, for socially useful work, for fundamental decency
and dignity'.[19]

Needham's response to the philosophers is, I think, less prob-
lematic than his belief in the inevitability of a socialist triumph.
Whatever is held responsible for the outcome of biological evolution, it is still humankind that will decide the future course of
social evolution. Upheavals there will certainly be. But whether
they result 'in a revolutionary reconstitution of society at large, or
in the common ruin of the contending classes'[20] will depend to a
considerable extent on the existence of a well-organised proletariat conscious of its oppression and determined to end it. Such
organisation does not arise spontaneously as a 'statistical
certainty'[21] in the wake of numerous social crises. Rather it must
be nurtured through the long-term theory and day-to-day practice of what is now a socialist minority. Yet to sustain this kind of
dedication requires a minimal assurance that human agency, not
cosmic necessity, determines whether social progress takes
place.[22]

A reliance upon a deterministic variety of evolutionary
Marxism[23]—one that undoubtedly gave hope at a point where
fascism was a more likely prospect for Europeans than socialism
—is one of the three main marks left on these essays by the time
and place in which they were written. A second is Needham's
notion that science and capitalism are irreconcilable. This was a
highly plausible argument in the conditions that prevailed in the
laboratories of Europe during the thirties. Now the issue is a good
deal more confused. After twenty-five post-war years of unprecedented scientific prosperity and expansion in the West, expenditure on research and development has at last again begun to tail
off. Unemployment and under-employment are once again
becoming a reality for many highly trained scientists. And unless
Western economies can recover their earlier taken-for-granted
stability, this new trend could well continue.[24] For the moment,
however, the striking feature of many capitalist societies is the

degree to which they display the repressive effects of scientific domination that Needham had once predicted as a slim possibility for socialist régimes.[25]

A final reflection of Needham's social milieu can be found in his designation of art, philosophy, history, science and religion as *the* great moulds of human understanding. To a Cambridge intellectual of the broadest possible sympathies, growing up at a time when the class divisions of his society were extremely acute and highly stylised, it was only natural to think of 'understanding' as an essentially intellective and élite process. Human 'desires', by contrast, were 'simple, natural, healthy' and belonged to 'the mass of mankind'. How the Cambridge context helped to sustain such a mentality is affectionately revealed in Essay One.

But why, for example, is 'socially useful work' identified as a 'desire' rather than as a significant context for 'understanding'? This is, on the face of it, a strange position for a Marxist to take. Marx himself felt that it is primarily through the work-experience that human beings have come to apprehend and control their relationship to Nature and to each other.[26] This is a view that Needham, too, has progressively come to adopt since his wartime contact with Chinese people from all walks of life. However, in these pre-war essays he stresses intellectual approaches to self- and social knowledge to the point of ignoring the habits of those 'men of practice', who 'learn their ideas and live their values in more experiential ways'.[27]

In the final analysis none of these (easily remedied) limitations should be allowed to obscure the strengths of Needham's great synthesis. His vision is ecumenical, drawing on a deep respect for all that is 'truly human' in the many types of experiences and peoples that have contributed to the course of social evolution. His outlook is progressive, designed to keep the goal of building a classless society clearly articulated and set off from the miasma of piecemeal reform and political setbacks. His message is timely, reminding us as it must that the problem of scientific domination presented itself well before the arrival of a war-born generation.

IV

As readers of *Moulds of Understanding* will soon discover, it is informed throughout by a warm and honest if somewhat shy personality. Yet even the most autobiographical of these essays,

'Cambridge Summer' and 'Metamorphoses of Scepticism', fail to convey an important aspect of Needham the man, namely his kindness and generosity to those who seek out his advice and support. Mine is a case in point.

I arrived in England in the spring of 1968 ready to interview a number of scientists who had been politically active in the thirties.[28] Dr Needham was of course high on my list. But before encountering him I felt obliged to study with some care all his published pre-war utterances. Hence I spent a solid week in the British Museum reading and taking notes on what turned out to be a daunting pile of material. By the time I had plucked up enough courage to write to Needham, I was in a pretty bad state. Now I knew that my 'subject' was not only a world-renowned scholar but also a social philosopher of some originality.

I was anxious enough about our meeting when I found myself in front of the austere entrance to the Master's Lodge of Gonville and Caius College, Cambridge.[29] Nor was my anxiety relieved by my first sight of Needham, who turned out to be a large man of great intensity. I discovered him hunched over a cup of tea deep in an earnest and erudite discussion of the merits of Taoist alchemy with two of his Chinese colleagues. Dr Needham looked up at me, and recognising how little I must have known about either Taoism or alchemy, proceeded to offer me a wonderfully compressed survey of the subject. To my great surprise I was then able to follow their discussion. And when it was over, the Master asked me to relate to his friends some of my own ideas about the social relations of British science in the 1930s.

It was a marvellous thing for an unknown student to be treated as an equal by such distinguished scholars. Yet Needham's generosity did not stop there. He later told me of an enormous cache of personal correspondence, political literature and unpublished documents that he had retained from the pre-war period. Would I care to return to Caius later on in the summer to spend the two or three weeks necessary for arranging and cataloguing this material? There could be no doubt of my reply, for it allowed me simultaneous access to the past and present of a key figure in my work.

As it happened, I was to become a regular visitor to the Master's Lodge at Caius. Each time I encountered Needham, his wife Dorothy, and Lu Gwei-Djen, his chief collaborator on the

China project, they had all grown in years and honours. Nevertheless, the same gentle and supportive hospitality has greeted me on each occasion. I was therefore well prepared a year or two ago to learn that one of Needham's favourite Confucian sayings was: 'Behave to every man as one receiving a great guest'.[30] No finer example of the identity between a man's thought and his actions could be imagined.

Notes

1. J. Needham et al., *Science and Civilisation in China*, 7 vols in 15 parts (Cambridge, 1954–).
2. By Theodore Roszak, among others. See Roszak's *The Making of a Counter-Culture* (London, 1970), which draws heavily on Herbert Marcuse's *One-Dimensional Man* (Boston, 1964). Also his later book *Where the Wasteland Ends* (New York and London, 1972–3).
3. The 'numinous' is a concept developed by the German theologian Rudolf Otto in his *The Sense of the Holy* (London, 1923). This work was influential in the development of Needham's own ideas about religion.
4. The latter phrase was the sub-title of an earlier collection of his essays: Joseph Needham, *History Is on Our Side* (London, 1946). Needham's *alter ego*, Henry Holorenshaw, describes 'The Making of An Honorary Taoist' in M. Teich & R. Young (eds), *Changing Perspectives in the History of Science* (London, 1973), pp. 1–20.
5. Needham, letter to David Grimshaw, formerly of George Allen & Unwin, May 4, 1973.
6. Needham, transcribed interview with the editor, May 21, 1968.
7. Hopkins' qualities are well brought out in J. Needham, 'Frederick Gowland Hopkins,' *Perspectives in Biology and Medicine*, v. 6 (1962), pp. 1–46.
8. See below, Essay Eight, p. 216-17. For a modern view of the General Strike, see Patrick Renshaw, *The General Strike* (London, 1975).
9. See P. G. Werskey, 'British Scientists and "Outsider" Politics, 1931–1945' in S. B. Barnes (ed.), *Sociology of Science* (Harmondsworth, 1972), pp. 231–50; and Gary Werskey, 'Making Socialists of Scientists: Whose Side Is History On?' *Radical Science Journal*, no. 2-3 (January 1975), pp. 13-50.
10. Needham's account of this event, together with my own analysis of the historical significance of the Congress, can be found in N. I. Bukharin et al., *Science at the Cross Roads*, 2nd ed. (London, 1971), pp. vii–x and pp. xi–xxix, respectively.
11. See below, Essay Five, pp. 140-1. This was the argument between 'vitalist' biologists, who argued variously that 'life' cannot be explained by or reduced to the operation of observable physical entities, and 'mechanist' biologists, who favoured such a 'reductionist' approach to the explanation of biological phenomena. Needham's position was that the vitalists were correct in their defence of the integrity of distinctively biological explanations, but wrong in their methodological pessimism. This was a controversy that preoccupied Needham much at the time, but it has since changed greatly in character. Hence his writings on the subject, notably in *The Sceptical Biologist* (London, 1929), have been omitted from this volume. But Needham's philosophy of biology is synoptically presented in his *Order and Life*, 2nd ed. (Cambridge, Mass., and London, 1968). For a survey of the problems of the philosophy of biology see C. H. Waddington (ed.), *Towards a Theoretical Biology*, 2 vols (Edinburgh

1968); F. J. Ayala & T. Dobzhansky (eds), *Studies in the Philosophy of Biology* (London, 1974); and A. Koestler & J. R. Smythies (eds), *Beyond Reductionism* (London, 1970).

12. Cf. J. D. Bernal, *The Social Function of Science*, 2nd ed. (Cambridge, Mass., and London, 1967).

13. Needham was active in the interesting revival of christian socialism in the 1930s, as witness his co-editorship of *Christianity and the Social Revolution* (London, 1935). Essay Nine, below, originally appeared in that volume. For a more contemporary book along similar lines see J. Klugmann & P. Oestreicher (eds), *What Kind of Revolution? A Christian-Communist Dialogue* (London, 1968).

14. E.g. by Holorenshaw, in Teich & Young (ref. 4 above).

15. Needham, letter to Grimshaw (ref. 5 above).

16. From the 'Prefatory Dialogue' to Needham's *Sceptical Biologist*, above, p. 12.

17. See below, Essay Nine, pp. 256-62. In Needham's social philosophy, religion and science form a symbiotic relationship almost analogous to that which obtains between the laws of thermodynamics and the evolutionary process: see Essay Six, below.

18. This has been urged in A. G. N. Flew's *Evolutionary Ethics* (London, 1967). Cf. C. H. Waddington, *The Ethical Animal* (London, 1960), esp. pp. 50–59.

19. Essay Five below, p. 160.

20. 'Manifesto of the Communist Party,' in Karl Marx & Frederick Engels, *Selected Works* (London, 1968), p. 36.

21. See below. Essay Eight, p. 220.

22. Obviously Needham is aware of the important role of human agents in history (see Essay Five, below, pp. 159-61). But he undialectically ascribes to 'objective' social contradictions (e.g. the social nature of production and the private accumulation of capital) the power to produce renewed struggle 'up to final victory'. The problem here is that contradictions have to be felt and perceived as such, and that requires the theoretical and practical intervention of organised socialists. Hence contradictions are phenomena, simultaneously subjective and objective.

23. The political consequences stemming from this Marxist tradition have been the subject of considerable argument. For critical and sympathetic accounts, respectively, see George Lichtheim, *Marxism; an Historical and Critical Study*, 2nd ed. (New York, 1965); and Sebastiano Timpanaro, 'Considerations on Materialism,' *New Left Review*, no. 85 (May/June 1974), pp. 3–22. On the issue of social determinism, Marx offers in his voluminous writings contradictory indications. Nevertheless, I would agree with Gianfranco Poggi that a deterministic position runs counter to the basic thrust of Marxian dialectics. See Poggi's *Images of Society* (London, 1972).

24. That economic de-stabilisation may well become endemic is the argument of Michael Kidron's excellent *Western Capitalism Since the War* (Harmondsworth, 1970).

25. See below, Essay Nine, p. 256, and above, ref. 2.

26. e.g. Karl Marx, *Capital*, vol. 1 (Moscow, 1958), pp. 183–84. On Marx's conception of work and its relationship to human nature, see Bertell Ollman, *Alienation* (Cambridge, 1971), esp. pp. 99–105.

27. E. P. Thompson, 'An Open Letter to Leszek Kolakowski,' *Socialist Register 1973* (London, 1974), p. 84. This quotation is making a general point about socialist intellectuals and does not refer to Needham specifically. It should also be added that in Essay One, below (pp. 43-5), Needham does show considerable appreciation for manual work as a mould of understanding. But this is never integrated into his more serious pre-war work.

28. This was part of my doctoral research programme. See P. G. Werskey, 'The Visible College: A Study of Left-wing Scientists in Britain, 1918–1939,

unpublished Ph.D. dissertation, Harvard University, 1973. An extensively revised and reorganized version of the thesis is now in the press as *Scientists for Socialism* (London, 1976).

29. Needham became Master of the College in 1965–6.
30. See Holorenshaw, in Teich & Young, p. 10. (ref. 4 above)

I

THE CAMBRIDGE CONTEXT

1

Cambridge Summer

(1932)

I

The mere idea of a university in vacation-time brings to mind the disquisition of Charles Lamb on the subject. No doubt the pleasure he got out of it was partly due to the fact that in ordinary life he had nothing to do with it, and so could easily imagine himself whatever he liked—a D.D. for ten minutes while walking through King's; a Reader in Pathological Entomology or what not while strolling up Tennis Court Road. But no less, for those who do belong to it in ordinary life, is pure pleasure to be found in vacation-time. The blessed absence of undergraduates releases the tutor from his hundred and one little jobs, and the scientist can get something done in his laboratory without having to worry about tomorrow's nine-o'clock lecture. In the evening, Colleges sit down to dinner in combination-room and not in Hall, with sevens and eights instead of twenties and thirties, so that conversation becomes more interesting, and dons who have belonged to the same college for years without time to see much of each other, can make some contact at last. Best of all if hot weather comes in August and September. The University is practically empty, and a sort of general lifting of clothes conventions makes itself felt. Eminent physiologists are seen passing along Trinity Street in shorts, and a historian in a Palm-Beach suit is no rarity.

It is at such times that one realises how well Cambridge is provided with places where one can swim. Even in the middle of the town there are good places in or beside the river, and the river itself upwards from Byron's Pool is one long and excellent bathing place. It was there that I used to experience, when a young student, a curiously vivid sensation of unification with Nature. One felt at first reluctant to dive in, thinking of all the creepy things in the river-mud, the decaying leaves, the insects on the surface; but all of a sudden an almost ecstatic identification of the clotheless self with the sum of beautiful coloured natural things around sent one flying into the river like a projectile. Long afterwards it seemed that perhaps Ludwig Feuerbach had felt the same. For he wrote, 'To bathe is the first, though the lowest, of virtues. In the stream of water the fever of selfishness is allayed. Water is the readiest means of making friends with Nature. Man rising from water is new, regenerate man.'

Happily the country round Cambridge, especially towards the north-east where the fens are, is wonderfully well provided with wild pools. To such places one may go off for a whole day, carrying two or three books, and with fair confidence that no one, except a few farm-workers, perhaps, will be met with. One of these pools lies very difficult to find in what is practically a piece of untouched fen. It is surrounded with reeds whose stems are almost white, but bear at the top their long green blades which stream unanimously out in one direction if there is a little wind. If you lie flat on the bank of the diving-place and look along the pool, you see a picture of reeds in the best Chinese manner. Then if you dive in, you find the water absolutely clear and beautifully brown, contrasting marvellously with the brilliant blue of the surface, reflecting the sun. Or at midnight, on one of those few nights of the year when the air and water are warm enough, it is lovely to swim through the moon and stars glittering on the water. Nor are excellent smells wanting, for the water-peppermint is about, and there is always a slight unidentifiable smell of fresh waters which delights those bathers, who, like myself, find nothing but disadvantages in the sea. Growing all round the pool you get ragged robin, purple loosestrife, scabious, and what Scottish friends call mouse's pea. And there in some convenient place you may lie, reading and swimming alternately, with your cells hard at work manufacturing vitamin D, and storing it, you hope, for your advantage in the coming gloomy Cambridge winter, abounding in cold and rain.

But meanwhile, wherever you look, the heart is rejoiced. In the distance, across the flat landscape, certain rows of poplars stand up, and an uninterrupted view of the whole sky can be had.

There are those who pretend that no landscape has virtue unless it contains hills; to please them, everything must be at an angle to the horizontal, and flatness is dull. But others, of whom I am one, find constriction in hills and freedom in the plain; moreover, if you are as interested in clouds as in anything else, only a flat country allows you to observe them. Hills, too, are distracting; they take off your attention from the small but beautiful details of your surroundings. Market Hill, with a gradient of about one in 10^6, is quite hilly enough for me.

Quy pool is not the only swimming place near Cambridge. Towards Fordham there is a deserted brick-pit which gives an impression of inconceivable depth, and where someone has fixed a high springboard. Tall derelict chimneys are reflected in the water. In 1919 there used to be a fine bathing place of white earth and bright blue water in the coprolite diggings near Hauxton, but after several years it was suddenly invaded one summer by a rapidly growing red weed which silted it up and spoilt it. And many another pool and stream could well be sung; celebrated as yet by no adequate poet.

It is surprising that Cambridgeshire has never had poetic justice done to it, and that no Matthew Arnold has arisen to deal with Madingley Hill and Bottisham Lode as well and faithfully as their Oxfordshire colleagues. Rupert Brooke, it is true, did something in this direction, but his praise was double-edged, for he found it necessary to vilify half the villages in the county in order to hand out compliments to Grantchester; a place pretty enough, indeed, but no better than many others. John Milton, I like to think, was speaking of Cambridgeshire in *Lycidas,* but no one will ever know, for he took no pains to make the references explicit, and the well-attir'd woodbine might have been growing any-where, though I hope and believe it was at Haslingfield. And there are 'cowslips wan that hang the pensive head' in great numbers near the chalybeate spring at Knapwell, if you choose the right time to go there, as no doubt Milton did when, with Edward King, his friend, he 'drove a-field, under the opening eye-lids of the morn.' Yes, on the whole, he must have been talking of Cambridgeshire: 'Mean while the Rural ditties were not mute, Temper'd to th' Oaten Flute : Rough Satyrs danc'd,' and so on—one remembers that Madingley and Comberton were 'desperate Morris places' right up to the middle of the last century. And the wooden Plough Monday plough still rests intact, though little used, at Balsham. And at Little Downham they expect the arrival of the dancers to 'do the droves'; they 'look for them to come.'

I suppose that one reason why so little has been written in praise of Cambridgeshire is that the county as such does not form an aesthetic unit. In the south, the hills around such places as Chishall are of a piece with Hertfordshire or the Chilterns; in the north, the valley of the Ouse (that lovely river) might well be part of Huntingdon; and in the east, the fens, with their geometrical drains and Dutch gables, are not confined to Cambridgeshire but stretch over into Norfolk and Lincoln. And yet one would have thought that the neighbourhood of Cambridge was beautiful enough to raise up ten major poets. Nor are historical associations wanting, as witness Bourne, where the Ferrar family lived after Nicholas had retired from the business of the Virginia Company in London, and before they moved to Little Gidding to found their illustrious religious house, the chapel of which is still standing, as beautiful as ever. To Bourne rode out one Mr Richard Crashaw from Peterhouse, making up verses probably, as he went, and happy to see there the ingenious Mr George Herbert, lately Orator of the University, and now vicar of Leighton Bromswold, just over the border into Huntingdonshire. Mr Herbert would tell them, doubtless, of the fine obelisks with which he was capping the repaired church tower at Leighton, and of the two panelled pulpits he was erecting (still there to this day), one on each side of the chancel arch, to show the people that the Book of Common Prayer was just as important as the preacher's sermon. And back Mr Crashaw would ride, to find, probably, bad news awaiting him in Peterhouse combination-room, some new political victory of the puritans, some new attack on the Church. Or if his luck was better, he might find his friend from London, Mr Abraham Cowley, come to spend a few days with him in that Society, and full of information about the doings of the natural philosophers, at Merton College, Oxford, and elsewhere, or ready to consider whether the Roman Church could be accepted if the English Church were utterly levelled by puritanism. In the end it was Crashaw who went and Cowley who stayed, to write :

> Pardon, my mother church, if I consent
> That angels led him when from thee he went,

For e'en in error such no danger is
When join'd with so much piety as his.
His faith perhaps in some nice tenets might
Be wrong : his life, I'm sure, was in the right.

Or again, go back some fifty years to another little theological
episode. In the 1580s Cambridge was in a condition of permanent convulsion, owing to the war between the puritans and the
orthodox Church of England men. They lectured against each
other in the schools, and preached against each other in Great St
Maries, they insulted each other at dinner and their student followers fought after dark in the streets. Of all the Anglicans, none
was more learned, wise and commendable than young Master
Lancelot Andrewes, the junior fellow of Pembroke, who lost no
opportunity of censuring the strict sabbatarianism of the opposite
faction. For this he was constantly preached at on Sunday afternoons in the University Church, but at last he had the best of it in
some such manner as follows :

'The puritan faction [says John Aubrey] carried themselves
outwardly with very great sanctity and strictness; they preached
up very strict observing the Lord's day and made damnation to
breake it. Yet did these hypocrits bowle in a private green every
Sunday after sermon; and one of their College (a loving friende
to Mr L. Andrewes) to satisfie him one time lent him the key of a
private back dore to the bowling green, on a Sunday evening,
which he opening, discovered these zealous preachers, with their
gownes off, earnest at play. They were strangely surprised to see
the entry of one that was not of the brother-hood.'

Paradise Gardens was the name of the place where the puritans
played at bowls, and Paradise still exists; a backwater of the Cam
between Cambridge and Grantchester. For hundreds of years the
gentle river-water has welcomed the men of Cambridge, towns-
men and gownsmen alike, coming out to swim on hot summer
days. William Stukely, the archaeologist, who went up to Corpus
in 1704, wrote in his diary :

'I used to frequent, among other lads, the river in Sheep's
Green and learnt to swim in Freshmen's and Soph's pools, as they
are called, and sometimes in Paradise, reckoning it a Beneficial
Exercise.'

And unlucky Walter Haddon, a student of King's, was drowned in 1567 while washing himself 'in a place in the river Cham called Paradise.'[1]

The other day, as I lay in the sun beside one of the fen pools, I had for companions two books little known today, but precious as containing the very essence of seventeenth-century life. One was Peter Heylyn's *Life of Archbishop William Laud,* the other Henry Isaacson's *Life of Bishop Lancelot Andrewes.* Nothing that has been written since compares at all, to my mind, with the prose of the seventeenth century, which has weight without the ponderosity of subsequent times, and grace without romanticism. How delightful it was to read Heylyn on Andrewes:

'This year we lost the stupendiously learned prelate, Dr Lancelot Andrewes, Bishop of Winchester, in the oriental tongues surpassing knowing; so studiously devoted to the Doctrine of the Ancient Fathers, as his extant works breathe nothing but their Faith; nor can we now read the Fathers more than we should have done in his very Aspect, Gesture, and Actions; so venerable in his Presence, so grave in his Motions; so pious in his Conversations; so primitive in all. The World wanted learning to know how learned he was; so skilled in all (especially the Oriental) languages, that some conceive he might (if then living) almost have served as an Interpreter-General at the Confusion of Tongues.'

An excellent conceit. Far away in the distance there was the implacable hum of a tractor, harvesting on a farm towards Horningsea, speaking a language symbolic of the future, a language of tremendous possibilities, but sometimes seeming too alien from the past and the ideas of the past. How difficult to translate into it the spiritual and intellectual beauties which the men of the past found it worth while to live for. The task would try to the uttermost, I thought, even the interpretative powers of Lancelot Andrewes. I turned to Isaacson, again both lovely and instructive:

'To Pembroke Hall, where he had been a scholar, fellow and master, Bishop Andrewes gave one thousand pound, to purchase land for two fellowships, and for other uses in that Colledge, together with a gilt cup and a bason and ewer, in all points, as weight, fashion, inscription, etc., so like to the cup, bason, and

ewer, given about three hundred years before to that colledge by
the religious foundress thereof, as that no *ovum ovo similimus*;
and these, he professed, he caused to be made and given, not for
the continuance of his own memory, but for fear that those which
she had given so long since might miscarry, and so her remem-
brance might decay.'

The tractor continued its background noise, as if straining
steadily towards another spiritual world. 'You look back too
much,' it said, 'and not forward enough; the future is there and
its colour dark or light as you help to make it.' Perhaps we find
ourselves at a term or period in the history of civilisation when
there is no virtue left in the old traditions and the new have not
yet been made. Lancelot Andrewes could look back to the
Countess of Pembroke with clear vision, certain that he belonged
to the same tradition as she. It was the medieval tradition, composed of rigid class distinction, duties from above to below, commerce controlled by theology, and life an antechamber to
Heaven. But just as Andrewes lay dying in the palace at
Winchester, divers resourceful and crafty merchants in the City of
London, who feared neither God nor man, were hard at work
laying the foundation-stones of that capitalist system of private
enterprise and usury which changed the face of Andrewes' world
and presently brought even the Church to submission. Andrewes'
chaplain could well preach in high Thomistic vein at Winchester
against usury—eighty years later any who should have challenged
the right of citizens to lend their money upon interest would have
been thought mad indeed. The Civil War transferred the right of
oppression from the Court to the City, where it still is today.

What traditions those will be that will arise in the classless
society of the future, who can tell? But we may hope that in the
end, when the dust has cleared away, some thoughts will return to
the seventeenth century and Lancelot Andrewes, who also, in his
day, prayed for social justice, though vainly thinking it could
come within the framework of the feudal classes and by the strict
prohibition of high finance.

I put down Isaacson and took up Heylyn. Royalist, Anglican,
reactionary though he was, he was very much aware of the talents
latent in the mass of the people. I decided to copy out a lively
passage of his which might be headed 'On Birth.' Archbishop
William Laud, he said:

'was not born therefore of such poor and obscure Parents as the publisher of his Breviat makes him, much less *e faece plebis* (out of the dregs of the People), as both he and all the rest of the Bishops were affirmed to be by the late Lord Brook (who of all others had least reason to upbraid them with it) in a book of his touching the nature of that Episcopacy which hath been exercised in England. But granting that he had been born of as poor and obscure parents as those Authors make him; yet must it needs add to the commendation of his Parts and Industry, who from so mean and low a birth, had raised himself into such an Eminent Height of Power and Glory, that no Bishop or Archbishop since the Reformation had attained the like. The greatest Rivers many times have the smallest Fountains, such as can hardly be found out, and being found out, hardly quit the cost of the discovery; and yet by long running, and holding on a constant and continual course, they become large, navigable, and of great benefit unto the Publick. Whereas some Families may be compared unto the Pyramides of Ægypt, which being built on great Foundations, grow narrower and narrower by degrees, until at last they end in a small Conus, in a Point, in Nothing. . . . Which brings to my mind the Answer made by Mr Secretary Pace to a Nobleman about the court of King Henry viii; for when the said Nobleman told him, in contempt of learning, that it was enough for Noblemans sons to wind their Horn, and carry their Hawk fair, and to leave study and learning to the Children of Mean Men; Mr Pace thereunto replied, Then his Lordship, and the rest of the Noblemen, must be content to leave unto the sons of meaner Persons, the managing of Affairs of State; when their own children please themselves with winding their Horns, and managing their Hawks, and such other Follies of the Country.'

A very subtle passage. Doubtless Laud and Heylyn were on the reactionary side of ecclesiastical feudalism, on the losing side; but in this stout affirmation of the career open to talents they were men of their age, a changing age, just as much as the merchants of the city or the officers and men who met in the Council of the New Model Army to debate the fundamentals of democracy. Of course, the encouragement of 'poor scholars' in the universities had had a long history previous to this, for the feudal system had been long decaying. This thought put me in mind of that charming description given by Dean Nowell of St Paul's about 1590 of the benefactions which Mistress Jocosa Frankland gave to my own College in Cambridge. I always like it for its genuine humanity, and moreover the tale repeated itself almost exactly in the history of the founding of Stanford University centuries later in far-away California.

'... One Mrs Jocosa Frankland, late of Herts., widowe [Dean Nowell was writing to Archbishop Whitgift], had only one sonne, who youthfully venturing to ride upon an unbroken young horse, was throwne downe and slaine. Whereupon the mother fell into sorrowes uncomfortable; whereof I, being of her acquaintance, having intelligence, did with all speed ride unto her house near to Hodgden to comfort her the best I could. And I found her cryinge, or rather howlinge continually, O my sonne, O my sonne. And when I could by no comfortable words stay her from that cry and tearing of her haire; God, I thinke, put me in minde at the last to say: Comfort yourselfe, good Mistress Frankland, and I will tell you how you shall have twenty good sonnes to comfort you in these your sorrowes which you take for this one sonne. To the which wordes only she gave eare, and lookinge up, asked, How can that be? And I sayd unto her, You are a widdowe, riche and now childlesse, and there be in both Universities so many poore toward youths that lack exhibition, for whome if you would founde certaine fellowships and schollerships, to be bestowed upon studious younge men, who should be called Mistress Franklands schollers, they would be in love towards you as deare children, and will most hartely pray to God for you duringe your life; and they and their successors after them, being still Mistress Franklands scholers, will honour your memory for ever and ever. This being sayd, I will, quoth she, thinke thereupon earnestly. And though she lived a good time after, yet she gave in her Testament to the College of Brasen Nose in Oxford a very greate summe, and to Gonville & Caius College in Cambridge she gave £1,540 in money, and annual rents besides.'

It was now after sunset. I closed up the books and departed from the pool. [....]

II

Those who do not know the Fen Country north-east of Cambridge have missed one of the most fascinating and specialised types of English scenery. The straight canals and high-chimneyed pumping-stations, like Holland (of which we are reminded by many Dutch names and traces of Dutch architecture, the relics of Sir Cornelius Vermuyden and his seventeenth-century engineers); the 'islands' standing out above the plain at Stuntney and Downham and especially at Ely:

> Ely the stately,
> Shining a landmark
> O'er the broad waters
> Gold-bright in sunrise
> Gold-red in sunset
> Grey in the waning
> Kissed by the moonbeams
> Glimmering through mist-cloud
> Magic and matchless,
> Tower of the Lord God
> Lord Everlasting
> Dreaming o'er Fenland
> Upland and Seaboard
> All through the ages.

There are innumerable delightful surprises in the Fens; the Wisbech and Outwell steam tramway, for example; but on a pumping-station between Pymore and Suspension-Bridge the following remarkable inscription is to be found, written in black letters on a white board in a style suggesting a date such as 1812:

> These Fens have oft-times been by Water drown'd;
>   Science a Remedy in water found;
> The Power of Steam, she said, shall be employ'd
> And the destroyer by itself destroy'd.

Pondering the reason for the strange charm of these rustic lines, far in the wilderness, with nothing in view but flat fields of black earth and a geometrically straight canal, it occurred to me that it echoes one of the favourite paradoxes of the great Latin hymns. The *Vexilla Regis* for example:

> On whose dear arms, so widely flung
> The Price of this world's ransom hung,
> The Price which He alone could pay,
> And spoil the Spoiler of his prey.

Or take a little country church hidden away in an unfrequented valley just over the border into Essex on Cambridge's south-eastern side—Hempstead. There is indeed a reason for pilgrimages to Hempstead, for none other than little Dr William Harvey, England's greatest physiologist, lies buried there. In long after years Hempstead's tower was struck by lightning, and such bells as remained were placed in a wooden campanile in the churchyard. Hence it is now easy for us to read on one of them the following verse, at first sight obscure, and even at second sight containing a false quantity:

BARBARA SIRENUM MELOS DULCEDINE VINCO

> I, Barbara, conquer with my sweet music
> the song of the Sirens.

Outsinging the singers, despoiling the spoiler, bringing death to Death and harrowing Hell, negating the negation. However sophisticated we become, the resurrection remains the symbol of the triumphant rise of humanity from the dark night of animality into the bright day of the heavenly city. And the cost of it is the voluntary sacrifice of that innumerable company of beings at all stages of social evolution who have given themselves for others in the assurance of a hope that often they only dimly understood. Of this sacrifice the Cross is the ever-enduring symbol. But the compassionate Kuan-Yin also turns back on the very threshold of Paradise, unable to leave the world of suffering while her ears are still assailed by so many little cries. Long may it be before we cease to appreciate the beauty of old words recording these things, such as the runes on the Ruthwell Cross, where the tree itself is speaking:

> Then the young hero, who was mightiest God,
>   Strong and with steadfast mind,
> Up to the Cross with steps unfaltering trod
>   There to redeem mankind.
> I trembled but I durst not fail.
>   I on my shoulders bore the glorious king.
> They pierce my sides with many a darksome nail
>   And on us both their cruel curses fling.

Or the most triumphant poetry of the resurrection ever made (by Master William Dunbar, sixteenth century, in Scotland):

Done is a battell on the dragon blak
   Our campioun Chryst confountit hath his force;
The gettis of hell are broken with a crak
   The signe triumphall rasit is of the croce,
The divillis trymmyllis with hidous voce,
   The saullis are borrowit and to the blis can go,
Chryst with his blud our ransomis dois indoce;
   Surrexit Dominus de Sepulchro. . . .

He for our sake that sufferit to be slane
   And lyke a lamb in sacrifice was dight,
Is likke a lyon risin up agane
   And as a gyant raxit him on hicht;
Sprungin is Aurora radius and bricht
   On loft is gone the glorious Appollo,
The blissful day depairtit from the nicht;
   Surrexit Dominus de Sepulchro.

III

Pacing along the grass-grown quays at King's Lynn on another summer day, I discovered the infallible formula for delightful places in which to spend one's days of rest and refreshment. Seek for the Abandoned Trade Route. This formula never fails, whether it be beside some overgrown canal piercing the Cotswolds, at a charming tavern where once the bargees used to pause for a drink before their long passage underneath the earth; or whether it be on the rocky coasts of Devon and Cornwall where certain quays, the haunt now of but a few rustic fishermen, used once to be the main channels of entry and exit to whole regions of inland country. So also in Cambridgeshire. Bottisham Lode and Twenty-Pence Ferry; Mare Way, Orwell and Foxhole Downs; Bourne Bridge station on the old Newmarket—Great Chesterford railway where the metals were taken up long since and only the cuttings and embankments remain; or the Via Devana rolling over the chalk; all have the nostalgia of human business over which the waves of many years have washed. And of such places, Clayhithe, down river from Cambridge, where the towpath ends, is rightly numbered. An old tavern, beside the only bridge between Cambridge and Ely, has grass sloping down to the river. One may sit there enjoying a cup of tea, while across on the other side a microcosm of industry dozes in the afternoon sunshine. A ghost of a quay, an official weather-beaten house with a large panel of printed matter concerning harbourmaster's dues, river conservancy rules, and so on. To the left, a ghost of a shipyard with a three-legged derrick, but with no appearance of having been used these thirty years.

Such is the place in which to meditate. Why not about the real world of industry today, in the midst of whose roar thought is more difficult?

Among the books I have read in leisure afternoons in that charming spot, none gave me more pleasure than those of Pierre Hamp. It seems that Hamp is a writer little known in this country. Perhaps he has not been translated into English owing to the technicalities of which his work is full—necessarily so, since he deals always with 'La Peine des Hommes,' the daily work of trades and professions. He sees that to be doing a job that one enjoys, *aimer son métier,* is the highest point of human felicity, but he also sees that in the modern world such jobs have become rarer and rarer, partly owing to the collapse of craftsmanship before mass-production, partly owing to the insensate lust for profits, and partly owing to the control of working conditions by administrators who have never been workers themselves.

Pierre Hamp's masterpiece, I believe, is *Le Rail.* Anyone at all acquainted with railway technology will have little difficulty with its terms, and will enjoy every page of this detailed account of the life of a large railway centre, for that is what it essentially is. The book contains almost no women and derives its fascination wholly from the description of the interplay of character between the officials and subordinate workers in the different departments. In its structure, too, the book is interesting, for just when you are beginning to feel a little of the monotony accompanying the daily attempt to accomplish the impossible, a serious accident to an express occurs, and with the unexpected suddenness of such events in real life, you are plunged into the immediate horror of it, and the havoc and disorganisation in the system which follow it. The latter part of the book is taken up with a brilliant description of a strike. And in this connection one gets a little enlightenment regarding anti-clericalism in France, for the so-called 'Catholic Unions' are set up side by side with the real ones, highly to the benefit, of course, of the company.

In a brilliant passage, Pierre Hamp exposes the value of conti-

nental Catholicism to the capitalist system. After the conclusion of
the strike, M. Griaux, the locomotive superintendent, is talking to
M. Bally, the engineer of the repair shops. The parish priest, the
abbé Heyndrickx, has furnished firemen and fitters to replace
those victimised by the company for their part in the strike, and
M. Griaux is taking leave to doubt the efficiency of the new
men.

'Never mind [says M. Bally], he takes pains to find us well-
affected minds. The way our moderate men were carried away by
the revolutionary hotheads shows that our percentage of Catholic
personnel was insufficient. It must be raised. Reflect, M. Griaux,
that the railway, like the army, requires absolute discipline. The
army can establish it by force and has no need of persuasion. But
for us such constraint is forbidden, and we must persuade. Now
where can we find a more perfect school of submission than the
Catholic Church? From one end of the hierarchy to the other, the
obligation is to obey, the layman to his priest, the priest to the
bishop, the bishop to the Pope, the Pope to God. Translate this discipline into terms of the railway, and you have the ideal organisation. And this has nothing to do, M. Griaux, with beliefs, with
faiths, or with this or the other dogma. They are without importance. It is the philosophy alone of the Catholic Church which is
important for us, and that philosophy is, Obey, Obey.'

What corresponds in England to the emotional force of
Catholic obedience in France would make the subject of an interesting investigation.

From *Le Rail*, I went on to *Marée Fraiche*, which describes
the passage of fish from the North Sea to the table of a city
restaurant, in terms of the conditions of work of the men
involved. How well the following passage illustrates the kind of
psychological clash which is so common :

'In the goods yard, the shunters' horns were ceaselessly blow-
ing. A long train had stopped before a danger signal. Beside it,
the inspector, while waiting for the signal to change, was delivering acid remarks to M. Ramblenne; an excellent man, nevertheless, who had been a shunter for fifteen years. Such work left
him ill-prepared to reply to the criticisms of an office worker for
whom everything amounted to figures on pieces of paper. The
habit of seeing all realities in terms of statistics had removed from

the inspector all conception of the indocility of matter. He would have liked everything done as quick as thought, and could not appreciate the difference between moving one's tongue to say 'thirty wagons' and actually getting them moved; tare : ten tons; total : three hundred thousand kilos.'

And then in *Vin de Champagne* there is a remarkable description of a glassworks where the bottles are made, and of the vineyards, their owners vainly struggling against the big merchant corporations. I read also *Mes Métiers*, in which Hamp describes autobiographically his apprenticeship to the trade of cook and confectioner.

Why have we no English Pierre Hamp? Grierson's documentary film, *Drifters*, was an attempt at a similar objective carried out in terms of the cinema for the English fishing industry, but it lacked the compelling power of a consciously proletarian sympathy, and gave only a cold analogy to *Marée Fraiche*. The trawlers were looked at, as it were, from a great distance, so far away that everything seemed happy and contented. Yet there is a vast scope for an English Hamp. Ernest Bevin once gave some particulars about the London bus-drivers. In 1926 the average horse-power of bus engines was forty, in 1932 it was ninety. In 1921 they drove a bus that carried thirty-four passengers, in 1932 there was room for sixty-five. Yet although the traffic conditions have become much more difficult and the number of passengers has practically doubled, the hours worked by drivers are exactly the same, and two conductors are not provided to do the doubled work. On the contrary, in 1932 we found general wage-reductions demanded in this industry. There would be no lack of work for an English Hamp.

IV

In whichever direction one decides to go out from Cambridge on a sunny summer morning, one will be travelling into the past as well as in space, so saturated with memories is the East Anglian countryside. One takes down, for instance, the footpath map. There, to the south, is a good direction, past Hauxton church (with its long hidden mural painting of St Thomas of Canterbury, that staunch friend of the people), diverging before Harston to Fowlmere and Thriplow. Fowlmere was the village where the charming, perhaps unique, May Day carol was found :

> Awake, awake, good people all
> Awake, and you shall hear
> That Christ has died for our sins,
> For he loved us so dear. . . .

> A branch of may I've brought to you
> And at your door it stands,
> It is but a sprout, but it's well budded out,
> By the work of our Lord's hands.

> Now my song, that is done, and I must be gone,
> I can no longer stay,
> So God bless you all, both great and small,
> And I wish you a joyful May.

Thriplow, with its cruciform church, has sterner memories. For it was on Thriplow's bare and wind-swept heath where Cambridgeshire borders on Hertfordshire that in June, 1647, the victorious New Model Army met in general assembly, and refused even to listen to the Commissioners of Disbandment sent down from Parliament. The Army's manifesto declared that it was not mercenary, but the free commoners of England drawn together and continued in judgement and conscience, for the defence of their own and the people's rights and liberties. The regiments (21,000 men) pledged themselves not to disband until security was obtained that 'we as private men, or other the free-born people of England, shall not remain subject to the like oppressions, injury, or abuse, as hath heretofore been attempted.' At this stage of the revolution Cromwell and Ireton were still able to lead the army as a whole. It proceeded to the occupation of London.

These were the regiments which elected democratic delegates to the Federal Council of the Army, known by the name of 'Agitators'—the first time the word was used. They were so called because they were appointed to *do* something (not hearers of the Word only), to see that the council carried out the wishes of the mass of the army. The council met first in the great church at Saffron Walden—another pleasant journey from Cambridge today, through Duxford and Roman Ickleton. A journey pleasant to me, since it leads into Essex and to the town of Thaxted, the very embodiment and incarnation of England, though the

England of More and Bunyan, Blake and Owen, not of Gresham, Pitt and Rhodes. For there *are* two Englands. As Tessimond has so well written :

> The generous smile of music-halls,
> Bars and bank-holidays and queues;
> The private peace of public foes;
> The truce of pipe and football news.

> The smile of privilege exultant;
> Smile at the 'bloody reds' defeated;
> Smile at the striker starved and broken;
> Smile at the 'dirty nigger' cheated.

> The old hereditary craftsman;
> The incommunicable skill;
> The pride in long-loved tools, refusal
> To do the set job quick or ill.

> The greater artist mocked, misflattered;
> The lesser forming clique and team
> Or crouching in his narrow corner,
> Narcissus with his secret dream.

> England of rebels—Blake and Shelley;
> England where freedom's sometimes won,
> Where Jew and Negro needn't fear yet
> Lynch-law and pogrom, whip and gun.

> England of cant and smug discretion;
> England of wagecut, sweatshop, knight,
> Of sportsman, churchman, slum-exploiter,
> Of puritan grown sour with spite.

> England of clever fool, mad genius,
> Timorous lion and arrogant sheep,
> Half-hearted snob and shamefaced bully,
> Of hands awake and eyes asleep.
> England the snail, shod with lightning,
> Shall we laugh or shall we weep?

But wherever you go, East Anglia's days of greatest seventeenth-century glory have left their mark. Out northwest, perhaps, towards Huntingdon and St Ives, or by way of St Neots to Bedford. There, a few miles out, is Childerly Manor, still retaining its medieval chapel by the lake, whither the New Model's general staff rode out for a conference with the captive King, newly apprehended by Cornet Joyce, and temporarily lodging at Childerley. Or on the left there is Toft, where in a large barn John Bunyan used later to preach, and where he fell into argument loud and long with the University Librarian (the Arabic scholar, Thomas Smith), who happened to be passing that way. Mr Bunyan in his youth, had been a soldier of the Parliament, a member of the revolutionary garrison of Newport Pagnell. At St Ives itself, of course, Mr Cromwell was himself for many years a farmer.

It was on this very Huntingdon Road that a couple of incidents took place of which I often think. Nothing shows the confused atmosphere of the early phase of the revolution so well as the account of two young Royalists, the Branstons (whose father was an eminent judge), who were riding from York to Essex in September, 1642 :

'In our return on Sunday, near Huntingdon, between that and Cambridge, certain musketeers started out of the corn and commanded us to stand; telling us we must be searched, and to that end must go before Mr Cromwell and give account of whence we were come and whither we were going. I asked, Where Mr Cromwell was? A soldier told us he was four miles off. I said, it was unreasonable to carry us out of our way; if Mr Cromwell had been there I should willingly have given him all the satisfaction he could desire; and putting my hand into my pocket, I gave one of them twelve pence, who said, we might pass. By this, however, I saw plainly that it would not be possible for my father to get to the King with his coach; neither did he go at all, but stayed at home till he died.'

About the same time, the Colleges, both at Oxford and Cambridge, were invited by letter to send silver and plate to the King's Treasury. The response at Cambridge was very poor, only two Colleges sending a consignment, and the waggons containing it were ambushed by Mr Cromwell and a troop between Cambridge and Huntingdon. The plate was thus safely lodged in Cambridge castle, and probably went to swell the funds of the Eastern Counties Association. The place where the ambush took place is traditionally identified with Lolworth wood, which marches with the main road just east of Lolworth village.

Those who are always searching for pleasant waters find them in plenty over from Cambridge towards Bunyan's Bedfordshire and Cromwell's Huntingdonshire. For there runs the valley of the Ouse, a lovely river already at Bedford, and improving as it passes under so many old stone bridges at St Neots, Huntingdon, and St Ives down to the border of the fens at Earith. The bridges, some of them so narrow that they have traffic lights on them now, echoed once to the hoofs of the New Model's troops of horse. And everywhere, as at Houghton Mill or the Hemingfords, there are excellent places where one can swim, or row a boat, or simply sit on the bank, chew grass-stalks, and read a book.

In such surroundings, in a moored boat with the water gently lapping, I read one year what I came to regard as one of the greatest books of our generation.

Among the literature of our time, so critical with decisions about the future of human civilisation, there is much that is escapist, much that is trivially realistic. Poets are face to face with serious dilemmas; the necessity of writing for the mass of the people on the one hand, and the desire to elaborate subtle poetic forms on the other. Causes for the decay of popular taste receive detailed attention, a decay which no one doubts but for which few can show, so long as present conditions continue, any remedy. Q. Leavis regards it as the escape from a life where *l'ouvrier ne chante plus*; and as the result of the pure play of the profit-making motive in the writing and publishing trade; N. Bachtin as the outcome of an atomistic society of competitive monads with absolutely no common purpose which the poet can express. Into all this there came a book reminiscent of John Bunyan's *Pilgrim's Progress*, or rather his *Holy War*, portraying the spiritual situation of today with unerring accuracy by means of a spacious allegory.[2] With justice I found inscribed on its first page—'For our contention is not with the blood and the flesh, but with dominion, with authority, with the blind world rulers of this life, with the spirit of evil in things heavenly.'

In one matter, at any rate, John Bunyan (whose ghost, I hope, was looking over my shoulder) had the advantage of Rex Warner. The spiritual truths which he was concerned to demonstrate by his allegory were the common property of the vast mass of his readers. But today the christian tradition, for better or for worse, has ceased to have the universal appeal which once it had, and the minds of the people are no longer conditioned to receive it. Hence Rex Warner was forced to construct a mythological framework of his own, and of course that made his allegory considerably more obscure than it would otherwise have been. But the general meaning of *The Wild Goose Chase* is plain. If Bunyan was concerned primarily with the struggle of the individual human being to attain blessedness, Warner proclaims that the individual's aim can only be attained through comradeship in the collective enterprise of humanity. This is in line with many great currents of christian thought, and if Bunyan emphasised the individual, that was the essence of puritanism and part of its historic task. But heaven is where there is fellowship.

The style in which *The Wild Goose Chase* is written is one of delightful simplicity which never jars on the reader, and the likeness to Bunyan is reinforced by occasional faint echoes of seventeenth-century prose. But Warner has drawn on many other sources of inspiration, such as the novels of Kafka with their atmosphere of subjection to mysterious and perhaps meaningless authority, and the work of the Surrealists in their nightmare juxtaposition of incongruous events and objects. In the beginning of the book three brothers set out from their home town, a provincial seaside resort, and after some adventures, pass across the space-time frontier into a new country in a search for the breeding place of the Wild Geese. This country has a rural population of enslaved, oppressed, and rather stupid peasants. In the centre is what is called The Town, a vast completely roofed-in concrete structure, hundreds of square miles in area, and surrounded by cloud-piercing towers and walls. Within the town there is The Government, working according to highly developed scientific technique with an organisation apparently perfect. Its servants are the ubiquitous Police, who wear crystalline helmets, carry electrically energised straw truncheons, and are constantly in touch with headquarters by wireless. One of their weapons is continual silly laughter, and the ridicule which they pour on anything real. All the manifestations of the Government and its servants convey in a brilliant manner that atmosphere of *slightly sinister irrationality* required to make a biting satire of most human governments today. The police keep in subjection, besides the peasants, large numbers of miners and industrial workers who live in caverns beneath the town. Their task is rendered the easier by the regimentation of the intellectuals, mostly hermaphrodites, who live in an enormous college, known as The Convent. Here are cultivated Science for Science's sake, and Art for Art's sake. In the Research Department there was 'a poet who had invented a new language, but could neither pronounce a syllable of it nor attach any meaning to any of its words. There was an artist who spent his time rapidly arranging fir cones on the floor of his cell, and sweeping them together with his hand when he was for an instant satisfied with their arrangement.' The inmates were encouraged to gratify every wish, however cruel, absurd, or repulsive to the ordinary mind. The Convent is indeed a satire of the degeneration which intellectual culture suffers when it cuts itself off from the life of the human collectivity in the processes of material production.

Introduced into the Convent, George (the best and the youngest brother) is asked to referee a football match between the Pros and the Cons, played on a rubber ground and finished off with machine guns and an armoured car, in spite of the fact that the score had previously been decided upon and announced by the Government. His attempts to referee fairly land him in trouble, but he appeals to the king. He is taken first to an aristocratic fencer, who speaks of Youth and Action, but turns out not to be the real king and passes him on to a scientist in a laboratory. In his search for the real king, he reaches at last the sanctum of the ecclesiastical business man with the piercing eyes, from whom he escapes only with difficulty, and whom he is not to meet again until the end of the book. This part of the allegory well depicts the uncertainty in which so many find themselves regarding the real seat of power in modern human societies. A quotation at this point may serve to give an idea of the book's whole atmosphere. George is about to referee the football match. 'Puzzled, he made his way back to the main entrance hoping to find the games master or some other person who could supply him with a whistle. ... I have been treated, he thought, in two opposite ways, with suspicion and contempt by the police, and with a certain amount of respect by the inmates of the Convent. How am I to account for a policy which appears self-contradictory? Have the Government perhaps given orders that I am to be treated well inside the Convent (though the behaviour of the students during my lecture was far from satisfactory) and badly outside, to the end that I may be induced to spend my life there, change my manner of thought, and perhaps undergo the operation? Or, for that matter, are the Government aware of my existence? If even their Chief

Statistician is unacquainted with them, how can I suppose that they are likely to have taken much notice of me? And yet the Headmaster, or at least some deputy of his, interviewed me from behind a rubber curtain, and the eavesdropping of the Rev. Hamlet is not a fact lightly to be dismissed. True, these men may be very subordinate officials, but they are in touch with their superiors, with whom I, through them, must also have something to do. But my time is slipping away, and so far I have achieved nothing notable.'

In the end George returns to the country, and realising that the Wild Goose Chase can go no further until the tyrannical Government of the town is overthrown, casts in his lot with the revolutionary movement among the peasants and miners. After some years a revolutionary army has been built up in secret, and during a series of exciting adventures and battles, the town is captured and the king driven out. All this part of the book, which is excellent, gives much scope for the delineation of typical revolutionary characters, and what with the defections of traitors, the quarrels over how much of the town's culture shall be built into the culture of the new order, and the deviations to left and right, a penetrating description of the choices before men today is given. In some passages of great beauty George discusses freedom with one of the Convent's intellectuals, Marqueta, who comes over to the revolutionaries, trying to show her that freedom is knowledge of necessity, the necessity of the regularities of Nature, and that of work in human community. Above all, he says, the king's Government 'waylaid adventurers and did not permit them to chase the Wild Geese.' In other words, true creative activity in all its forms, carried on by all those who are capable of doing so, will never be achieved until the essential material relationships between human beings have been set right, until the satisfaction of fundamental human needs has been assured to all; and the only course open to the adventurer (or pilgrim) is to join forces with those who are working and fighting for this end. Seek ye first the kingdom of God, and his *justice*, and all these other things shall be added.

Bunyan's trumpets are not absent. The Town had contained, of course, its Cathedral, the 'Anserium,' in which the sacred cult-object had been a *stuffed* goose, not a live wild one. The book closes with a mass-meeting, celebrating the successful conclusion of the revolution, in the Anserium. 'What our old leaders most

respected,' said George, concluding his speech, 'we chiefly despise
—the frantic assertion of an ego, do-nothings, the over-cleanly,
deliberate love-making, literary critics, moral philosophers, ball-
room dancing, pictures of sunsets, money, the police; and to what
they used to despise we attach great value—to comradeship, and
to profane love, to hard work, to honesty, the sight of the sun,
reverence for those who have helped us, animals, flesh and blood.
Let us live, comrades. Long live the Revolution !' And then the
trumpets sounded (in a metaphor), but what it was that actually
happened, I shall leave to the book's thousandfold readers, both
old and young, to discover. For this is a book profoundly germane
to the individual of today, and will be understood and treasured
when much that now receives praise has long been little regarded.

Notes

1. A. Austen Leigh, *History of King's College* (London, 1899), p. 64.
2. Rex Warner, *The Wild Goose Chase* (London, 1937).

II

UNDERSTANDING

2

Religion in a World Dominated by Science

(1930)

I

When we stand aside from our individual preoccupations and meditate on the progress of affairs in the world of thought, we can sometimes feel the presence of the great forms of human activity, struggling like leviathans in the upper air with tremendous conflict, or standing over against one another with almost imperceptible subtle hate and opposition. No opposition has been more violent and long continued in the past than that between the organised apprehension of the world's ultimate mystery, which we call religion, and the organised investigation of the world's apparent mechanism, which we call science. Whole shelves of books have been written about this opposition, and it is easy to dismiss it by lightly giving in one's adherence to one aspect as if to some parliamentary party or local group. Yet it possesses a profoundly tragic side, and no inconsiderable part of the world's evil must have been apportioned in the torments of those who, as if caught between the upper and the nether millstone, wore out their lives seeking for some rest in the confusion and not finding any. And I do not, of course, suggest that to these people the philosophical difficulties appeared in any clear or well-defined form, for the strange thing about life is that philosophical propositions of an apparently academic character have a habit of disguising themselves as problems of everyday life, and presenting themselves to the ordinary man as he goes about his business in the shape of moods which may be very vague indeed. Such moods of dissatisfaction or disgust may act as subtle irritants, leading him to the conviction that something is wrong with 'things in general,' though what it is he cannot tell, and to actions which he may himself afterwards regret.

We obviously live in a world *dominated by scientific thought*, or rather, not by scientific thought itself, but by a popular version of the state of mind natural to the scientific thinker. A great organised form of experience such as science carries with it a mass of subsidiary ideas, feelings, beliefs, and conventions, which you can easily strip off from it when you begin reducing it to its essence, its minimum claims. Thus it is not necessary for a scientific worker to hold absolute determinism, or, in other words, the opinion that everything that happens had to happen just so and not otherwise, going back by an endless chain of causes to the original first cause, which may, of course, have a purely naturalistic and non-theological explanation. It is not necessary for him to hold that no matter how chaotic a realm of things may seem, patient searching and experimentation will one day triumphantly arrive at general laws covering the whole of its operations. He may get on well enough without such beliefs, but nevertheless you find, taking a wide view of the history of science, and examining the intellectual atmosphere of present-day laboratories, that they tend to be universal, and that you have to reckon, not only with science in the usual sense, with the contents, that is, of the books which summarise the knowledge that has been won, but also with the typical state of mind of the scientific worker. It is as if the minimum claims of science were surrounded by a wide fringe, which you cannot get away from as it seems to be required for the functioning of the essential units of progress, the scientific workers themselves. And the acceptance of a somewhat distorted version of this fringe as their basic assumption by the vast majority of men in every occupation at the present day is the kernel of the situation which we have to consider.

II

On all sides we see the domination of the scientific way of thought. It is indeed a banal commonplace to say that we live 'in a scientific age,' but how deep-reaching this statement is may very often not be realised, and it is worth while to make some effort to do so. The most obvious characteristic of our time is the extraordinary power over natural processes which has been put into our hands by advances in scientific technique. It would be super-fluous to enumerate instances of this, for we are constantly being reminded of it, not only in a practical way, wherever we go, whether in our homes or out of them, but also by the great company of writers who provide us with what is called 'popular science,' and who try, often vainly, to explain the working of pieces of apparatus which many of us use every day, and which we should hardly know how to do without. In this way the roots of mankind, which in earlier times went deep down into the earth, are now insulated, as it were, by layers of steel, glass, and concrete, from any living contact with it. And let us not deceive ourselves into supposing that this process has come nearly to its conclusion already—far from it, the future probably holds out nothing but a long succession of further pseudo-triumphs, further acquisitions of power over Nature, further temptations to sever all living connection with her. I will only give one instance of this, an instance which concerns me particularly as a biologist, namely this, that we are as yet only at the very threshold of an undreamed of control over living things, including ourselves. It is already clear that what we might call a biological engineering will grow up. Who would have thought a century ago that man would be able to set a thief to catch a thief in the animal world, and by liberating one kind of insect from captivity to destroy myriads of another kind. Yet economic entomology[1] is now one of the most flourishing branches of applied science, and the growth of the prickly pear, a kind of cactus, which some years ago threatened to make vast areas of Australia absolutely unfit for cultivation, has been completely checked by the liberation of a little insect from another country which is known to prey upon it and in the end kill it. The most obvious instance of biological engineering nearer home, and as applied to ourselves, is, of course, birth control, and the position of those who oppose it on theological grounds is precisely similar to those country parsons who, in the middle of the last century, protested loudly against the use of anaesthetics in childbirth on the ground of quotations from the Old Testament.

But, as is so often said, the scientific age which gives us these powers, gives us no corresponding indication of how we are to use them. The land is only redeemed from the prickly pear in order to become immediately the source of a bitter quarrel between Australian and Japanese; the control of the number of persons entering the world leads at once to differences between racial, national, and religious groups, so that the general outcome is disharmony and inequality. Other religious bodies, with that worldly wisdom in which the English Church has always been so lacking, find any argument good enough as long as it prevents birth control among their adherents, and so increases continually their numbers.

III

No doubt the greatest effect which applied science has, however, is in filling the sails of that frame of mind which is sometimes called millenarianism, or in other words, the belief that there's a good time coming, actually here on earth, and at no distant date. This is indeed a characteristic concomitant of scientific progress. In classical antiquity the world was by no means a pleasant place to live in, and if we were transplanted forthwith to the eighth century in the West, or even the Western middle ages at the height of their glory, we should be acutely miserable. The Hellenistic philosophers described the world as *paideuterion tēs theognōsias psychōn logikōn didaskalion* a 'school for rational souls to learn the knowledge of God,' and the quality of life was such that later thinkers saw no reason for modifying the phrase. As late as the nineteenth century, the medievalist poet, J. M. Neale,[2] could write of earthly pains and sorrows,

> What are they but the ladder
> Set up to Heav'n on earth?

But with the rapid increase in human comfort, brought about as a result of scientific knowledge, this mystical attitude towards the problem of evil faded into the background, and the more active efforts of the social improver took its place. His fundamental postulate was and is that *by human effort*, evil may be caused to play a constantly diminishing part in human life. It is here that we come upon a fundamental source of antagonism between science and religion, for millenarianism and mysticism are nothing but the mirror images of the two great forms of experience. Hence the sort of person with whom we are all familiar, whose religion is a mixture of kindness to animals and vague hopes for 'social betterment,' is not a religious person at all, but a muddle-headed well-wisher, oscillating in a vacuum between two poles of spiritual energy, the meaning of neither of which is known to him. Hence the legitimate contempt in which we may hold 'egg services'[3] and other boneless manifestations of a dying religiousness; for a virile mysticism will know how to estimate the golden promises of a scientific millennium at their true worth. Beauty is transient, death inevitable, and escape will never be possible from the essential tragedy of life.

It is possible, of course, for millenarianism to be virile too, and the place where it can be studied best today seems to be in the influence of militant communism. Can we be surprised that a collision with traditional religion has occurred in Russia? The more interested you are in the other world, the less so you will be in this, and as the communist is very interested indeed in this world, can we be surprised that he does not agree with the mystic? The communist is in one sense the direct descendant of the nineteenth-century scientist, detesting mystery and determined to control the material world in the interests of man. As for opium, there are several sorts. There is much truth in the well-known assertion that religion is the opium of the people, but we do not get very far by simply conferring this distinction on science instead.

IV

Power over external Nature is a crude attribute of science, and it is not difficult to find other attributes of a more subtle kind, which yet exercise a tremendous influence throughout the modern world. The principle of abstraction is one of these. Anyone who is at all intimate with the method of pure science realises that its fundamental procedure of classification and indexing is the assertion of the abstract, the assertion of the group or class, and the absolute forgetting, at one and the same time, about the individual instances which have gone into the class. If I were to take an illustration from my own work in order to make the point clearer, I should refer to an investigation which I made a few years ago[4] into the amount of sugar which is contained in the body of the embryo of the chick as it develops within the hen's egg. Chemical analyses had to be made on each day throughout the three weeks which comprise the incubation-time of the chicken, but it was not sufficient to analyse one embryo for each day, on the contrary, it was important to analyse a great many, and from the results to calculate averages, standard deviations, etc. Only in this way could we begin to approach our scientific aim, namely propositions about the amount of sugar in chick embryos in general. But once the calculations were made and the crude figures of the individual experiments subsumed into the final curve, then the former were forgotten, and the results for the individual cases ceased to be of any scientific interest.

Nothing can be more profoundly characteristic of the scientific method than its stern overlooking of the individual. Science is through and through statistical. In some cases even its individual instances are statistical wholes, in that they are compounded, as we believe, of vast swarms of units, such as the particles of a gas, no one of which can ever be isolated and studied as such; but even where the units do form unbreakable wholes, their individuality quickly disappears as they go through the mill of scientific treatment, issuing out as the sausage-like general law.

'There can never be,' as D. H. Lawrence says somewhere quite rightly,[5] 'an exact science dealing with individual life', For the very fact of its being exact, and a science, would mean that it had gone far beyond the realm of the individual. It is quite thinkable that we should have statistical sociological laws from which we can read off how many people are going to be killed in railway accidents in England during the next six months, and the statistics which we have practically permit us to do it, but unfortunately we have no means of knowing which of us are going to be involved therein, chosen, as it were, like the tribute which the Athenians in the legend had to send every year to King Minos in Crete. Questions which are of the highest importance to the individual, then, may not be of the slightest scientific importance. And conversely, for all we know, molecules and atoms may possess a high degree of individuality, an individuality which we never see because we are forced to treat them in immensely large congregations and can never isolate them for close inspection. With this idea in mind, we see in a new light the common description of factory workers as 'hands', clocking in and clocking out with soulless precision, sinking their human individuality in the productive whole of which they form a part, communism may be in this respect just as deeply influenced by science as capitalism. The ideal of some writers seems to be a social condition resembling that of the communal insects, such as bees and ants, in which each individual is utterly subservient to the requirements of the State as a whole, even to the extent of profound physical modifi-

cations adapting the worker for his particular job. Admirers of H.
G. Wells' earlier manner will recall in this connection his account
of the inhabitants of the moon, who combined human intelligence
with insect form and an ant-like community of highly specialised
creatures.[6] Certain modern biologists, such as W. M. Wheeler,
openly advocate an approximation to this way of life for man.
Robert Bridges, indeed, suggests that the bees first of all had
reason but afterwards lost it, suffering an atrophy of the individual in proportion to the hypertrophy of their state.[8]

> For among Bees and Ants are social systems found
> so complex & well-order'd as to invite offhand
> a pleasant fable enough: that once upon a time
> or ever a man was born to rob their honey-pots
> bees were fully endow'd with Reason, and only lost it
> by ordering so their life as to dispense with it;
> whereby it pined away and perish'd of disuse,
> which, whether it were or no, if men can judge of bees
> well might be in their strange manner of life—so like it is
> with what our economical bee-minded men
> teach as the first intelligential principle
> of human government, wellfare, and happiness.

But all I wish to insist upon in this connection is that we can
trace a powerful influence of scientific abstraction on everyday
life, an influence which is not likely to diminish but rather to
increase, and which yet is fundamentally and bitterly opposed to
the characteristic viewpoint of the religious spirit. Just as the
interference of science with the course of Nature weakens the
appeal of the mystical attitude towards life, so the habit of
abstraction common to all scientific procedure weakens that
attention to the individual and unique which always was and
probably always will be an essential part of religion.

v

Next we may say something of what is called the ethical neutrality of science. The one thing the experimentalist is anxious to
do is to 'let Nature speak for herself', and he is very suspicious of
any appearance of dictating answers to Nature. Theoretically the
scientific worker should be absolutely indifferent to the result of
any experiment; it should be all one to him whether the litmus

turns red or blue, whether the rabbit is born with black hair or white, whether the moulds grow on the prepared medium or whether they do not. In practice, of course, he cannot help a certain bias one way or the other, because he is usually in the middle of a long series of experiments, and the result of one trial may easily mean that he has been completely wasting his time for the previous three weeks. Indeed, no small part of the training of a research worker consists in accustoming oneself to such disappointments. It is impossible for an outside onlooker to conceive how careful the scientific worker has to be to prevent himself unconsciously giving an experiment a tip in the right direction, and so obtaining the result which he would prefer.

But this is not the only aspect of the ethical and aesthetic neutrality of science. We expect the scientific worker not to be deterred by his subject-matter, however unpleasant it may become; the anatomist must deal with the dead body, the pathologist with gruesome and disgusting materials, the chemist with all kinds of dangerous compounds. In itself this detachment from the normal likes and dislikes of men is an excellent and, indeed, an extremely noble thing, but it has the effect of letting loose on the world certain things that the world would be better without. In the course of chemical investigations on the dichlorethyl compounds, somebody stumbled on the substance we now know as 'mustard gas', and in spite of the properties of this substance, no doubt felt it both his duty and his pleasure to go on investigating it and even to prepare a number of compounds very similar to it or even worse. At this point the men of evil will stepped in, the military intelligence came into operation, and the forces of disunion, envy, hatred, and malice, which are always walking up and down the world, found a little corner admirably adapted for them to lay their eggs in.

In short, for the scientific worker ethical neutrality is an indispensable aim, and he must at all costs strive to attain it, but for the whole man it is by no means an unmixed good. It is as if the house of the spirit, which was previously inhabited by the genius of religion, always preoccupied about God, Man, the Good, the Holy, the Right, were thoroughly spring-cleaned, swept, and garnished, leaving nothing but the empty rooms and bare walls of scientific ethical neutrality, whereupon seven other demons, all worse than the first, including war and pestilence, enter in and take up a permanent residence there. It is evident that the scien-

tific worker, *as such*, cannot possibly claim any right to adminis-
trate human societies, for the basis of any administration must
be a set of ethical judgements, a set of views about what is wrong
and what is right, and one of the most refreshing things about the
scientific worker is that he thinks nothing wrong and nothing
right, save only the perpetual accumulation of verifiable knowledge, and the progressive formulation of scientific truth. It is not
his fault if poison gases, explosives, etc., come into being to
oppress mankind; these things were thrown out by him, it is true,
from Nature's storehouse, along with a lot of other miscellaneous
luggage, and if evilly-disposed persons come past and carry them
off, he cannot be held responsible, and is usually much too busy to
notice that anything has happened. But the point is that his
ethical neutrality is diametrically opposed to the point of view of
the religious man, who is vitally concerned with the problems
involved in an association of souls. And just as the abstraction
inherent in the scientific method tends to weaken the respect for,
and interest in, the individual, which is so marked a characteristic
of religious feeling, so the ethical neutrality natural to a large,
influential, and continually growing section of the community
tends to abolish the distinction between good and evil, and to
weaken the homage paid to the traditional conception of the good
by the religious mind. Not only does it do this, but it leaves the
way open for evil applications of scientific knowledge, applications
which, as is so often said, stand a very good chance of destroying
the whole of our civilisation, and ourselves with it, unless somebody awakes from this enchanted sleep in time.

Now it is legitimate for the scientific worker to lay ethics aside
as irrelevant to his special pursuits, but when his state of mind
becomes the keynote of a whole epoch, as is the case today, the
average man tends to lay ethics aside too, often in the interests of
mere enjoyment or personal gain. Traditional morality is thus
adversely affected by the ethically neutral attitude of the scientific
worker. Not only is he indifferent, at any rate theoretically, as to
which of two results turns up in an experiment, but he is also
indifferent as to which of two forms of human behaviour is put
into practice, unless he can see some strictly scientific reason for
preferring one over the other. Traditional theological sanctions
are nothing to him. It follows from the dominance of science in
our modern world that experimental morality will more and more
come into being—a fact which I do not regret, although unfortu-

c

nately it puts added difficulties in the way of organised religion. These difficulties are by no means insuperable, but my point that religion holds a very difficult position in such a world is illustrated again.

VI

Another outstanding characteristic of science which imprints itself everywhere around us is its preoccupation with the quantitative, that is to say, with sets of figures. The scientific worker is not interested in mere facts or mere phenomena, he is interested in precisely defined facts and exactly described phenomena. But precision is impossible without sets of numbers or symbols, and logic tends more and more to become mathematical logic. In various ways this preoccupation with the measurable and the numerable, admirable and necessary though it is in its own place, filters through to the affairs of everyday life, where it is neither admirable nor necessary. It accounts perhaps to some degree for the extraordinary ideas which some people entertain about happiness, assuming as they do, to judge by their actions, that it can be purchased in the market, without other activity on the part of the purchaser.

When science, under the name of economics, applies itself to the study of human societies, it has to adopt some form of measurement, and several eminent economists speak of the 'measuring-rod of money.' Lawrence Hyde has vigorously attacked the use of this idea.[9] It is, he writes, 'like saying that the classification of pictures by area or of statues by weight would introduce a satisfying element of accuracy into the obscure subject of aesthetics.' Qualitative non-numerable values are supremely important in life as we have to live it, and just as the ethical neutrality proper to the scientific worker's attitude tends to weaken the ethical certainty on which religion must insist, so the scientific emphasis on the numerical, the quantitative, weakens the interest which we ought to take in the more impalpable, intangible qualities important for religion.

Obviously this factor introduces itself into practical life largely through the wide realm of engineering, for the engineer is only the scientific worker disguised. R. L. Stevenson, in his *Records of a Family of Engineers*,[10] speaks thus of his father, 'he once stood and looked on at the emptying of a certain oil-tube; he did so watch in hand, and accurately timed the operation; and in so doing offered the perfect type of his profession. 'The very term mensuration sounds engineer-like' I find him writing, and in truth what the engineer most properly deals with is what can be measured, weighed, and numbered.' But whereas in past times, this assertion could be made with little misgiving, owing to the fact that the vast majority of people were not engineers, the position is very different now, when the vast majority are rapidly tending to become so. Every time a plough-team is replaced by a tractor, every time a typewriter supersedes a pen, events march a step further forward towards the domination of the quantitative and the collapse of religious feeling.

On this account it has often been urged that a reaction against machinery is necessary, e.g., by the Morrisites and Samuel Butler in this country, and by the Narodniki, with whom Lenin quarrelled, in Russia. But nothing can come of a mere backward movement. Technological unemployment, which has caused so much machine-wrecking in the past, has really nothing to do with machines as such, but attends inevitably upon a capitalistic system of production. What is required is the formation in the minds of men of some kind of immunity mechanism against machinery, or rather against the peculiar mental bias associated with a life surrounded by machinery.

When Elmer Rice, in his play *The Subway*, wishes to indicate the most dreary and hopeless element in the atmosphere of our time, he introduces a man sitting at home in the evening after his day's work, reading monotonously pieces out of the newspaper such as '3762 cases of divorce were tried in the State court during the past year, Judge Smith stated in an interview today', '22,345 bathers made use of the city swimming-bath between 12 p.m. last Monday and this morning, it is computed.' This continual appearance of arbitrary facts expressed in quantitative form, and absolutely devoid of living interest, can be seen everywhere around us. It is as if the human mind were fascinated by the coils of accurate nonsense which it is for ever spinning. And as commerce becomes more and more 'scientific', so this atmosphere of meaningless precision will more and more overspread the world. In view of the fact that the overwhelming majority of men are, and always will be, engaged in some form of commerce, it is obvious that the future is extremely gloomy. For the old prestige of Church, Aristocracy, Classical Learning, etc., etc., has gone and can never return; it has, in fact, transferred itself to the so-called 'captain of industry' and the controller of the movements of money. Through these channels the scientific spirit imposes itself upon the mass of mankind, which, although quite unconscious of the direction in which it is being pushed, continually throws up to the surface indications of the opposite tendency—Nature-cults, Youth-movements, Folk-revivals.

It has been argued, apparently with much justification,[11] that one of the most notable of these indications is the wave of 'fundamentalism' in the Southern States of North America. On this view the ill-educated provincials, in their revolt against the teaching of evolution, were inarticulately engaged in objecting to a world dominated by the scientific mentality, and in asserting value as against origin. The popular philosophy against which they were fighting, although itself wholly belonging to the high-ways and by-ways of life, 'has academic connections through the laboratories of science, from which it flows as a disregarded by-product.' And in attacking the factual basis of the evolution theory, which is quite impregnable, the rustic religionists of Tennessee missed their real objective, namely, the psychological conclusions drawn from the evolution theory and from science as a whole, which are by no means impregnable.

VII

But if the scientific mind exercises a domination over our life in this way, there are other ways in which it is no less operative. As I pointed out at the beginning of this paper, the principle of determinism can theoretically be dispensed with by the scientific worker, but in practice it never is. Some form of determinism must, for his purpose, hold good everywhere, and it is an obvious commonplace that this conflicts with the subjective impression of free-will which the religious man is particularly concerned to retain. There are, it is true, philosophic methods whereby this opposition may be explained away, but logic is not psychology, and the spirit refuses to accept the pacifications of the intellect. It is clear that when determinism is the indispensable daily tool of a body of men whose mental outlook is setting the style, as it were, of the whole period, it will inevitably colour the whole period, even apart from the fact that there are always a certain number of scientific workers who think that their axioms and postulates are finally and ultimately true, and are prepared to impose these on the rest of mankind. In this way we see how the sense of sin, which at any rate used to be thought of as an essential ingredient in the relation of Man to God, is bound to suffer a subtle decay. The concept of sin has no scientific meaning, for the words right and wrong have no scientific meaning, and actions can only be scientifically judged on the biological basis of material injury or benefit done to the society of individuals within which the action takes place. Sin has to be regarded as an inferior term for an anti-social action, and the person who sins cannot be regarded as responsible, for his action is the joint product of his genetic constitution, and the environment of his developing years.

Moreover the scientific outlook, pressing further than this, involves the notion of legal responsibility, and it is difficult to see with what justice any man can be condemned to punishment for whatever action, if we regard all his deeds as irrevocably determined, and dependent, in the last resort, on the chain of causes going back without a break to the creation of the world. Scientifically speaking, there can be no such thing as personal responsibility, and all that can be done is to disembarrass society from its undesirable elements by killing them off. Let us note that this was the course adopted both by the French Revolution and by the Russian Revolution, and let us note that both these upheavals were distinctly under the influence of the scientific view of the world.

On the other hand, it is a curious paradox that when scientific determinism is not dictating a wholesale abolition of one group of persons by another more powerful group, it throws its influence wholly on the side of mercy, mitigating the rigours of a justice based on theology or idealistic philosophy. When scientific determinism saps the strength of legal responsibility, it gives the criminal the benefit of all the doubts, and in the United States, where these tendencies have gone further than in Europe, it often affects the decisions of the courts. 'The tribunal that condemns to death once in 7 years is a murderous tribunal. Rabbi Eliezer ben Azaria said "If it condemn once in 70 years." Rabbi Akiba and Rabbi Tarfon said "If we were members of the court no man would ever be condemned to death." ' This quotation from the Jewish Talmud[12] (first century AD) embodies what is often the attitude of the scientific worker to justice. Once again the influence of the scientific mind, spreading imperceptibly throughout our time, finds itself in opposition to religion, and here we may perhaps be glad that it is so. 'It must needs be that offences come,' but the scientific spirit does not always add 'woe to him by whom the offence cometh.'

VIII

In this light we see the scientific mind as particularly beneficent and merciful, and it is most interesting to remember that in its origin science was regarded as specifically conferring *peace of mind*. Early Greek science, about the fourth or fifth century BC, differed from later Western science in that it was not experimental, but contented itself with speculations of a scientific character concerning natural things. These speculations were recommended to men on the ground that they conferred 'peace of mind,' rescuing them from the belief in gods or demons, ranging from divine and splendid beings who rode upon the planets in their celestial journeys, to the small deities of wayside spring or forest tree, benevolent enough for the most part, but liable to spring out and kill you if you forgot to propitiate them with the customary rites. Thus Epicurus, writing a summary of his scientific opinions to a friend,[13] said, 'Some of those on the way to being perfected can obtain from this summary a hasty view of the most important matters without personal instruction *so as to secure peace of mind*'. Epicurus was far from denying that the gods existed, but he maintained that they were removed from human affairs, far above the concerns of men. This comes out delightfully in another passage where he says, 'The regularity of the periods of the heavenly bodies must be understood in the same way as such regularity is seen in some of the events that happen on earth. And do not on any account allow the divine nature to be introduced at any point into these discussions, but let it be preserved free from burdensome duties, and in entire blessedness. For if this principle is not observed the whole discussion of causes in celestial phenomena is vain.' This polite but very definite statement shows how, even at that early time, Epicurus realised that the provinces of science and religion cannot be mixed, but must be kept most sharply separate. Peace of mind was to be attained by reflecting on the natural construction of the world, the ceaseless interplay of atoms, and by realising the through-and-through naturalness of all that goes on around us. I care nothing, the Epicurean might have said, if I am killed tomorrow in some catastrophe, I thank the gods from afar for the pleasures I have enjoyed in my life, for the love of my friends, and for the work that I have been permitted to do; and I snap my fingers at the brutish forces of the world, for I understand their inner nature, and by knowing what the world is made of and what the atoms do, I am superior to it, and the despiser of them. This peace of mind is essentially congenial to the scientific consciousness, and has genuinely upheld an untold multitude of persons from the time of Epicurus onwards. Its greatest expression occurs, of course, in the poem of Lucretius, *De Rerum Natura,* on 'The Nature of Things.'[14]

Very little insight is required, however, to see that it is not the same thing as the 'peace that passeth all understanding.' It is, indeed, neither better nor worse, but profoundly different. For the Epicurean or scientific attitude implies a position of defiance towards the universe, a total lack of reverence, a complete absence of awe, although these are precisely the qualities which are indispensable for the religious position. The religious position, as Schleiermacher said,[15] is one in which the individual is conscious of, and fully recognises his dependence upon, a superhuman Power, which may be an impersonal force as in emergent evolutionism, a personal will as in Christian theology, or the universe as a whole, the One, as in Neoplatonism. Such a subjection of the individual person, without which there can be no sense of the holy, is obviously quite inconsistent with the scientific state of mind. 'Religion without awe' as Kohnstamm says,[16] 'is a contradiction in terms.' Yet if it was possible for Epicurus and his followers to stand in no awe of the universe, how much more possible is it for the scientific worker of our own time, with a vast succession of practical and theoretical triumphs behind him. In Kohnstamm's words, 'The more the conviction prevails that human power can control the universe, or even a small part of it, the more we get an attitude in which awe and reverence would be absurd, as the materialistic systems of the past two centuries illustrate. And it is, of course, impossible to change this attitude by pure theoretical reasoning, for it is considered as a truth *a priori* that no argumentation is valid which would undermine this subjective conviction.' It was all very well for Goethe[17] to say that all social and moral conduct finds its root in a threefold reverence for that which is below man (the infra-human organic and inorganic world), that which is on the same level as man (our neighbour), and that which is above man (the spiritual world). But the very fibre of the scientific mind runs in a direction contrary to reverence. In the pursuit of that abstraction which we call scientific truth, we have to be prepared to subject anything to accurate investigation according to the rules of the game, and each generation in turn is shocked by the savage violence of the scientific mind, dragging out into the light one hidden thing after another. In the Middle Ages the investigation of inorganic nature was invested continually with an unholy glamour, and even as late as the dissolution of the monasteries by Henry VIII, acquaintance with alchemy was likely to be an added indictment against some unlucky Prior. In the last century biology in general occupied the same place, and at the present time psychology comes in for a great deal of suspicion.

Here, perhaps, we have the most striking of the ways in which the scientific outlook exercises an influence throughout our time, antagonistic to that of religion. It must be frankly admitted that the sense of the holy cannot flourish in the atmosphere of defiance, power, irreverence, and impiety, which science quite legitimately has to cultivate. Those who have in any degree experienced both the Epicurean peace and the Christian peace are well aware that in passing from the laboratory to the holy place, or vice versa, a spiritual transformation has to occur, even sometimes to a painful extent, as if a skin had to be thrown off and a new one grown. And just as scientific determinism inevitably leads to the decay of the sense of personal responsibility, so the Epicurean or scientific attitude of independence of divine power makes the cultivation of the sense of the holy more and more difficult in our time. Epicurus was not misjudged by subsequent centuries when they set him down as an atheist, for his gods, in spite of his insistence on their reality, are no more than words, lingering on in the empyrean for ornamental reasons.

IX

What can religion do in the midst of all this? In what has gone before I have tried to define some of the ways in which a civilisation dominated by science attacks the life of religion. I am not deceived by the interest in religion which has marked the opening years of the present century, for I believe it to be a wholly temporary and minor phenomenon. The 'emptiness of the churches,' about which we hear so much, is attributed by some to the antiquated formulae which persist in the liturgy, and by others to the widespread ugliness which the naturally conservative religious mind permits to envelop its houses. But though all this may be true, there are deeper reasons for the decline of religion, and the lowest depth has not yet by any means been reached.

Considerations of this kind lead conveniently to a historical discussion. Some people have very strange ideas about history, and this is not surprising in view of the appalling methods of teaching it which have long been in use in this country. Some people suppose that history is little more than an arbitrary series of the names of kings, together with an acquaintance with the battles and wars which have disfigured the past of every nation. Others, taking a wider view, regard history as the narrative of a continuous progress, starting with primitive man, going on to the early civilisations of Assyria, Crete, and Egypt, and so reaching our own time by way of the so-called 'dark' ages. Each civilisation, it is thought, represented a stage on a continuously rising scale, so that if we were to pass backwards in time we should observe steadily increasing degrees of barbarism. But there is a much truer view of history than this, namely, that each civilisation has had its period of youth, its flowering-time, its senility, and its virtual death. Looking at the facts in this way, we can draw a remarkable parallel between the history of classical antiquity from the earliest Greek days to the fall of the Roman empire, and our own Western civilisation from that time onwards. Let me put it briefly.

It seems that the present dominance of science over our lives is a phenomenon something very like which has occurred before, namely, in the Hellenistic Age, the period from about 200 BC to AD 300. That was the time when the great scientific schools of the ancient world, such as Alexandria, were in their prime, and if the science of classical antiquity did not issue out in the command of Nature which we have today, it was only because of its incurably speculative character, and because certain special factors, such as the prevalence of slavery, discouraged that desire to save labour, which is the mother of invention. By the time that Alexandrian science was at its height, what we might call the Classical 'middle ages' were quite over, the great religious period had gone, and the Gods of Olympus had faded into the purely honorary position to

which Epicureanism and Stoicism alike consigned them. So it is
with us. Our religious period has gone, and gone for good. The
Christian middle ages can never return, and we may as well make
up our minds to admit it. To build cathedrals is not the fundamental urge of modern men, but why should the religious mind
complain? It had its high summer, when it decided what the very
aspect of European towns and cities should be like; it had its hey-
day, when it dominated the thoughts and actions of Western men,
just as science dominates them now. It dictated the forms of their
function to philosopher and scientific man alike, it crushed without remorse every opposing factor, it saw to it that the Epicureans
held their tongues. It moulded into its own kind of beauty nearly
all the poetic upspringing of the time, and knew how to use for its
own ends every grain of artistic genius that the age produced.
How precious to us now are those scraps of secular feeling that
have come through to us from the Middle Ages: the *Summer is i-
cumen in* of Brother John Fornsete of Reading Abbey, the song
about Henry of Agincourt, the poems of the wandering scholars,
the aubades of the Provençal troubadours. I am not undervaluing
the magnificent treasures of poetry and art which the medieval
Church has left us, I am simply remembering the domination
which it then exercised, and which it will never exercise again.
For the religious age of Western man will not recur.

X

Why then, one may say, not slide with the current of history, why
not abandon ourselves entirely to the domination of the scientific
consciousness and give up our efforts, so hard and costing, to
maintain religion in an irreligious age? There are two reasons why
not, one concerning the group and the other concerning the individual. The tyranny of one form of experience over the others in
any given age can only be softened by the unyielding witness of
those few persons who are not overborne by the prevalent spirit.
In most cases these persons, perhaps fundamentally of more value
to their age than the greater men who swim with the tide, never
leave any memory behind them, but sometimes they gain a perpetual prominence, and then we say of them, as of Leonardo da
Vinci, that they were born 'out of due time' or 'in the wrong
century.' But this is not so.

If now, as individuals, we give up religion, we hand ourselves over like passive logs to the flood-waters of history, and transform ourselves into fundamentally one-sided creatures. And our deepest self realises that man was not born to throw away his several powers, man was not born to be hypertrophied in one special direction. In the Middle Ages men 'made themselves eunuchs for the kingdom of heaven's sake,' and in the future the same invitation will be extended to us to suppress our sense of the holy, to stamp it out, and to confront defiantly a world denuded of awe and of mystery. Such a deicide will be a homicide too. The best man is the man who is friendly to, even if he himself cannot enter into, each one of the great forms of human experience, and the worst man is the man who is willing and desirous of throwing all but one form of experience on to the scrap-heap. But it is not as if fanatical men of religion were the danger in the Middle Ages, it is not as if fanatical men of science were the danger now; it is rather that in any given period the dominant form of experience subtly interpenetrates the whole of life, insinuating itself into logic, introducing its own concepts into practical affairs, and colouring the whole situation with its own particular tint. This is why it seems to me that it is now more necessary than ever before to participate actively in religious rites, and to maintain firmly the fundamental validity of the religious experience as a characteristic activity of the human spirit.

'To argue in this way,' wrote Lenin in a letter,[18] 'is to admit the basic principle of priesthood.' He was perfectly right, and there is no reason for denying that once this admission is made organised religion follows automatically. But the mention of Lenin brings up the interesting question, which I raised before, whether Russian communism is really as anti-religious as it seems. We hear a great deal about the "Godless League" and similar theatrical exhibitions, but it may very well be that what is being destroyed in Russia is the traditional orthodox form of Christianity, and not religion itself. For, as a recent writer in the *Hibbert Journal*[19] has pointed out, there are indications that some forms of communism, at any rate, may be held in a manner which strikingly approximates to a religion. We must frankly face the fact that throughout the world today, a persecution of communists is going on which is patently reminiscent of the first Christians. The first Christians refused to sacrifice and pay the proper honours to the divine Emperor, and it was almost entirely for political reasons of this kind that they came into conflict with the Roman police. Theologically there was no reason why they should not believe whatever they wished, and they were, in fact, regarded as an unimportant sect of Jews, as far as that was concerned. If, then, a new religion is coming into being in Russia, we have an extraordinary example of mysticism breaking through the cracks, as it were, of millenarianism. Although communism as a political programme concentrated its interest on the distribution of wealth and the benefits of wealth in this world, communism as a religion must be building itself on that profound sympathy of one worker for another, that 'love of a man for his mate,' which plays so much larger a part in everyday life than outside observers are usually willing to concede to it. Perhaps the sense of awe and reverence which, as we have seen, is inseparable from religious experience because it is the typically religious reaction to that which is felt as utterly other than, and superior to, the individual, may be turning itself upon the community of human workers as a whole, in which case the conclusions of the Cambridge philosopher, M'Taggart,[20] would come to an extraordinary fruition. For M'Taggart, though technically an atheist, and advocating a philosophy which dispensed with the idea of God in the traditional sense, spoke of the universe as being made up of finite souls bound together by love. Of one thing we may be certain, religion will never die, although the form of it which is so familiar to our eyes may very well do so: 'The foundations of the Lord's City are strong, they shall never be moved.'

To draw together the threads of this paper, it may be said that probably religion as a whole, and certainly the Christian religion, is in for a bad time during the next four or five centuries. We are still in a transitional period, so that science is not so dominant over our lives now as religion was in the Middle Ages, but a kind of inverted middle ages is almost certain to come. These things are rooted in the constitution of the world, and we cannot escape them, but we can keep before ourselves continually the conception of the harmonious man, the man to whom science and religion, though always antagonistic, are equally necessary methods of attaining contact with what lies at the core of the world. To such a man history has no terrors, but he will always have to run counter to the age in which he lives, if not in one respect, then in another. He may not be honoured in his generation, but having seen and considered the parts of human nature, he stands as the only guardian of its wholeness.

As usual, we find the seventeenth century a period of profound interest with regard to these conflicts. And that remarkable man, Sir Thomas Browne, though commonly remembered simply as a master of English prose, was a figure of much greater importance than this. He occupies a position in the history of biology which has been considerably underrated; he was one of the first investigators in England to study the systematics of birds, and in his laboratory at Norwich the first experiments on chemical embryology were carried out. But while thus taking part in the foundation of exact biology he remained at one and the same time a person of real piety and a literary artist of the very first class. He is therefore of particular interest to us as a perfect example of harmonious interior life.

'The great question[21] of the seventeenth century, which controls the undulations of Montaigne and the impatient optimism of Bacon, which fires Donne to despair and smoulders in the humorous melancholy of Burton, which is at the root of Browne's *Vulgar Errors*, and throbs in the most exalted musings of his *Religio Medici*, this question is the disputed extent of human ignorance and human knowledge. How much do we really know? How much can we ever know? And when these questions had been answered, if they were answerable, how were we to comport ourselves accordingly and patch up a truce with faith? Very different answers were given, and very different conclusions were drawn from them as to our consequent behaviour. But on one point there was a fairly general agreement—that we knew for certain extraordinarily little. It had been a shock to discover just how little.

'It had been supposed, for example, for a millennium and a half that the earth was the stationary centre of a finite universe, and that the sun went round it. It was now asserted, and indeed proved—though the majority of thinking men, with Francis Bacon and Thomas Browne amongst them, refused to be convinced—that the earth was not the centre of a finite universe, but only one among innumerable revolving bodies in a vast immensity of space; nor was it stationary, but revolved about the sun. We can but dimly imagine the shock of these assertions, of this terrestrial dethronement, to learned and devout men; for the "new

philosophy" hit both learning and religion. It was the pride of the
Catholic middle ages to have forged into one system the
Ptolemaic and Christian universe, and so compactly riveted them
together that one, it seemed, could hardly fall without the other.
It was a wedding, as tight and fast as a learned Church could
make it, of science and religion. We cannot wonder, then, that
Copernicus, the Polish Canon, concealed his discovery of the
revolutions of the heavenly bodies until the year of his death, and
only published by entreaty, in 1543, what he had discovered
thirty-five years before; or that his successor, Galileo, continued
to teach the old errors from his chair in Padua, and delayed his
revelations until the appearance of a new star, in the year 1604,
set all the heads of Europe shaking, and supplied him with a
text.

'It was a great event, that star. You find it in Bacon, in
Donne, in Burton, in Browne, in Jonson; everyone talked of it,
and drew, or shrank from drawing, his own conclusions from it. It
was not, indeed, the first occurrence of the kind. Early in that
same generation, in 1572, when Bacon was a Cambridge fresh-
man, a new star had appeared, as bright as Jupiter, and then had
incontinently gone out. It was hoped that it would be the last of its
species, that Nature would recollect herself and relapse into her
preordained decorum. But here, within a single generation, was
another! It may be asked by a modern reader, why all this fuss?
They should have been interested and pleased. They were
certainly interested. For by these two extravagances of Nature
another cherished belief had been upset. It was an axiom of the
Christian astronomical theology, and had been an axiom for
centuries, that the Firmament is Unchangeable and Incorrupt-
ible; and here were these very heavens suddenly lighting up, and
presently extinguishing, in the very region of the Immutable, one
new star after another, protesting by signs and wonders against a
cardinal doctrine of the old natural philosophy, which was also,
by incorporation, a doctrine of the Christian Church. Can it be
wondered that on these, as on other grounds, some men turned
sceptics? How do we know that we know anything? Or that some
had already turned reformers of method, like Bacon? For clearly,
if real knowledge be possible (and he fervently believed that it
was), the true method had not been found. Or that others, like
Burton, turned amused and melancholy spectators, watching men
"run, ride, turmoil, and macerate themselves" for what?, he,

meanwhile, "laughing at all,'', but with a smile a little twisted?
Or that yet others, such as John Donne, turned revilers of the
world, bitterly disillusioned to find their science thrown away,
and all the proud interpretations of man, together with that
magnificent centrality of his, crumbling, perhaps, into words and
fable? Thus he wrote:[22]

> The New Philosophy calls all in doubt,
> The Element of Fire is quite put out;
> The sun is lost, and th' Earth, and no man's wit
> Can well direct him where to look for it.
> And freely men confess that this world's spent,
> When in the Planets, and the Firmament
> They seeke so many new; they see that this
> Is crumbled out againe to his Atomies.

Donne turns with contempt from a declining world to the pitiful
spectacle of human impotence:

> In this low forme, poor soule, what wilt thou doe?
> When wilt thou shake off this Pedantery,
> Of being taught by sense, and Fantasie?
> Thou look'st through spectacles; small things seeme great
> Below; but up into the watch-towre get,
> And see all things despoyl'd of fallacies;
> Thou shalt not peepe through lattices of eyes,
> Nor heare through Labyrinths of eares, nor learne
> By circuit, or collection to discerne.
> In heav'n thou straight know'st all, concerning it,
> And what concerns it not, shalt straight forget.

The despairs of great poets are never valueless; but Donne, the
anti-Baconian, parts company here from the best hopes and
prospects of his century, and shows himself the inferior of the
Norwich doctor, not only in the science of this world, but in the
wisdom of the next.

Montaigne was as idle as Donne was hasty, dissatisfied, and
despairing. 'Go easy,' says the Frenchman; 'though nothing is
certain, there is always the art of life; as for man being the motive
of the universe, if you pursue that fanaticism you must expect
despair; just listen for a moment to my goose:

'Why should not a goose say, "Every part of the Universe is

made for me; the earth is for me to walk upon, the sun lights me, the stars shed their influences upon me, I find such conveniences in the wind, such others in the water, the vault of heaven regards nothing so favourably as me. Indeed, I am the darling of Nature. Does not man keep me, lodge me, serve me; does he not sow and grind for me? And if he eats me, he eats his fellow-men as well, and I eat the worms which eat him".'

'Browne was quite at home with such irony; his distinction was that he combined it with an undamaged religious temper, *and* with the new courage of the Baconians and experimental science. Alone of all the men who have been named, he was also able to join the *meditatio mortis* and the philosophy of human vanity with a cheerful, sceptical, a truly scientific and undismayed pursuit of knowledge, and to round his piety with an art of life as delicate and nicely ordered as Montaigne's.'[23]

Notes

1. See *e.g.* W. R. Thompson, *The Biological Control of Insect and Plant Pests* (London 1930).
2. J. M. Neale, *English Hymnal*, p. 597.
3. [At the time this was written, such variations on the 'harvest festival' theme were being introduced by parish clergy who relied for congregations more on gimmicks than on explanations of what liturgical religion really was.]
4. J. Needham, *Journ. Exp. Biol.*, 1927, **5**, 6.
5. In *Kangaroo* (London, 1930), p. 330.
6. H. G. Wells, *The First Men in the Moon* (London).
7. W. M. Wheeler, *Foibles of Insects and Men* (New York, 1928).
8. R. Bridges, *The Testament of Beauty* (Oxford, 1929), II, ll. 1188 ff.
9. L. Hyde, *The Learned Knife* (London, 1928), pp. 71 ff.
10. R. L. Stevenson, *Records of a Family of Engineers* (London, 1912), p. 82.
11. By J. M. Fletcher of Tulane University, New Orleans, *Hibbert Journal*, 1931, **29**, 239.
12. Quoted by L. Lewisohn, *Mid-Channel* (New York 1929).
13. See C. Bailey, *The Extant Remains of Epicurus* (Oxford, 1926).
14. Many English translations exist, *e.g.*, that of W. E. Leonard (London, 1916).
15. F. Schleiermacher, *Reden ü. d. Religion*, 1799 (Göttingen, 1906); also *Der Christliche Glaube*, 1821 (1884).
16. P. Kohnstamm, *Proc. VIIth International Philosophical Congress*, Oxford, 1930.
17. In his *Wilhelm Meister* (die pädagogische Provinz).
18. V. I. Lenin, quoted by V. Marcu, *Lenin* (London, 1928).
19. Anonymous contributor, *Hibbert Journal*, 1930, **28**, 385.
20. J. E. M'Taggart, *Some Dogmas of Religion* (London, 1906).
21. In delivering the lectures I ventured to quote this and the following paragraphs from a brilliant but anonymous essay on Sir Thomas Browne, in the *Times Lit. Supp.*, 1928, No. 1373.

22. In *An Anatomie of the World*, 1611.
23. Sir T. Browne's writings have been published three times in collected form, by S. Wilkin (London, 1836), by C. Sayle (London, 1904), and best by G. Keynes (London, 1928).

3

The Limitations of
Optick Glasses

SOME OBSERVATIONS ON SCIENCE AND RELIGION

(1927)

*To my discourse about the Dioptrick Tubes, the Telescope and
Microscope, the Reverend Disputer replied—that our glasses
were all deceitful and fallacious.* Crosse of Chew Magna in
JOSEPH GLANVILL'S *Plus Ultra*, 1688.

I

Probably everyone would admit that to deal properly with the
intellectual contrast between Victorian days and our own many
large volumes would be necessary. A beginning has already been
made by Robert Murray, but he concerned himself with a theme
which was wider in time than the nineteenth century, and only
dug in that ground to unearth illustrations for it. There seems to
be no book which deals with all the Victorian manners of thought
in relation to those of other times. Here will be found only the
slightest sketch contributory to such a work. But there is one
mental turn which I specially want to discuss, for it seems to me to
have been highly characteristic of the mind of the nineteenth
century. I mean the clear-cut distinctions, the final definitions,
and the vehement simple antagonisms in which that period
delighted.

It is very likely that there are many other characteristic traits of
the time, tacit orientations of thought which could by a skilful
draughtsman be well contrasted with our own more complex
features; but perhaps no one of them could be thought more
fundamental than the one in question. In the nineteenth century
one either was, or was not, on the side of the angels; there was no

possible middle course, and the individual battle-front, like a sword separating soul even from body, bisected all fields of study without exception.

It ought not to be necessary to give a multitude of illustrations of this naïve attitude, for when once stated as a characteristic of the Victorian period, it seems to me to carry conviction immediately. A little reflection serves to call up pictures of elderly clergy going about Oxford, pointing at the New Museum and alluding to it as 'the cockatrice's den.' One thinks of such bodies as the Rationalist Press Association, their headquarters humming with a missionary enthusiasm, and pennies rolling in from poor young men anxious to equip a pre-Raphaelite world with the opinions of M. Voltaire and Mr. Thomas Hobbes of Malmesbury, in the form of cheap reprints. To counter these wicked and atheistical activities other growths appear; the Catholic Truth Society arises as an equal and opposite force. It sets forth in small pamphlets of a vigorous style: 'What Science owes to Catholics' ... 'What Men of Science say about God and Religion' ... 'Modern Science and Ancient Faith.' In turn to counteract this field artillery of orthodoxy, enterprising freethinkers publish weekly journals—machine guns, to continue the metaphor—designed to carry the consolations of scientific naturalism to the home of every working man. Christian Evidence Societies compete in Hyde Park with Anti-Superstition Leagues, and 2000 people gather to listen to Father Ignatius arguing in public with Mr Charles Bradlaugh.

But all this is down among the valleys and lower passes of the hills of thought; if you go up higher, you find that just as strikingly it is believed that black is black and white is white and that the twain shall never meet. In 1863 the Archbishop of Paris, preaching in Notre Dame, spoke thus:

'In recent times some thinkers have tried to base their views as to the antiquity of the world on physical observations and researches in natural history. Particularly there have been alleged the displacement of the sea, the number and age of volcanoes, the multitude of fossils found in the earth, and the pretended incandescence of our globe. As for the erudition displayed on these matters, it is a pure loss, and can only serve to dazzle a few ignoramuses or to flatter some of our modern infidels who do but seek excuses and motives to continue in their irreligion.'

These violent opponencies and tremendous takings of sides had, of course, their amusing aspect. In 1868 a pamphlet was published in Aberdeen which may serve as typical of the time. Thus ran its title : 'Protoplasm, Powheads, and Porwiggles, and the evolution of the horse from the rhinoceros, illustrating Professor Huxley's scientific mode of getting up the Creation and upsetting Moses.' Since Huxley had just been proposed as Rector of Aberdeen University, the sub-title ran :

Advice to Electors
In choosing Lord Rectors.

The work itself consisted of humorous verses in the style of Hudibras ridiculing science as a whole and Huxley in particular. The occasion was shortly after Tyndall's address to the British Association at Belfast. 'We have recently had,' says the writer of the pamphlet, 'an abominable burst of infidelity from Mr Tyndall, at Belfast. "Protoplasm" has turned out to be a losing horse, so the game with him is now up, and Mr Tyndall has taken to driving tandem with the ribbons on "Organism" and "Environment." ' This atmosphere might be supposed to have been current in the provinces or among unintelligent people. No, Disraeli in addressing the Commons on Gladstone's Dublin University Bill, remarked : 'We live in an essentially material age, when young men prattle about protoplasm and young ladies in gilded saloons unconsciously talk atheism.' From the pulpit of the University Church in Oxford Dean Burgon thundered against the scientists, grouping them with such public dangers as Ritualism, Co-Education, and the undergraduate lodging-house system of the time. 'Infidelity,' he said in 1878, 'is very rife among us. The facts of Christianity are openly flouted, the very foundations of all Faith and Hope are openly denied by men calling themselves philosophers, and in the name of science.'

Among all the clouded issues and conflicting ideas of the struggle there is one point upon which our attention may with advantage be fixed. It is the 'all-or-none' attitude which the protagonists so clearly exhibit. Either one could be a supporter of traditional religion, or one could be a follower of science; white or black, a sheep or a goat. Superstition or atheism were the only alternatives, and though a few moderate minds might feel that so sharp a contrast of opposites could not in the nature of things be the last word, they never succeeded in making themselves articulate.

A few further quotations will make clear the mental state. We may take as representative Charles Bradlaugh's editorial in the *Investigator* for 1858: 'There is no middle ground between Theism and Atheism. The genuineness and authenticity of the Scriptures themselves are questions relative to secularism.' That is the true Victorian attitude, and in the prologue to the *Essays on Controverted Questions* Huxley wrote as follows:

'The phraseology of supernaturalism may remain on men's lips, but in practice they are naturalists. Among the watchers of the course of Thought, some view with delight, and some with horror, the recrudescence of supernaturalism which manifests itself now among us, in shapes ranging along the whole flight of steps which in this case separates the sublime from the ridiculous, from Neo-Catholicism and Inner-Light Mysticism at the top, to unclean things not worthy of mention in the same breath at the bottom. The extant forms of supernaturalism have deep roots in human nature and will undoubtedly die hard, but in these latter days they have to cope with an enemy whose full strength is only just beginning to be put out, and whose forces, gathering strength year by year, are hemming them round on every side. This enemy is Science, systematised natural knowledge, which during the last two centuries has extended those methods of investigation the worth of which is evident by daily appeal to Nature, to every region in which the supernatural has hitherto been recognised.'

Jacques Loeb, the American biochemist, only lately unhappily lost to science, remained all his life a true Victorian when he ventured outside his laboratory.

'It is well enough [he once wrote] for a romanticist to state that the domain of exact science is limited, and that he is acting as a guide outside scientific boundaries; what guarantee have we, aside from his own assurance, that his statements have any value? Why does he not prove the superiority of his intuitional method over that of the mechanist by competing with the latter in the solution of one of the more limited problems of physics or exact biology, where the correctness of the result can afterwards be ascertained by the rigorous tests to which the mechanist is accustomed.'

Such a paragraph might also have been written by the author of *The Riddle of the Universe.*

'The true revelation [said Haeckel] must be sought in Nature alone. Every intelligent man with normal brain and senses finds this true revelation in Nature on impartial study, and thus frees himself from the superstitions with which the "revelations" of religion have burdened him.'

Nothing could be clearer than the mental attitude which these quotations reveal. Let your yea be yea, and your nay nay, was a saying which the Victorians treasured up, followed out, and perhaps carried altogether to excess.

> One answer from our armies,
> One watchword through our lands,
> No dealings with Diabolus
> As long as Mansoul stands.

Only the men of imagination, the very few, such as Matthew Arnold and Thomas Carlyle, had a good word for the poor devil.

II

The changes which have come over the frontiers between science and religion have been in the last fifty years, as is generally admitted, of the greatest importance. In those days it was Geology, Zoology and Biblical Criticism which were felt to be the subjects bearing most importantly on our conceptions of science and religion. It has been pointed out by several observers that organised religion had so specially hard a time in the last century because attacks came upon it from so many quarters at once. It was indeed remarkable that within thirty years questions of the greatest import for theology and religion all sat up at once; questions which nobody had ever asked before. In the first place the comparatively new science of geology, itself founded by a Catholic bishop, Nicholas Steno, suddenly began to maintain that a universal great deluge was at any rate a great improbability. It was also very likely that the age of the earth was far greater than had previously been supposed. In themselves these shocks would have been serious enough, but to them was added before long the mass of evidence collected by the evolutionists. The fixity of species was a myth, and the principle of Natural Selection not only did away with the necessity for a Special Creation of animal forms, but also upset that detailed teleology which had been so familiar an inhabitant of the intellectual world ever since the time of the Bridgewater Treatises.[1] If geology and zoology together could show that the Book of Genesis was not literally true, then lies were inherent in God's word itself, and Absolute Truth, committed once for all to the Saints, could not be found in the Bible. Thoughtful people feared that if Genesis was criticised, the Gospels would receive the same treatment and nothing be left of the historical Christ. Indeed, it was not only the natural sciences which had remarks to make on the subject of religion, but quite new studies such as scientific Archaeology and Egyptology contributed their share of adverse criticism. In a short time biblical criticism attained very large dimensions, and so strained was the atmosphere that a mild critical work like that of Bishop Colenso drew upon itself showers of abuse. In France it was this phase of the struggle rather than any other which upset the equanimity of religious people, as may be seen in the writings of Renan and the historical work of Houtin.

This was by no means all. The predominant philosophy at the time in England was that of Herbert Spencer, a philosophy which, well-articulated and riveted firmly together in every part, seemed to issue fully armed from the brain of a master-engineer. The supporters of religion were in the position of infantrymen during the first Tank attack; they had no idea how to deal with the monster, though later on, indeed, they acquired their own tanks as, for example, Dean Mansel. Finally, it must be remembered that the leaven of the Copernican hypothesis had been working for two hundred years, and the medieval conception of man as the centre of the universe was as dead as any thought can ever be.

Moreover, the religion of the time was even fuller of internal dissensions than religion usually is. It was, perhaps unfortunately, the nature of the Church which was at the time uppermost in the minds of theologians. They were not very far away from Catholic Emancipation on the one hand and the creation of independent Roman Catholic sees in England on the other, and the most hormonic influence of all was the Tractarian controversy.[2] Surely it was very unfortunate that, just at the time when the most spiritual and mystical conception of religion would have been valuable, theologians were discussing how far anyone who subscribed to the Thirty-nine Articles might go in support of private confession, and exactly what the Ornaments Rubric could mean when it said the 'second year of King Edward the Sixth.' The Nonconformists were in as bad a way as the Church of England, for they were even more enthusiastic about the literal inspiration of the sacred writings, and they inherited a narrower Protestantism.

In due course positions of compromise and equilibrium were attained. Alfred Wallace, for example, refused till his death to believe in any evolution of Mind. Allegorical interpretations of the Book of Genesis found favour with many, and I can remember my own father telling me that if you substituted the words 'thousands of years' for the word 'day' in the creation-narrative, you could adapt it very satisfactorily to the requirements of modern geology. By 1905 the equilibrium seemed very firm, but it was not really so, because it was founded on a tacit agreement among thinking men to keep their science and their religion in separate mental compartments. This method has always had its followers; probably its greatest exemplar was Louis Pasteur. But such a proceeding lends no unity to our idea of the universe, and P. N. Waggett, in 1904, described the state of affairs as being a mutual ignorance in which scientific workers and theologians were as isolated from each other as 'the Catholic provincials and the barbaric Arians of a Frankish kingdom of the fourth century.'

Such a separation could not last. As time went on new branches of learning came to the fore in discussions about science and religion. Perhaps the most important of these was Physiology. Philosophical physiology had played comparatively little part in nineteenth-century polemics, for though Huxley, for instance, did adopt epiphenomenalism[3] as part of his general position, he said as little as he could about it and considered himself on safer ground when dealing with the evolution of animal form and the incredibility of New Testament miracles. The mechanistic theory of living matter had been held by many physiologists, Ludwig, du Bois-Reymond, and Virchow, but quite as many had adopted a distinctively vitalistic position, as, for example, von Baer, Johannes Müller and Claude Bernard. The methods of physiology and chemistry were, moreover, too crude to carry things very far in theoretical regions. 'Medicine,' Burdach had said, lecturing in 1838, 'will certainly always be able to dispense with the aid of chemistry.' But as time went on, and the methods of physics and chemistry improved, an astonish-ing transformation began to appear. Physico-chemical methods became more and more usual, and what seemed to be a new science, biochemistry, sprang into being. So surprising and so numerous were its successes that many had no hesitation in predicting the possibility of complete description of all the processes of life in a physico-chemical way. Such researches as those of Atwater and Benedict, it was held, proved the total subservience of the organism to physico-chemical laws. These workers constructed a large and exceedingly delicate calorimeter, with the aid of which they were enabled to determine the total amount of energy taken in by a living organism and the total amount put out. They found that the results exactly balanced. The law of the conservation of energy held as rigidly for the animal body as for any concatenation of purely inorganic processes. Energy cannot arise out of nothing, nor be dissipated into nothing, and to this the animal body signifies its assent by not retaining any and by not producing any.

Thus Biochemistry and Biophysics rapidly attained the position of importance which they hold at the present day. It is interesting to note that in the Fundamentalist controversy in America the mechanistic theory of life is the bone of contention rather than the theory of evolution. Closely allied to these went other tendencies, all engaged in altering the intellectual climate. If physics and chemistry were so successful when applied to the individual mechanisms of the body, why should they not be applied to the reactions of the body as a whole? In this way arose the study of Tropisms, which, initiated by Jacques Loeb, attained very rapidly great dimensions. In the higher animals these problems were attacked in a similar way. Investigators devoted themselves to the understanding of the paths in the nervous system of the higher vertebrates and greatly extended our knowledge of reflex action. It was found that the laws which govern reflex action, such as Facilitation and Fatigue, were applicable also to many actions usually thought to be intimately and causally bound up with consciousness. Nowhere in the brain could any discontinuity be observed; at no point is there a gap between the incoming afferent feeling impulse and the outgoing efferent acting impulse. The brain can be considered a mass of reflex arcs like an enormously complicated but automatic telephone exchange. All this naturally raised the question whether mental activity could really be considered of any importance to the life of the animal.

Such positions as these, if adopted, meant the acceptance of a crude epiphenomenalism, but a similar type of theory, which was not necessarily committed to that opinion, found a home in Psychology. Behaviourism maintained that it was possible to tell all that is in the mind of an organism simply by studying its behaviour when reacting with its environment. The older introspective psychology lost ground and experimental psychology flourished as never before. Then the Great War brought in masses of material which added to our knowledge of psychopathology, and out of it grew the psycho-analytic schools of Freud, Adler and Jung. The interest which in Victorian times had been given to biblical criticism now became devoted to these subjects, as is described in the last chapter of Burkitt's book *Christian Beginnings*.

But here again, just as in dealing with the Victorian period we directed our attention to one special characteristic, so also in the trend of thought since that time there is one to which special attention ought to be given—the criticism of the scientific method.

III

The earliest pragmatists took certain steps in this direction. Concerned as they were to minimise the capacity of the human intelligence to attain to truth, they pointed out that if, as the evolutionists said, man's mind had been evolved out of *Urschleim* in the struggle for existence, it could hardly be said to be adapted for such high enterprises. It had been primarily of importance in enabling him to get food, to reproduce his species, and to avoid or overcome his enemies. What a tool with which to pick the lock of the main entrance to Truth! As Flecker puts it in the play:

> Don Juan. I trusted to Reason. It was all I had.
> The Statue. It was so very little.

But a general criticism on these lines did not go deep enough nor was sufficiently detailed to induce scientific workers to lay aside the extravagant claims which they had inherited from their Victorian predecessors. Much more was coming.

The history of what came has been written in Aliotta's book,

The Idealistic Reactions against Science. Ernst Mach was, perhaps, the first of the group. He maintained that science has a biological purpose, to guide men through a maze of facts in which they would otherwise be lost. 'Mechanical laws,' he said, 'are, though still valuable modes of describing phenomena, quite fictitious; and to place the laws of physics actually in external nature is to hypostatise an abstraction of purely human origin.' Boutroux and Bergson maintained that instead of taking us towards reality, the scientific method actually leads us away from it, because by its constant employment of the statistical method it omits consideration of the individual. Le Roy showed that though an isolated fact has no real existence, the scientific method proceeds by dissecting out facts from the body of reality, and since the process of choice of facts for dissection is purely mental, the scientific universe is purely a mental construct. Poincaré, to take another instance, maintained that in geometry there exist no general principles possessed of universal, self-evident and objective value in preference to all others; there are only conventions established by the mind which have been made more or less habitual, and their convenience is the only thing capable of discussion. Not very different from this point of view is that of Wilbois, who pointed out the close relationship between aesthetic experience and scientific work. Facts are selected because they fit our mind's desires, the Universe is shaped to fit our mental structure, not we to fit its plan. The process of a scientific discovery bears a strong resemblance to a work of art and is in no minor sense a work of creation.

The most recent interpretation of the scientific method on these lines is that of A. S. Eddington. Describing the terminology and methods of modern theoretical physics he points out how 'potentials' are defined in terms of 'intervals,' 'intervals' in terms of relations between pairs of events measured by a scale or clock. In turn, scales and clocks are found to be composed entirely of matter, and matter on examination turns out to be the embodiment of three measurable entities—mass, momentum and stress. These are certain analytical expressions containing various combinations of potentials. Potentials we have already defined; in fact, we have come round to our starting-point. Thus theoretical physics, the most fundamental of all the sciences, turns out to be a sort of circular construction of conceptions, each of which can only be defined in terms of the others, and all of which are dependent on mental activity. If anyone said that he knew what a clock or a scale was, at once mind would be coming in. This is well illustrated by Eddington.

'The nineteenth-century physicist [he says] knew just what he was dealing with when he used such terms as matter or atoms. The atoms were tiny billiard-balls—a crisp statement which was supposed to tell you about their nature in a way which could never be achieved for the transcendental entities of the world, such as pain, beauty, personality, or consciousness. But we know now that what physics studies is the linkage of atomic properties to other terms in the physicist's vocabulary, each depending on the other in an endless chain with the same inscrutable nature running through the whole.'

In another place he asks what it is that distinguishes the world from many other possible worlds consistent with the laws of Nature.

'Let us take two worlds [he says], A, the actual world, and B, a world which might have been. That is to say, B is ruled by the same laws of Nature but with different and differently distributed stars, planets, cities, animals. How can a physicist test (by his own resources) that when I am describing the world B I am not describing a real world. I refer to a piece of matter in the world B; it is not real, but what right has the physicist to call it unreal? It attracts every other particle of (unreal) matter according to the law of gravitation, since the usual natural laws are observed in B. With my unreal matter I construct unreal scales and clocks which measure wrong intervals between unreal points; but the physicist cannot say that they are unreal unless he has previously shown my matter to be unreal. If once we could demonstrate the unreality of any element in B the whole structure would collapse, but we cannot do this as long as we keep to the cycle because the cycle of unreal qualities is just as perfect as the cycle of real qualities. The unreal stars of B emit unreal light, which falls on unreal retinas and finally reaches unreal brains. At last there is a chance to expose the deception, for the next step takes us outside the circle. Is the brain disturbance translated into consciousness? That will prove whether the brain is real or unreal.'

The position to which we have come is not badly expressed by a reviewer of the book of essays in which Eddington's contribution appeared :

'We are no more and no less in bondage to the laws of the physical world than we are to the law that a circle cannot be drawn whose circumference is six times its diameter. We can go no further. These primary entities have been selected by the mind which has been guided in so doing by the search for something permanent, but the material universe which it perceives is in a sense an arbitrary selection from what exists. And having made its choice, the laws of Nature are the necessary consequence of that choice; they are laws which could quite conceivably have been different. The alien universe of the Victorian scientists with its iron laws has no longer any terrors for us, for we are far more responsible for them than we had ever supposed.'

Goethe wrote in *Faust* :

> By eternal laws
> Of iron ruled
> Must man fulfil
> The cycle of
> His destiny.

That is the conception we are discarding.

It is, indeed, a question whether the scientists of Victorian times would have fought as they did for the place of science in education and in public life if they had believed the somewhat pale-blooded doctrine which we are now compelled to hold. Its acceptance would have taken a good deal of the wind out of their sails. We have here another case of that unfortunate phenomenon observed first by L. P. Jacks—namely, that the universe is full of secrets which fulfil their purpose as long as they are kept secret, but which cease to do their appointed task the moment they are found out. The Hedonist is best advised not to tell his friends his secret, and William James' chess-player, once the cat is out of the bag, 'rises from the table not without addressing a few uncomplimentary remarks to his consummate antagonist.'

In any case, the entelechy[4] of the universe would seem to be well instructed in the art of staging plays, and theories, like men, possess their exits and their entrances. Order is always maintained, and only when the proper cue has come can an event in thought occur. Dramatic irony, too, that great spirit perfectly understands; and we shall note carefully how parallel with the rise of mechanistic biology has grown the criticism of the scientific method.

IV

Let us examine for a moment the changes that have taken place in religion. Tremendous works of research will be needed to detail their true history. Perhaps it can be said, however, that the emphasis has tended to shift from the Church to the individual. By this is simply meant that since the last century more interest has been taken in religious experience, the here and now of faith, and less in the historical and corporate aspect of it.

It was not only that the Tractarian movement directed attention in theology towards the Church and away from the individual, but it also affected deeply the type of piety of the time, and that among the Nonconformists as well as in the Church of England. The earlier Evangelical revival had concentrated attention on the events of the inner life, and Charles Simeon's teaching was not far removed from that of William Law. But an

'austere reticence [as Clement Webb puts it], a distrust of sentiment, a delicate reverence in speaking or even thinking of holy things, were pre-eminently characteristic of Tractarian piety. And with this went a revulsion from preoccupation with one's own feelings, even one's own experience, from *what the philosophers call subjectivity to a reliance on what is regarded as objective*, as independent of our moods and views and theories, upon historical facts, upon an authoritative ministry.'

The italics are mine, and this is a most pregnant sentence. There was, though few might at first suppose it, a strange subterranean linkage between the Tractarian and the Victorian scientific worker, for both were permeated by a strong vein of outward-lookingness. In the light of this comparison, it does not surprise us that the only theologians in Oxford who were in favour of voting the money required for the building of the great New Museums, in 1857, were the Tractarians. And old-fashioned rather Evangelical divines, like J. W. Burgon, were unconsciously acting in accordance with the deepest currents of human nature when they preached against Puseyites and Huxleyites with equal vigour.

For, each in their own way, the adherents of those two great leaders were looking outward to the world rather than inward to themselves, and the atmosphere of the other temperament was bound to be in diametrical opposition.

I have not the requisite knowledge even to sketch briefly the theological movements which have taken place since that time. But it is likely that the Anglo-Catholics of the present day differ from the Tractarians as much in their acceptance of the terminology of conversion as in anything else. An Evangelical Catholicism has grown up, and it represents, perhaps, in another mirror the change which has previously been described. More important, however, is the remarkable revival of interest in mysticism which has occurred in the last twenty-five years. To the controversialist of Tyndall's time the word 'mysticism' was an active irritant, synonymous with 'obscurantism' or 'occultism.' We have learnt much better since then, and the process of our learning can be gauged by the steady increase in the number of books on that subject which have issued from the press. Religion, like science, has made a return to a more subjective standpoint, but to one that differs from its predecessor in that St. Theresa and Julian of Norwich are studied now instead of John Bunyan. The psychologists have added their efforts to this tendency. The expression 'religious experience' itself was practically introduced by the title of William James' great book.

This little assessment of the alterations in the climate of the intellect since Victorian times is now completed. Not, indeed, complete. But there is ground for maintaining that the pre-eminent mark of the time has been a universal subjectivation of the two great fields of human experience, which were once so objective and so mutually incompatible.

v

We might now express the position by saying that science and religion have been brought together by being reduced to the same place. It seems likely that far from being, as the Victorians thought, two opposing, incompatible and mutually destructive theories of the universe, they are two states of mind, two attitudes, and there is no reason to suppose that they may not co-exist in the same person at different times. The two are, to use the familiar phrase, 'in the same boat.' Moreover, they complement and reinforce each other. As Aliotta says:

'From science and philosophy to religion, from religion to science and philosophy, this is the eternal rhythm of the process of the spirit, which rises from life to thought and returns from thought to life in a progressive enrichment, a progressive attainment of ever higher levels of reality and truth. There is a flash of mystic intuition at the roots of all philosophy, there is a philosophic exigency at the basis of all religious rapture.'

What has happened to science is that the concept of Revelation has been removed from it. For, in effect, Victorian science was definitely committed to the belief that by a sort of revelation we knew that the external world as shown to us by the scientific method was objectively real. We have already heard Haeckel on the subject. The Victorian exponent of science laughed at the religious man for believing that God's will for men descended from refulgent clouds inscribed on tablets of stone, but he was himself committed to an exactly similar belief. 'Thus there are two books,' Sir Thomas Browne had said, 'from whence I collect my Divinity; besides that written one of God, another of his servant Nature, that universal and publick Manuscript which lies expans'd unto the eyes of all.' The Victorian scientist rejected the former, but only for a like faith in the literal inspiration of the latter. A philosophy based alone on the data of science might indeed be materialistic, but only very few would now attempt to build such a structure. A greater humility has come into being and religion and science start level upon a common basis. 'We must put on one side,' says Aliotta, 'the old intellectualistic conception of Reality as a Thing in Itself, and of Truth as the correspondence of our ideas with this existence in itself.'

The subjectivity of the religious and scientific attitudes brings various considerations in its train. In the first place, it leads us to face the fact again that all men are not alike as two peas and cannot usefully be treated as though they were. The 'reasonable man' complete with all instincts, faculties and features in perfect balance is a legal fiction.

It has been Jung's great achievement to recognise this in the sphere of psychology. In his *Psychological Types* he has attempted to give preliminary rules for the individuation of minds. Now it would obviously be absurd to try to show that Jung's types of extraversion and intraversion can be crudely applied to the individuation of minds from the point of view of the scientific and the religious habits of thought. To say that a distinctively scientific mind is extraverted and a religious one introverted would be absurd and likely to be as far from the truth as are all such crude correlations. But no one can fail to be impresssed with the importance of such individual differences for all questions of thought, and it is at any rate impossible to maintain that the scientific and the religious attitudes stand outside the mental mechanisms which produce the types.

The state of affairs to which we have come, therefore, involves important corollaries. If science is in essence as subjective as is religion, there ought to be little real question of 'conflict' between them. Both are trying to express their thoughts in their own languages, tongues whose appalling inadequacy we are only now coming to recognise. Our tolerant state of mind must be based not upon an exact delimitation of boundary lines, but upon the realisation that we have to deal not with two contradictory theories of the universe, but with two states of mind, both legitimate, both inadequate, and both valuable to man. It may be in the future fewer thinkers will support extremist views and hold that one or other realm of human experience is the solitary gate into the realm of the Real.

On this view there are no limits whatever as to what may be approached by the methods of science and of religion. Nothing is in its nature incapable of treatment by either genius. What we must be careful not to do is to expect from one what the other alone can give us. It is in this way that the classical watertight-compartment attitude contained its grain of truth. But whereas many minds, like Louis Pasteur, arbitrarily divided up the universe into a part which the scientific method could tell us about, and another part which it was quite incompetent to deal with, we ought rather to think that methods are limited by their nature and not their scope. We are, after all, accustomed to forego the entertainment of smelling noises and listening to odours. Similarly, while we are inside the closed circle of the scientific method we rightly conceive of the universe as mechanistic, but when we are outside it, in other circles, we rightly adopt other views.

The recognition of the importance of the individual leads, of

D

course, to the conclusion that since no two of us are alike it is not much good expecting mystics to appreciate the universe of science, nor to hope for therapeutic effects when religious feeling is injected into the unwilling naturalist. People who are not musical are not, in polite circles, made to listen to music, yet no one, strangely enough, questions the right of the religious man and the naturalist to pray for each other's conversion. Let each rather pursue his course in peace. Yet the last interpretation that the word 'peace' should have would be a mutual ignorance and unconcern. Side by side with the spirit of tolerance there ought to go a notion of goodwill towards other experiences, which, if we cannot share ourselves, we ought to listen to with respect.

VI

It is obvious, of course, that no final problem is solved by the subjectivation of science and religion, for their relative positions as interpreters of reality to us remain matters of discussion, as do their affinities with philosophy and aesthetic feeling. Any possible combination of opinions might be adopted. Science might be regarded as possessing an end of a purely practical nature; so Nietzsche would have regarded it. With A. E. Taylor religious mysticism may be considered as capable of grasping the One, the Absolute; or with F. H. Bradley, God may be thought of as the highest conceivable entity, but not the Absolute. Aesthetic experience may be considered the profoundest or the most superficial of experiences. Philosophical speculation may be considered our only mode of dealing with the Real, and science a subsidiary matter concerned only with a part of the universe instead of the universe as a whole. Or the fundamental dichotomy may be set between ratiocination and intuition, and philosophy and science may be considered as representing the one with mystical and aesthetic experience upon the other side. Higher or lower values may be placed upon all these conceptions. But one characteristic they all have, one thing about them is always the same, their dependence for their form as well as their existence upon the minds that think them and the spirits that feel them. None of them come in from outside us, shaped already, possessing immutable self-evidence and superhuman authority; the 'optick glasses' through which we darkly see the universe, we cannot lay aside. Man has, to quote Henry More, 'no pair of spectacles made of the crystalline heaven, or of the *coelum empyreum,* to hang upon his nose for him to look through.' He must never forget that he is wearing glasses of an inferior quality.

Perhaps we shall find that neither philosophy, science, nor religion in themselves are directly in contact with what is real, but only through those moments of insight, of mystical experience, closely allied to the appreciation of the beautiful, which all three of them give us. When, like Mozart, we see in an instant of time, all the sonata of the universe circling round the point from which we started—a profound theory in science, a meditation in religion —then we may say that we are, though in the midst of time, in our eternal home.

With the Victorians, then, we may admit that science is in essence definitely 'materialistic,' but unlike them we may realise that science has no more claim to supreme authority than any other department of the activities of the human spirit. The Victorian man of science despised the 'morasses of metaphysic,' the 'superstitions of religion' and the 'quicksands of poetry.' He drew attention to the imposing universe of 'iron' laws in which he himself believed. But we have come to see that the being responsible for these metallic ordinances is neither the Creator nor blind necessity, but simply ourselves. There is, after all, no Man Friday, the 'footstep on the sands of time turns out to be our own.' The universe of science is a construction of our own imaginations; it is deterministic, but we unconsciously reject what would make it otherwise. It is orderly, but we select, out of the infinite number of facts, facts to set in order. It is rational but so are we, and we make it so.

And in order to correct the aberrations of vision which we must of necessity suffer when we employ the method of science, we ought to know how to employ other methods as well. A narrow specialism brought about the lack of understanding between scientific and religious people. In the later times of the Renaissance men knew better; Humanists flowered on every hedge. Of one of them, Pico della Mirandola, it was said that he

'believed that nothing which has ever interested living men and women can wholly lose its vitality—no language they have spoken, no oracle beside which they have hushed their voices, no dream which has ever been entertained by human minds, nothing about which they have ever expended time or zeal.'

Notes

1. [These essays appeared in 1833, the result of a bequest of £18,000 in the Earl of Bridgewater's will to support the advancement of natural theology.]
2. [The Tractarian movement arose in the 1830s with the threat of the Church of England's disestablishment. It served thereafter as a basis for the revival of Anglo-Catholicism.]
3. [A reductionist theory in which the human mind is said to be an incidental effect of brain processes.]
4. [Literally, the informing teleological spirit.]

4

Religion and the Scientific Worker

(1930)

I

If any excuse is necessary nowadays for a discussion of such a subject as this, it must simply be that some of us happen to be still interested in it. The common expressions 'reconciliation of,' 'relation between,' and worst of all 'synthesis of,' sound very distastefully in modern ears, and more nonsense must have been written under these headings than under any other two, perhaps, put together. Yet I think there are several things of value which have not yet been said, and among these the principal, as it seems to me, is an emphasis upon (a) the necessity of both forms of experience in the individual life, and (b) the difficulty of passing from one to the other. Formerly, of course, there would have been no point in emphasising such a difficulty, which was familiar to everyone, but in our day, when we are all so anxious to agree among ourselves, and so kind and accommodating to any belief, some of us tend to minimise the differences between experiences beyond what is allowable. From the uninstructed person who informs us that we are all 'seeking for the same thing' to the philosopher who can see no difference between religion, science, and philosophy except degrees of clarity and truth, the pinnacle of which is reached by the last-named discipline, all are on the wrong track, and confuse what is fundamentally disparate. Again, the demonstration that faith, for instance, is a necessary ingredient of all experience, although often supposed to bring science and religion close together, has no such effect in practice, and can hardly claim to be more than a platitude, since the concept of authority is common to both realms. All these attempts at 'reconciliation' fail because in spite of their utmost efforts the passage from one form of experience to the other remains supremely difficult in practice, as much as to say that something more deep-reaching is necessary.

Now I am not concerned, except incidentally, with the actual attitude of scientific workers to religion at the present day, for such an inquiry would only be a part of comparative religion, and would have to include the very interesting question of the impingement of natural science on the religions of the Orient as well as upon our own. Thus I am informed that in Japan Buddhism and Western scientific thought are by no means taken as antagonistic. Shintoism, which I suppose is the association of the numinous[1] feeling with a place set apart for the souls of heroes and ancestors, seems to have fitted in still better, for every laboratory has its shrine dedicated to Galileo or Pasteur, and, according to my informant, the Professor of Physiology in the University proceeds once every year, attended by his staff and research workers, to a spot sacred to what there was of soul in the numerous frogs sacrificed during the year for the increase of learning; and at this spot the appropriate ceremonies are performed, the saké is drunk, and the propitiatory prayers are said. This may or may not be called superstition; it seems to me, at any rate, an admirable myth.

I propose to deal, then, with what ought to be the attitude of the scientific worker to religion, and also, inevitably, with the converse of this question. It seems to me that the ideal attitude can be looked at from several positions, of which the three most important are (a) from outside, (b) from inside, and (c) from above.

II

The first of these is found when the scientific worker looks at religion without, as it were, leaving his laboratory, and we then get not religion, but the science of religions, in which data about other people's religious experiences at all times and places are collected, sifted, filed, and boiled down into generalisations which might eventually be susceptible of mathematical formulation. Such a science of religion cannot be too sharply distinguished from religion itself, as the example of Professor George Marsh, in

L. P. Jacks' *A Psychologist among the Saints*,[2] so vividly shows us. To know so much about the religious experience as to be incapable of having it himself was George Marsh's unhappy condition, and so it will always be for those who confuse the outer husks of theology, even if it be scientific theology, with the inner light which they surround. Nor is it fantastic to recognise that there is another side to the matter, and to admit that there may be a religious aspect of science. Can we deny a certain participation of the numinous in the state of mind of a biologist who examines, for instance, the manuscript notes of William Harvey,[3] written half in English, half in Latin, with the immortal monogram scattered here and there, marking the observations which the writer considered original? Or can we differentiate between the ethical satisfaction afforded by actions invested with religious sanction and that which the scientific worker derives from his ruthless suppression of artifacts or vitiated data, and his unceasing efforts to attain the degree of exactitude which we call scientific truth? The two forms of experience have ideas of each other, as it were, which differ considerably from the idea which each has of itself.

Precisely parallel with the relations between science and religion are those between science and history. We have had, not long ago, a remarkable instance of the confusion which may arise between these two disciplines in the work of Oswald Spengler,[4] published in this country under the name of *The Decline of the West*. Armed with a vast learning and a high degree of sympathetic insight into manners and customs alien to the European soul, Spengler took universal history for his theme, and gave us a picture of the rise and fall of civilisations, each with its youth, its middle age, and its period of senility and decay. The most primitive condition of a 'world-soul' is called by Spengler a culture; there the form of life is pastoral, the towns few, manners simple, a superstitious religion or mythology dominant, and the intellectual life sporadic or almost non-existent. Slowly the culture ripens into a civilisation; the monster cities come into existence, and the country, the haunt before of arcadian shepherds or warlike marauders, becomes widely cultivated first by free men, afterwards by slaves or mechanical appliances. As religion dwindles, science becomes predominant, for the city-soul has no use for the former and is fundamentally sceptical and cynical. And all these processes are of course immensely complicated, immensely involved, so that Spengler's book is fundamentally a dissection of history in the attempt to show this very skeleton underneath the maze of facts which dazzle at first the eye of the beholder and make him think that no structure exists at all.

Not only, according to Spengler, does history consist of the separate revolutions of the world-souls, each with its own circular structure, but the structure is the same in each case, so that any event may find its precise homologue in every one of the other cultures or civilisations. The battle of Chaeronea, for instance, in the middle age of what he calls the Apollinian world-soul, will correspond to some battle at the same stage of evolution of the Chinese or the Egyptian world-soul. The discovery of printing in the European West will correspond to the same or a very similar discovery in the history of China, and will occupy the same place, as it were, on the time-scale of a graph, each world-soul being allotted a zero hour, from which onwards they unroll in a super-imposable fashion. The second religiousness, as Spengler calls it, came at a certain point in the development of the Egyptian, Indian, Apollinian, and Mexican world-souls, and will come, he ventures to predict, at a certain point in our own (the Faustian) development. The tyrant- or emperor-period occurs, he finds, at a corresponding degree of ripeness in each cycle, and we may there-fore expect it in our own so many centuries ahead. It was not without reason that professional historians observed that this was not the kind of history they were used to. This new kind of history showed three very suspicious characteristics: first, it was nothing if not given to wide generalisations; secondly, it betrayed a lean-ing towards graphical presentations on co-ordinate diagrams, and thirdly, it ventured to predict what is going to happen. These facts should have given the game away at once; it was not history at all, but the science of history. The cultures and civilisations were as alike as two peas, or rather, not two peas, but two mathematical units, only differing from each other by virtue of their mere existence as two entities, and precisely similar to the more or less artificial units which science is always concerned with, no matter what its subject. Julius Caesar and some Chinese general, whose name we are not, unfortunately, very familiar with, were not, on this view, fundamentally different, for each played a practically identical part in his civilisation, conquering here and being defeated there, and might for all intents and purposes be regarded as a reincarnation of one and the same person, if so scientific a history were not naturally averse from speaking of another world. Now all this is no disparagement of the science of history; on the contrary, nothing could be more important for other scientific minds, such as chemists and biologists, for if the ultimate aim of scientific work is to describe the universe in one single equation, as no doubt it is, history and pre-history will have to be included, and Spengler has shown how it may be possible to bring this about.

True history is the knowledge of individual and unique events, things that only happen once, consonant with Rickert's aphorism, *Die Natur ist nur einmal da.*[5] To mould historical events into mass-produced spare parts was Spengler's great achievement, and there was no cause for surprise in the distaste which ordinary historians had for it. Yet the kind of history which will eventually be included in the world-equation will equally be, from the historian's point of view, history with most of its juice left out, and this will be a regrettable but typical case of the way one form of experience treats another. From the historical point of view what is wrong with Spengler's presentation of the facts is that he deals with a whole epoch or culture, as well as lesser units, by means of one single idea, tendency, or feature, which he regards as 'characteristic' of the entity in question, oblivious of the fact that this must involve its opposite, which was existent in a kind of subterranean antagonism all the time. This procedure enables him to shift groups of historical events about in his schemes as if they were, to use the famous phrase, scientific pointer-readings. They become atomistic, like points on a graph, and this is why the relations between different cultures are so evilly treated by the Spenglerian style, for the scientific historian is unwilling to trace more actions and reactions among the monadic world-souls than he can possibly help, inasmuch as to admit these links would be to detract from their atomistic character. There must be no continuity between Apollinian mathematics and Faustian mathematics, no influence of Egyptian architecture upon Apollinian architecture, and so on. The world-souls ripen and decay like chemical systems in separate beakers, each independent of the rest, and uniformly predictable, so that if you return after three hours you will find that so much aldehyde has been formed, or if after three centuries that socialism is giving place to imperialism. This is indeed the science of history.[6]

On the other hand, it is sure that we can have true history

applied to science, for we have many accounts of the historical development of individual sciences, and some even of science as a whole, such as the recently published work of Dampier-Whetham.[7] Here the successive discoveries and perennial effort of scientific workers are related without any attempt to generalise or to equate the individual facts with one another. This contrast between the science of history and the history of science, then, is only introduced to indicate the same kind of contrast which exists between religion looked at from the scientific worker's point of view and science numinously apprehended. On this level the scientific mind remains scientific when it considers religion, merely taking the latter as the substrate for a variation on its usual theme. It is clearly looking at religion from the outside.

III

There is more to be said for looking at it from the inside. Once inside the skin of the other form of experience, as it were, everything looks entirely different, and the attention of the soul, which before was given to certain constituents of its environment, is freed from them and fastens itself upon other very different ones. Only thus has the scientific worker some chance at last of seeing what religion meant when it said such curious, and even absurd, things about the world. It will be worth while to consider for a moment why everything looks different according to the standpoint which you have taken, and to do this we must, if we can, describe first what we may call the notes of the scientific view of the world. The first of these must undoubtedly be the preoccupation of natural science with what is *quantitative*. The primary impulse of the scientific mind is to describe *metrically* the processes of nature, and hence arises the *classificatory* frame of mind. Natural objects and natural processes have to be torn first of all from the matrix of simple sense-experience, and the facts so obtained have to be sorted into boxes according to what we are interested in at the moment, all their properties being subordinated to the one property upon which we are focusing our attention. It is often said that the word fact is a remarkably appropriate one, for it means *factum est*, something made or done, but not made or done entirely by Nature; on the contrary, made or done largely by us, and not merely collected by us. After all this, science emerges with a collection of round hard balls, capable of functioning as units in mathematical calculations and differing fundamentally from the unique events which they represent. The concept of identity is paramount in science; identical effects, it is said, follow from identical causes; get all the conditions of the experiment right, and what will happen will be what happened before. Yet all this cannot be more than mere approximation, for it is obvious enough that no experiment can ever be repeated under exactly the same conditions; everything is changing, and the experiment is surrounded by a sea of complicated swarms of events. However, experiments can be repeated well enough for science, which is another matter; there are chances in the world so small that research workers and insurance agents can neglect them, but not philosophers.

Having got the facts into a form which can be included in a table of measurements or expressed as a curve upon a graph or nomogram, the business of science can begin. The incredible richness of the so-called real or raw world which furnished the metrical data remains out of the scientific field of vision, and what it is is no part of the scientific worker's aim to decide. He can get on with his job while completely ignoring the nature of the background behind the metrical data. 'All that can come from the ultimate scientific analysis of the material world,' as Dingle says,[8] 'is a set of numbers, and the only god that science could recognise would be a *deus ex aequatione* with the character of an arbitrary constant.'

The quantitative character of the scientific method was not, of course, always so well recognised as it is today. At the very beginning of the modern phase in Western Europe, Francis Bacon, who thought that he, if anyone, knew what was wanted in natural philosophy, quite overlooked this fundamental point, and under-estimated such workers as William Harvey, whose principal argument in favour of the circulation of the blood was a quantitative one. On the other hand, their contemporary, Joachim Jungius, realised to the full the intimate association between science and mathematics, and in his *De Matheseos praestantia, dignitate, et usu,* which appeared in 1609, did not fail to point it out as the best means of advancing natural knowledge. With Robert Boyle the demand for the mathematisation of Nature came not from the logician, but from the laboratory worker, and in the *Sceptical Chymist* it was demonstrated that neither the four elements of the peripatetics nor the *tria prima* of the alchemists were suitable as hypotheses with the aid of which exact measurements could be made. The chemist, just beginning to extricate himself from the purgatory of clumsy glassware, crude furnaces, and impure reagents, turned naturally to the 'corpuscularian or mechanical hypothesis' for help in the interpretation of his exacter experiments. And by so doing he took a step of immense consequence, for the Epicurean atoms, which after the neglect of a thousand years had been re-introduced by Jungius and Gassendi, were unobservable. This employment of unobservable entities to systematise the results of observation might indeed cause no great change in scientific thought as long as the entities were easily imaginable. The Epicurean atoms were not unlike seaworn pebbles. But as time went on the unobservable entities became more and more unimaginable, corresponding to nothing in everyday experience, and proceeding from ethereal vortices to nuclei of electricity and so to quanta, divorced themselves more and more from everything save sets of figures. This is why we now find ourselves abandoning all models of physical unobservables, and likely to abandon biological models too.

It is superfluous, probably, to say that science has always a leaning towards the *mechanical* and the *deterministic*, for these concepts are so obviously involved in the scientific frame of mind. It is no coincidence that science, invention, and technical engineering are so closely intertwined in every civilisation, no coincidence that scientific workers work with their hands and that technique is one of the foundation-stones of pure science. The reciprocal motion of cranks, the thrusts of piston-rods, and the intricate stress and strain conditions of static machines are the background of the scientific worker's mind, although nothing nearly so crude may enter into his hypotheses, which may be confined to subatomic phenomena. Many a biologist is an engineer *manqué*. And if we often speak of mechanism or of causality being given up in modern science, it is only in recognition of the fact that the most fundamental laws, such as the laws of thermodynamics, are now seen to be statistical. The scientific worker no longer believes that if we knew enough about the physical world we could predict the movements of individual particles; he considers rather the odds on their movements and admits the unavoidable escape of everything individual and unique through the meshes of his net. Nor does he believe that any familiar model can be made to imitate the entities he deals with, but rather that sets of figures and equations are all he is likely to get out of the physical world. Yet nevertheless the engineer's attitude is still there, and to replace determinism by statistical determinism is to evoke no change of heart in the scientific worker. As for the causal postulate, he can give you no reason except the pragmatic one for believing in it, and will continue to assert that, for his purposes at any rate, if two crystals dissolve in solution A and only one of them in solution B, then there must have been a difference either between the two solutions or between the two crystals, and that this is correlated with the observed fact of solution on the one hand and non-solution on the other.

The *analytical* aspect of science is also very fundamental, and arises, of course, out of the qualities we have already mentioned, not merely on account of a kind of prying curiosity, but because no system can be understood until it is taken to pieces and its details, which are hidden from view in the intact whole, made observable. This necessity gets the scientific worker into great difficulties when he has to deal with units possessing a high degree of intrinsic organisation, such as living animals and plants, and at the present time our apparatus for analysis is probably much more efficient than our arrangements for synthesising in thought what we have taken to pieces. As Claude Bernard said, the physicist and the chemist are inside the organism which they are studying, namely the world, and can hardly hope to see it as a whole, but the biologist is outside the organisms which are his province, and his problem is how to attack experimentally the working of the parts without injuring the whole.[9] His hope lies, no doubt, in the rapidly increasing refinement of biological method, both technical and logical.

The world of science, then, is *orderly*, and *generalisations* can be made about it. But it has nowadays nothing in common with the world of laws of the eighteenth century, which was thought to have been set in motion by a law-giver and to be constantly administrated by his magistracy. 'It would be very singular,' said Voltaire[10] in his *Ignorant Philosopher,* 'that all Nature, all the planets, should obey eternal laws, and that there should be a little animal, five feet high, who in contempt of these laws, could act as he pleased, solely according to his caprice.' And 'Laws which never shall be broken, for their guidance he hath made,' sang the anonymous hymnographer of the Foundling Hospital in 1796;

but modern science attributes to itself the creation of the laws, and thinks of them as guiding us, not the phenomena of nature. Nothing, in fact, can be more different than legal law and natural law, whatever their origins may have been. This is why a miracle is a contradiction in terms for the scientific worker, for if persons are not in accord with legal laws, so much the worse for the persons; but if phenomena are not in accord with natural laws, so much the worse for the laws. A miracle for the scientific worker can only be a very uncommon occurrence, and the laws must be re-stated so as to cover it. No doubt in the popular mind the confusion still exists, and investigators are supposed to be gradually unearthing the tables of stone on which is written the code of laws which regulate the world. Not long ago, when I was visiting some of the cliff-dwellings in Arizona, I fell into conversation with an old man in a hut about the tall cactus plants which grew everywhere around, and, discussing their rate of growth, he remarked slowly, 'Well, the Government has just decided that sahuaro cactus plants grow half an inch a year.' I was charmed with this confusion of the Government with its botanist, of natural with legal law, and could not help speculating on what punishment would be awarded to a cactus plant which failed to come up to the minimum requirements of the legislature.

Now a law is, or should be, written plainly down, and those who love law hate mystery. Nothing is more characteristic of the scientific mind than its intense desire for clarity and rigidity, its antagonism to mysticism. It is hence profoundly incompatible with poetry, religion, metaphor, and symbol. A mystery stimulates a scientific worker to clear it up, not to worship it, and the fact that 'God moves in a mysterious way, his wonders to perform' is almost sufficient reason for his having a disrespect for the deity. Hence it comes about that scientific schemes are often what the French call *simpliste*, over-simplified, and the life of science may be said to consist largely in the proposition of an over-simplified hypothesis by one worker, followed by the discovery of previously unrealised complexities in the phenomena by a second, and the consequent abandonment of the hypothesis. This tendency to over-simplification accounts for the superiority which religion often feels as regards science, much the same as that which some old shepherd, in Collingwood's comparison, would feel for a young cocksure motor mechanic with all the outlook of the townsman. The scientific worker hates unnecessary complexity because it renders his task ever more difficult, and he casts from him therefore every unnecessary postulate. In psychology this may even be the mind itself. In biology it leads to a typical preoccupation with the limitations imposed on living creatures by the universe, rather than with their attempts to overcome the limitations. Accordingly there are often painful strains between those biologists who carry traces of philosophy and religion with them into their laboratories, and those who are careful not to do so. Thus a friend of mine confessed to me that when first he heard at a meeting the celebrated dictum of Barcroft that haemoglobin was the substance that made the mammals possible, he almost fled from the room, so nauseated was he at what he felt was a fundamental lack of comprehension of living things. What limitations they possess, he felt, are of their own making, and if the *élan vital* had felt inclined to produce mammals, it would have done so whether the haemoglobin molecule was chemically possible or not. But to the truly scientific mind the limitations have the greater attraction, and I myself have followed Barcroft's example in trying to show that uric acid was the substance that made the terrestrial oviparous animals possible. It all depends what you want, complexity or simplicity, mystery or clarity, cornucopiality or manageableness. In physics also emphasis on the limitations of nature is met with, and we believe that the reason why no atom heavier than uranium is met with on the earth is that it would be too unstable to persist.

As for the biologists, one sort accuses the other of having no feeling for the nature of life, and he retorts by saying that his friend has no conception of the scientific method or of the aim of science. But we may leave them at this stand, and remark only that the scientific mind, when it does face at last the meaning of the universe as a whole, can but assert that it has no meaning. The only gods it could recognise would be those of Epicurus, remote and unimaginable beings, who having for some obscure reason created the atoms out of nothing, were preoccupied with their own concerns and having nothing to do with us.

Its aversion from mystery, again, perhaps as much as its propensity for measurement, keeps it through and through *anti-teleological*. The purposes of the world are only part of its mystery; to the scientific mind there can be no conceivable reason why things should be as they are, except because matter is what it is, and it is absurd, as Santayana says,[11] that the form which things happen to have could be one of the causes, or even the principal cause, of their having it. The concept of purposiveness is distasteful to the scientific worker, for in the world of science it is impossible to see why anything should want to be other than what it is. Nor has anyone so far suggested a mathematical formulation for a final cause which should prove itself of any practical value in investigating Nature.

It is often said that science is *impersonal* and studiously avoids any consideration of the possible destinies of man, his fears, hopes, and premonitions of other modes of existence. It is true that the scientific worker pays no attention to any human desires, excepting only one, the desire to squeeze the universe into a few pages of print. His principal pleasure is to go about the world saying, 'O yes, this is only a special case of that,' 'this is merely an instance of such and such a rule,' 'this follows the general law of so and so, modified in an interesting way by such and such conditions.' It is a kind of wrestling with the universe; the scientific worker has a bottle beside him, and he means to get the djinn inside, and given sufficient time, he knows he will.

Whether the world would be 'worth living in' afterwards is a matter which he, quite rightly, never considers. No doubt this is the meaning of E. R. Eddison's remarkable work of imagination, *The Worm Ouroboros*,[12] in which 'after the drums and tramplings of three conquests' in an entirely imaginary geography and chronology, the cruel dynasty of Carcë is overwhelmed at last: but now there is nothing more to do, and on the very last page an unexpected miracle of miracles is performed which restores the world to its original condition and the conflicts begin again from the beginning. To emphasise the peculiar value of the activity as opposed to the end-products of that activity would be to digress too far from the present line of thought, but the existence of the 'dialectical tension of opposites' may be noted here, the existence of Carcë being necessary for the existence of her enemies, the existence of chaos in Nature being necessary for the development of scientific order.

It is certainly true that science is impersonal in this sense, and therefore also *unethical* and strictly unconcerned with all questions of moral level. It has, of course, an ethic of its own, involving honesty and unselfishness in research, but this is merely the oil upon its cams and cogwheels, without which it would not be able to function at all. Nothing irritates the scientific worker more than to hear natural events discussed ethically, for he is very suspicious of the imposition of purely human values upon non-human phenomena. 'I see and I tremble, I neither mock nor judge,' said Bishop Nigel of Ely,[13] and the scientific mind approves of this, only it does not do much trembling, regarding emotional responses as a waste of time; it sees, changes the conditions and sees again, notes the result in quantitative form, and publishes its conclusions in the appropriate journal. To such phenomena as parasitism, for example, the scientific worker does not wish to allot any ethical adjectives, for from his point of view a parasite such as a trematode or a bacillus is admirably adapted to its environment, and simply happens to be smaller than the animal on which it feeds, instead of being larger, as is more usual. And what the world finds intensely repulsive and terrifying will be to the scientific mind a 'beautiful stillborn specimen of phocomelia.'

IV

Could anything be more different from all this than the universe as seen through the eyes of the man to whom religion is the profoundest part of existence? It would be impossible to imagine any pole more diametrically removed from it. And first, with respect to *mystery*, the world to the religious state of mind is nothing if not mysterious, for to fathom its nature is as impossible as not to worship the maker of it. The religious man knows that in the last resort 'the whole creation is a mystery,' as Sir Thomas Browne said,[14] and that there is nothing logical or rational about the universe, except the logic and reason of the gods, whose ways are not our ways nor their thoughts our thoughts. Why things are as they are and not totally different is the rock upon which science perpetually splits without knowing it. 'The alogical core of the world,' in Tennant's words,[15] 'is not a residuum of haze that science, when ideally perfect, shall have dissipated,' but a fundamental property not unknowable or inexplicable, but incapable of being dealt with on any scientific basis of argument. 'The world, or the reality behind it,' he says, 'has been conceived as it must be conceived if it is to be pervious to thought, but that it must be as it is conceived to be is groundless dogma, assignable only to the pride and prejudice of the human intellect. And what is perhaps offensive to this pride and odious to this prejudice must, in the interests of psychological truth, be spoken, namely, that the demands of thought, and of what is called disinterested science or non-anthropomorphic philosophy, are dictated by human interests.' Now although one human interest forgets about the alogical core and cannot indeed function at all unless it does so forget, there are others which make it their business to remember. Nor is it surprising that religion, which realises that in the last resort everything is a mystery, should cultivate and embrace mysteries of a lesser order united organically to the *mysterium tremendum*. In these times it will be well for us to remember that the essential component of religion is mystery and mystical experience, for we are threatened on the one hand by an exsuccous deism, brought in to account for the original winding up of our so improbable universe, and on the other by a set of bloodless ethics, all that remains of the Christian religion, apparently, after the prolonged histolytic treatment which this and that movement have given it. The numinous sensation of shuddering fear and joy, the sympathetic understanding of all creation, the dark night of the soul, the supernatural sense of peace and illumination, the peculiar beneficent effect of rites, the whole range of experience, in fact, which makes up religious mysticism is what we have to deal with when we speak of religion. It is nonsense to talk about the 'dangers of modern psychology' for religion, for if psychology proposes to treat religion it can only do so like any other science, and the peculiarities of science, with its dependence upon induction, statistics, measurement and mathematics, are far too glassy to permit of its throwing stones at other people. It is a mistake, again, to under-estimate the importance of rites and liturgical observances, for they act as so many stimulants to the numinous sense, and to go about the church at Easter-time with a green bough tied to the processional cross is to invoke the most profound meditations in any beholders. Nor is it worth while to prune laboriously the words of the liturgy itself, for at the best they cannot possibly say all that they mean, and are better left untouched with their numinous associations clustering about them. How unpleasing it is, again, to see ancient ecclesiastical ornaments in museums, for they are so many triggers which can release the numinous feeling, and should be used in the purposes for which they were designed, not kept behind glass for the occasional examination of some archaeologist who is probably profoundly ignorant of the religious view of the world.

It need hardly be said, I suppose, that religion is *antagonistic to measurement,* not merely indifferent to it, hence comes that slight flavour of blasphemy which the measuring and weighing spirit has always carried with it. To weigh the mountains in a balance or to measure the heavens with a rod was deemed impossible, and a good thing too, for he that should try such operations would be derogating from the dignity of the sublime regions around and above us. Thus Greeks, Hebrews, and Egyptians alike banished their lay astronomers. And when religion thinks at all, it puts all its emphasis upon individual things, unique things, incalculable and spontaneous things, qualitative entities having no exact counterpart anywhere in the universe. It is thus wiser than science and akin to history. We cannot quite say that it is non-causal, because it remains for the most part below the argumentative level until it secretes for itself a theology and enters the syllogistic arena disguised as a philosophic theory of the world. But without doubt its favourite cause is the final cause, the divine idea of the completed process, the pulling force of the end-in-view. Nothing is so characteristic of the religious view of the world as this pre-occupation with the purposes of things; why everything should be as it is, why evil should exist, why God should have made the world, are primarily religious questions, and only afterwards become philosophical ones. The scientific worker leaves them on one side as insoluble conundrums in which he is not interested. In a polytheistic world the apparently different purposes of various natural processes were thought to be due to the wills of different gods, and monotheism was as much a scientific hypothesis as anything else, unifying phenomena and reducing purpose to one all-embracing purpose, one single inconvenient question, which science could the more easily avoid. Writers such as Aldous Huxley,[16] therefore, who counsel us to make a return to poly-theism, will encounter strong opposition from an unexpected source, namely the scientific workers, who will not wish to give up easily the ground they have won. Nevertheless, now that the scientific mind has completely disembarrassed itself of all teleo-logical questions, there would be less difficulty from this quarter and various possible arrangements might be made, such as a college of five senior gods representing the five highest forms of human experience, with about ten junior gods and goddesses representing the passions. It appears that Aldous Huxley would be prepared to consider such a pantheon.

'There is but one first cause, and four second causes of all things,' said Sir Thomas Browne,[17] 'some are without Efficient, as God, others without Matter, as Angels, some without Form, as the first matter; but every Essence, created or uncreated, hath its final cause and some positive End both of its Essence and Operation; this is the Cause I grope after in the works of Nature; on this hangs the providence of God; to raise so beauteous a structure as the World and the Creatures thereof, was but his Art; but their sundry and divided operations, with their predestinated ends, are from the Treasure of his Wisdom. In the causes, nature, and affections of the Eclipses of the Sun and Moon, there is most excellent speculation; but to profound farther, and to contemplate a reason why his providence hath so disposed and ordered their motions in that vast circle as to conjoyn and obscure each other, is a sweeter piece of Reason, and a Diviner point of Philosophy; therefore sometimes and in some things, there appears to me as much Divinity in Galen, his books *De Usu Partium,* as in Suarez, his *Metaphysicks.* Had Aristotle been as curious in the inquiry of this cause as he was of the other, he had not left behind him an imperfect piece of Philosophy but an absolute tract of Divinity.' In this wonderful passage we see as well as we could anywhere the association of teleology with piety and religion. Browne's reference to Galen is exceedingly interesting, for Galen's book *On the Uses of the Parts* occupies a central position in the history of biology. Written about AD 160, it set out to demonstrate in the course of seventeen books the value and purposive significance of every structure and function in the bodies of men and animals, and to show that being perfectly adapted to its end it could not be other in shape or nature than what it is. At the conclusion of this massive work, with all its ingenuity and labour, he wrote, 'Such then and so great being the value of the argument now completed, this final section makes it all plain and clear like a good epode, I say an epode, but not in the sense of one using enchantments,[18] but as in the melic poets whom some call lyric, there is as well as strophe and antistrophe, an epode, which so it is said, they used to sing standing before the altar as a hymn to the gods. To this, then, I compare this final section, and therefore I have called it by this name.' Now this is one of the half-dozen most striking paragraphs in the history of biology, worthy to rank with the remarks of Hippocrates on the Sacred Disease. Galen, as he wrote the words, must have thought of the altar of Dionysus in the Athenian or Pergamene theatre, made of marble and hung about with a garland, but they were equally applicable to the altar of a basilica of the Christian church with the bishop and his priests celebrating the liturgy at it. What could be more charged with significance than this? At the end of the antique epoch the biology of all the schools, Crotona, Akragas, Cos, Cnidus, Athens, Alexandria, Rome, is welded together and deposited, as it were at the entrance into the sanctuary of Christendom. It was the turning-point, in Spengler's terminology,[19] between Apollinian civilisation and Faustian culture. Galen's words are the more extraordinary, for he himself can hardly have foreseen that the long line of experimentalists which had arisen in the sixth century BC would come to an end with him. But so it was to be, and thenceforward experimental research and scientific speculation were alike to cease, except for a few stray mutations, born out of due time, until in 1453 the city of Byzantium should burst like a ripe pod, and distributing her scholars all over the West, as if by a fertilising process, bring all the fruits of the Renaissance into being.

As for Aristotle, a closer attention to teleology might have commended him more highly to the somewhat exacting piety of Sir Thomas Browne, but would have probably destroyed his position as the greatest of all biologists. Had he, on the other hand, been more of a Democritus, he equally might not have made so many great discoveries. But to quarrel with the constitution of the genius of great men, sent to us as ambassadors from the gods from time to time, is to invite calamity and confusion. If Aristotle was curious in the inquiry of the final cause it was no doubt in part because teleology is essential heuristically in science, like all the other aspects of common sense, and we may remember that William Harvey told Robert Boyle, in conversation, that he was led to certain important considerations by meditating upon the final cause of the valves in the veins.[20] But science can never give the last word to teleology. And those attractive shady places which Aristotle, guided by his genius, quickly passed through on his perpetual journeys into the hot sunlight of research and speculation, were so many traps for those who followed him. He himself knew how to change rapidly from metaphysician into physicist and back again, how to bow politely to the final cause and press on with the dissection, but the later peripatetics had no knowledge of this art, nor had the patristic doctors, nor the medieval

Aristotelians, who all remained, sleeping quietly, in the shade of the will of God. But although Aristotle knew very well from the sea (to come to Bacon's metaphor at last) the look of the Circe country of teleology, he never visited it for a long time, being an authentic Odysseus, unlike so many later heads, who, following the example of Plato, 'anchored upon that shore,' and, dropping their hooks to the sound of plainsong, there rode, never to hoist sail again.

Our assessment of the religious view of the world must not omit to say that, in direct opposition to science, it finds the *complexity* and cornucopiality of untouched nature highly congenial to it. The innumerable hosts of angels, the cohorts of the fathers, the cloud of witnesses, all exemplify this characteristic, and in religions other than our own the fertility of pious spirits has peopled heaven with gods, heroes, and saints. And not content with reproducing their kind in the ordinary way, these hordes of holy ones, especially in China and India, have budded in all directions with superfluous limbs. How the Mexican mystics, for example, must have revelled in complexity, vying with the untouched jungle itself in their creation of monstrous forms, each bristling with symbolism and requiring endless expositions. The richness of imagination seems always to accompany the sense of the holy and to be utterly alien from the austere realm of the scientific spirit, which is continually subsuming one thing under something else, and arranging the myriad phenomena of Nature in hierarchies of importance and laws of ascending generality. It is in this way that religion is akin to art, and especially to poetry, being profoundly *non-analytical* and *concrete*, content to accept objects and events as they come and caring nothing about their relations with other preceding or succeeding events.

v

After all this commentary it is not hard to understand why the difficulty of passing from religious experience to scientific experience and back again is enough to deter most of us from ever leaving the realm where we happen to be most at home. Some people try to persuade us that our difficulties here are purely logical and that a little clear thought will quite remove them. This introduces the third way of regarding the attitude of the scientific worker to religion, *i.e.* from above, from a region in which philosophy is being so good as to turn its attention to our difficulties, and to resolve the thesis of religion and the antithesis of science into a higher synthesis. In this manner we come to the conception of the spiritual life of man as constructed on the plan of a cathedral in which the high altar is dedicated to metaphysics and one each of the side-chapels to art, religion, science and history. These side-chapels, though beautiful enough in themselves, are nothing but forms of error, by which a large proportion of us is permanently retained, leaving only a minority to pass on up the chancel-steps into the presence of a truth as true as we are ever likely to know. I should not like to call such a metaphor an unsuitable one, for I think it is fairly well chosen, but the difficulty is that although we ought to be able to pass readily from one form of error to another, this is not in actual fact our experience. Thus we may say that science attends solely to the metrical aspects of the universe, and neglects both the alogicality and individuality in it; we may say that history neglects the former and attends to the latter, and we may say that religion resembles history rather than science, but has no intellectual business to do, and is concerned with the sense of the holy just as art is concerned with the appreciation of the beautiful. But all this is so true that it is not very interesting, and even when we have got everything straight in this way and sorted, as it were, into box-files, the practical questions remain as acute as before. We may know that no opposition exists anywhere, and may firmly believe in this philosophic faith, but we find it as difficult as ever to take off the armour of faith and put on our laboratory overalls.

Doubtless this arises from the fact that all our forms of experience are surrounded by fringes, as it were, views of the world which grew out of them and are practically inseparable from them. The philosophical procedure is to shear them off, to throw them away, and to reduce our forms of experience to their lowest level, their minimum claims, after which, a howling wilderness having been made, peace is proclaimed and the metaphysicians go off to their own place. In this way a properly cemented, external, formal synthesis of all contradictions may be possible, but only at the cost of sacrificing the frame of mind proper to each kind of experience, together with the fringe which it has secreted round itself as it gradually rose up out of the unformed primitive potentialities of man's spirit. It may be possible, and in a sense correct, to sacrifice these frames of mind, but is it politic? Do they not represent the very creators of the experiences themselves, and could anyone whose mind was tidied up in the manner proposed ever get anything done, thought, or felt in any of the realms at all? It is more likely that we shall do better to accept, for instance, a sort of materialism inherent in the scientific mind, rather than strip it remorselessly of its favourite errors and demonstrate how weak it fundamentally is. We shall do better to follow each road out to its farthest end, and to accept the Lucretian estimate of the world in the laboratory as well as that of St Augustine or St Teresa at other moments and in other places. All alike are partially false, none means exactly what it says, save only that of philosophy, which, unfortunately, can say practically nothing. The histologist who looked up from his microscope and remarked that he was thinking God's thoughts after him, is a ridiculous figure; nothing could be more irrelevant than divinity to a microscope or a serial section. Cohesion and coherence seem to involve inevitably attrition and erosion; why should we not, then, dispense with them? Who wants coherence? It is flatly impossible to give a coherent account of the universe which shall include what all the forms of experience have to say about it; such an account can only be given by philosophy, which sets about its task by blithely destroying everything which the rest had said, and Aldous Huxley was perfectly right to bring back to our memory the lines of William Blake:

> Do what you will, this life's a fiction
> And is made up of contradiction.

This is what is meant when people occasionally protest that only one fiction should be allowed to hold the floor at the same time. The kind of synthesis which is implicit in the words of Sir Thomas Browne,[21] 'Those that hold that all things are governed by chance, had not erred had they not persisted there,' though almost made palatable by his lovely cadences, is yet fundamentally nauseous, and all his jam cannot diguise his pill. For to say that the will of the gods is operating through and by the means of the laws of chance, is to satisfy nobody; it offends the religious spirit who is not interested in the means so long as the end is worshipful, and it offends the scientific spirit who is not willing to admit the right of any divinities to interfere with the machinery of the world. Thus there is no logical opposition necessarily here, but a vivid psychological one, not to be overcome by any mediator, even though he knew what song the sirens sang and could wring delight from gardens of symmetrical vegetables. 'The prime intellectual difficulty of our age,' it has been said,[22] 'is that true beliefs may make it impossible to act rightly; that we cannot think without verbal fictions; that they must not be taken for true belief, and yet must be taken seriously; that is essential to analyse beauty; essential to accept it unanalysed; essential to belive that the universe is deterministic; essential to act as if it were not.'

In still more practical fields these oppositions are met with again. The other-worldliness of the religious mind, which occurs univerally in persons intimate with the numinous, and arises directly out of the ethical and individual character of that experience, tends to scorn the happenings of this life, for its treasure is elsewhere. By explaining the alogical core of the world in a teleological manner and describing the universe as a school for reasonable souls, it proves itself superior to science, but in so doing it comes up against the social reformer, who is not as much interested in the other world as he is in this. It is probable that this attribute will bring about the death of organised religion in the West within the next two or three centuries, for millenarianism is likely to sweep all before it, and will perhaps produce a maximum population of contented bodies inhabited by discontented souls. We have not nearly finished yet with the domination of science over everyday life and thought, and it will probably go a great deal further before the wheels come full circle once again and the altars of the gods are lit up once more.

We may admit, then, that the synthesis of experiences is not at all desirable, for the scientific view of the world, for instance, satisfies finally certain types of mind, and also more balanced minds in some types of moment. Our problem is, in fact, to stimulate, if we can, the production of these balanced minds, minds which can summon up at intervals not too widely spaced the spiritual energy to cross and recross the boundaries of thought, greeting their friends in the realm of science and being at home in Syon. It is evidently owing to these oppositions that we have the possibility of constructing character and personality. Here the Greek view of education assists us, for, as Lowes Dickinson says,[23] 'Virtue in their conception was not a hard conformity to a law felt as alien to the natural character; it was the free expression of a beautiful and harmonius soul. Character, in the Greek view, is a certain proportion of the various elements of the soul, and the right character is the right proportion.' This is the clue to what I have already referred to as the necessity for the two forms of experience. Ultimately the question seems to be an ethical one, for the best human community, as I see it, would be that which possessed the largest number of harmonious souls within it, the fewest fanatical ascetics, the fewest hide-bound, hard-boiled, scientific minds, the fewest aesthetes cultivating art for art's sake, and perhaps, but I am not sure of this, the largest number of philosophers. At the same time it would be a mistake to do violence to natural temperaments, for some seem to be naturally framed and constituted wholly in one direction, and however we hold up our harmonious ideal, the infant saints will continue to pursue their lop-sided aim. Lop-sided, I repeat, even although we recognise, as we must, that without this lack of harmony some of the most forceful beings would never have existed. It is at this point, if we are not careful, that we fall into the platitude of saying that fanatical persons are necessary as effective agents in the world, constituted as it is, and certainly those who were fortunate enough to be at school under Sanderson of Oundle[24] can never forget this emphasis on the 'obsession' necessary for creation of whatever sort. But we may admit the right of individuals to press on along some chosen way, while at the same time exhorting them to keep alive within themselves their potentialities for following other ways. Indeed, no misunderstanding of what is here proposed would be more acute than to suppose that any diminution of intensity of the kinds of experience is intended; on the contrary, the whole argument is designed to recommend as vigorous a following out of each kind as possible during such time as it is holding our attention. Dilution is what we do not want, dilution of one experience with another, or worst of all, the mixing of them into one grey mass, wherein science is not very scientific nor religion very religious. If such an ideal of harmony between irreconcilable disciplines should ever come to be generally held, a state of affairs which I should regard as exceedingly improbable, extraordinary changes would occur in the affairs of the world, for as there would be no tendency to overestimate or overcultivate one field of experience at the expense of the others, there would be no following reaction, and with the disappearance of the pendulum motion with which we are so familiar would go the disappearance of the Spenglerian cycles. Stability would replace instability, and the world would become an antechamber to heaven, all its inhabitants being engaged in exercising their souls in accordance with virtue. In Milton's words:

> For if such holy Song
> Enwrap our fancy long,
>   Time will run back, and fetch the age of gold,
> And speckl'd vanity
> Will sicken soon and die,
>   And leprous sin will melt from earthly mould,
> And Hell itself will pass away,
> And leave her dolorous mansions to the peering day.

This is not likely, as the politicians say, to happen in our time.

It is probable that the conception of fringes which I have outlined will not be welcome to many of those who are interested in these questions. No follower of Spengler, for instance, could admit them, for he would be concerned to assert that no connection exists between ancient science and modern science, that these structures grew out of separate world-souls, and mirrored their origin in themselves so perfectly as to be utterly incommensurable. With this, however, I cannot agree, for I think that in a very real sense modern science is directly connected with the science of classical antiquity, with that of China and India also, and possesses traceable links of continuity with them. Mechanism is no fad in science, nor is materialism; they are necessary concomitants of that particular form of experience, and will arise, as they have in the past arisen, wherever the form of experience itself is cultivated by human spirits. In the remote future, for instance, after many revolutions in science, and during some temporary dominance of idealism and piety, they will surprise and shock all but the historians by suddenly turning up again as if nothing had happened, and as if they had not winced under a thousand exorcisms. Again some of our more advanced students of scientific method take pleasure in describing the great differences between modern and ancient science, in order to add point to their accounts of the changes that have recently been taking place, but when the dust has blown over and we have settled down to the quantum theory and the new mechanics, I fancy it will appear that Lucretius, Erasistratus, Herophilus, Aristotle, and Anaxagoras stand where they did as the originators of our experimental science. I believe that there is something fundamentally identical in their outlook with that of the biophysicist of AD 2000, something which sharply differentiates them and their descendants from Plotinus, Augustine, and theirs, and which would closely unify them with those Mayan and Mexican scientists whose names and achievements even are unknown to us.

Must we then conclude that the outward manifestations of two such forms of experience as science and religion can have no influence upon one another, and that ecclesiastical superstitions of all sorts have nothing to fear from the advance of the scientific consciousness? I fear that in some sense this is the case, for it hardly becomes science, which has so many superstitions of its own, to attack those of religion. Nevertheless, this kind of tolerance will not happen in practice, for we always observe that in an age when science is dominant religion apologetically purifies itself, and even where it retains as much of its historical clothing as it can, it interprets its actions in a modernistic spirit. Such a process is inevitable, and we are never seriously faced with the strict water-tight compartmentism represented, for instance, by the opinions of Anatole France's Abbé Lantaigne.[25] 'I hear that there are priests', said the head of the high seminary, conversing with M. le Prof. Bergeret under the elm-trees, 'regarded as eminent, who maintain that science ought to agree with theology. I detest this impertinence, I will say this impiety, for there is a certain impiety in making the immutable and absolute truth walk in harmony with that imperfect and provisional truth which is called science. This madness of assimilating reality to appearance, the body to the soul, has produced a multitude of miserable, baneful opinions through which the apologists of our age have allowed their foolhardy feebleness to be seen. One, a distinguished member of the Society of Jesus, admits the plurality of inhabited worlds; he allows that intelligent beings may inhabit Mars or Venus, provided that to the earth there be reserved the privilege of the Cross, by which it again becomes unique and peculiar in the Creation. The other, a man who not without some merit occupied in the Sorbonne the chair of theology, which has since been abolished, grants that the geologists can trace the vestiges of preadamites and reduces the Genesis of the Bible to the organisation of one province of the universe for the sojourn of Adam and his seed. O dull folly! O pitiable boldness! O ancient novelties, already condemned a hundred times! O violation of sacred unity! How much better to proclaim that science and religion ought no more to be confused with each other than the relative and the absolute, the finite and the infinite, the darkness and the light.'

While there is no reason, for instance, why the Tridentine doctrine of indulgences should not co-exist in the same civilisation with the equations of Einstein, there is every likelihood that in the long run it will cease to do so, withering at the roots as if by a secret disease. However far the realisation spreads that we cannot combine into one account of the world the language of religion and the language of science, yet at the same time the languages cannot help infecting one another, and the recessive one borrows words and concepts from the dominant one without wishing to, and often without being aware of it. Thus it was that teleology infested all the science of our own Middle Ages, and not teleology only, but also even ethics, which furnished spurious arguments to astronomy based on the varying degrees of perfection and geometrical figures. In embryology, Albertus Magnus argued,[26] about AD 1250, that male birds hatched from those eggs which were most spherical, as the sphere was the most excellent of all the figures in solid geometry, and he was neither the first nor the last to emphasise this point. And Thomas Aquinas, again, while mainly reproducing Aristotle's *De Generatione Animalium*, remarks,[27] 'The generative power of the female is imperfect compared to that of the male, for just as in the crafts the inferior workman prepares the material and the more skilled operator shapes it, so likewise the female generative virtue provides the substance, but the active male virtue makes it into the finished embryo.' How admirably this expresses the dominating sentiment of the Middle Ages! Aristotle might make a distinction between matter and form in generation, Galen might embody the forces concerned in faculties or virtues, but it remained for the medieval mind, with its perpetual hankering after value, to enquire which of the two was the higher, the nobler, the more honourable. And this was because the medieval mind was, above all, a religious mind. In our day and the days which are soon to come, the whole situation is reversed, and religion will borrow even its atmosphere from science, not only on the crude level typified by the bishop who hoped that some experimental investigation might be made of the spiritual efficacy of the blessed sacrament, but to the extent of minimising attention to value, concentrating effort on ethical counsels, and deprecating theology. This is the very reason why, in a scientific age, we must beware of the danger of religion borrowing too much, the very reason why Leonardo da Vinci stood almost alone in his time maintaining silently the right of science to be scientific.

In seventeenth-century England we see the fascinating picture of the balance trembling on a poise of equal weights, Faustian religion having lost little of its ancient power, Faustian science having gained its first magnificent victories. To have been a gentleman of leisure, acquainted with the virtuosi of the Royal Society and the group of remarkable divines which the Church of England then produced, with such men as John Mayow and Charles Scarborough on the one hand, and Lancelot Andrewes and Nicholas Ferrar on the other, would have been to inhabit the precise turning-point, the decisive moment, in our Western civilisation as it expressed itself with us in England. This happy fate was more or less reserved for Abraham Cowley, among others, confidential secretary to the king and decipherer of the royal cryptographs, inferior but persevering poet, friend of the Royal Society's historian, Thomas Sprat, and the only man, probably, who ever wrote an ode to that noble institution. In those times not a few hopeful spirits busied themselves with schemes for the foundation of colleges in which the new or experimental philosophy should be represented, sometimes fantastic, after the manner of Bacon's Solomon's House, sometimes realisable, and within the bounds of practical possibility. Among those of the latter class comes Abraham Cowley's 'Proposition for the Advancement of Experimental Philosophy.'[28] A college was to be built two or three miles from London, and if possible near the river; it was to consist of three large courts, a hall, a chapel, a gallery, and many elaboratories for natural operations, including an anatomy-chamber. There were to be twenty 'professors, or philosophers,' of whom sixteen were to be always resident, the remaining four abroad, collecting the rarities of Asia, Africa, and America. There were, furthermore, to be as many scholar-servants, allotted one to each of the philosophers as his apprentice, and a master and treasurer over all, together with a sufficient provision of messengers, gardeners, cooks, bakers, and other attendants, with four old women. Here the professors were to cultivate every branch of natural and speculative philosophy, to make experiments with plants and animals, to advance physics and chemistry, and to write down their results in a big book kept under lock and key. The gallery was to be filled with a fair array of pictures and statues, and the chapel was to be well appointed and furnished with a chaplain, who should read the services of the English Church with the philosophers and administer the holy sacrament to them every month at the least.

It all has a quaint but very attractive air, and I have nothing to add to Cowley's description of his college save that if it had ever secured a benefactor to bring it into actuality, it would have found itself in difficulties as time went on, utterly different from those that had been foreseen. The philosophers, who had at first hoped to pass with ease and rapidity from experimental plot or laboratory to art gallery, and from there to chapel, and so on, would have found upon the thresholds invisible bonds, invisible restraints, putting a brake upon their free entry. With the passage of time they would have learnt that these invisible bonds were not of one piece with the buildings, not of an external and magical character, but wholly existing within themselves, and due to the fact that they themselves were not such simple units as they had thought. Doubtless they would have had recourse to many palliatives for this difficulty, but they would have found only one cure, namely, the acceptance of each form of experience *cum grano salis*, with a sceptical reserve. And in this scepticism they would have been as assiduous in their laboratories as in their chapel, where we may leave them, saying with their chaplain,

Attingit ergo sapientia a fine usque ad finem fortiter et omnia suaviter disponit.

For Wisdom reacheth from one end to another mightily, and sweetly ordereth all things.

Notes

1. [Refers to the sense of the holy: see above, p. 14.]
2. L. P. Jacks, in *Philosophers in Trouble* (Williams & Norgate, London, 1916.)
3. W. Harvey, *Prælectiones Anatomiae Universalis*, Facsimile Edition (London, 1886.)
4. O. Spengler, *The Decline of the West*, (London, vol. i, 1926, vol l. ii, 1928).
5. H. Rickert, *Die Grenzen d. naturwissenschaftlichen Begriffsbildung* (Leipzig 1902.)
6. This point has been put, with all his usual brilliant incisiveness, by R. G. Collingwood, *Antiquity*, 1927, **1**, 311 and 435.
7. Sir W. Dampier-Whetham, *A History of Science* (Cambridge, 1930).
8. H. Dingle, *Hibbert Journal*, 1928, **27**, 35.
9. Claude Bernard, *Experimental Medicine* (London, 1927), p. 88.
10. Voltaire, *Oeuvres Completes* (Paris, 1879), vol. xxvi, p. 56.
11. G. Santayana, *Dialogues in Limbo* (New York, 1925), p. 183.
12. E. R. Eddison, *The Worm Ouroboros* (London, 1922).

13. Quoted by R. Kipling in *Rewards and Fairies* (London, 1910), p. 332.
14. Sir Thomas Browne, *Religio Medici*, I, § 44.
15. F. R. Tennant, *Philosophical Theology* (Cambridge, 1930), vol. i, ch. 13.
16. A. Huxley, *Do What You Will* (London, 1929).
17. Sir Thomas Browne, *Religio Medici*, I, § 17.
18. In the Greek there is a pun on the word epode here.
19. O. Spengler, *op. cit.*
20. This was related long afterwards by Boyle in his *Disquisition about the Final Causes of Natural Things* (London, 1688).
21. Sir Thomas Browne, *Religio Medici*, I, § 21.
22. By William Empson, *Oxford Outlook*, 1930, **10**, 477.
23. G. Lowes Dickinson, *The Greek View of Life* (London, 1896).
24. See *Sanderson of Oundle*, a collective work (London, 1923,) and H. G. Wells, *The Story of a Great Schoolmaster* (London, 1924).
25. Anatole France, *The Elm-Tree on the Mall* (London, 1924), p. 76.
26. Albertus Magnus, *De Animalibus, libri xxvi* (ed. Stader, Münster, 1916).
27. St Thomas Aquinas, *Summa Theologica*, Part III.
28. In Abraham Cowley's *Collected Works*, ed. Hurd, vol. i, p. 219.

III

PROCESS

5

Integrative Levels:
A Revaluation of the
Idea of Progress

(1937)*

The flower of humanity, captive still in its germ, will blossom one day into the true form of man, like unto God, in a state of which no man on earth can imagine the greatness and the majesty.

HERDER

> It is certain we shall attain
> No life till we stamp on all
> Life the tetragonal
> Pure symmetry of brain. DAY LEWIS

Statement of the Theme
Disquisitions without summaries are among the worst trials of the intellectual life. Only too often, on occasions such as the present one, when a scientist or a philosopher has the honour to stand before you, as now I have, forming one of a succession of plain thinkers who offer their conclusions for comment and criticism, he is content to leave his audience and his readers to gather his meaning as best they may without the assistance of any summary. In this case, however, a summary shall be provided, and instead of leaving it until the end, when your patience would have been, perhaps, severely taxed, it shall be given at the beginning in the form of a statement of the theme.

The theme of integrative levels is not one which we can approach without considerable hesitation, since the field which it

* ['Integrative Levels' is reproduced here as it appeared in *Time: The Refreshing River*; it had been given first as the Herbert Spencer Lecture at Oxford, and was slightly revised later in 1942 or 1943.]

covers is so wide and deep, no less than the whole nature of the world we know, and the way in which it has come into being. No one thinker can hope to do justice to this theme, and the only apology which may be offered for treating of it is that interest must always attach to what a specialist in any field of research may say when he abandons for a moment his speciality and looks boldly out to consider the world. Moreover, in taking the whole world for his province, your lecturer may the more easily, though a scientist, escape the condemnation of philosophers, who have always been rather interested in the world as a whole. The subject, then, to which our attention is to be given is the existence of levels of organisation[1] in the universe, successive forms of order in a scale of complexity and organisation.[2] This is a theme which that great man whose name we have in mind today, Herbert Spencer, the 'synthetic philosopher,' would at least have appreciated.[3] Today it is no longer necessary, as it was in his time, to devote any effort to convincing people of the existence of evolutionary development in the world's history.[4] The cosmological changes which eventually produced a number of worlds, probably rather small among the galaxies, suitable for the existence of massed and complicated carbon compounds in the colloidal state, have become a commonplace background of our thought. So also the conception of biological evolution, in the course of which the many-celled animals and the plants arose from single-celled organisms probably somewhat resembling the autotrophic bacteria of today. A sharp change in organisational level often means that what were wholes on the lower level become parts on the new, e.g. protein crystals in cells, cells in metazoan organisms, and metazoan organisms in social units. Lastly, the anthropologists and ethnologists have familiarised all of us with the idea of evolutionary development in sociology, where we see the gradual development of human communities from the earliest beginnings of social relationships to the conception of the co-operative commonwealth now dawning upon the world.

But this great sweep of vision needs further elucidation. First, if we look carefully at the steps between the successive levels of organisation we find that the sharp lines of distinction are only made all the more sharp by the 'mesoforms' which occur between them. Thus between living and non-living matter the realm of the crystalline represents the highest degree of organisation of which non-living matter is capable. It approaches, moreover, quite closely to the realm of the living in the phenomena presented by the so-called 'liquid crystals,' states of matter intermediate between the random orientation of a liquid and the almost absolute rigidity of the true crystal. These 'paracrystals,' with their internal structure and their directional properties, are closely related to living systems. Living systems, indeed, almost certainly contain many components of a paracrystalline nature. The viruses again, minute ultramicroscopic particles, probably represent some kind of intermediate form between living and lifeless.[5] But these forms of existence, the more clearly we understand them, will all the more clearly serve to bring out the essentially new elements of higher order which characterise the form of organisation we call life.

Secondly, there follows from the developmental nature of social organisation a conclusion which some thinkers, though otherwise clear-minded, have not been so ready to see, namely, that we have no reason to suppose that our present condition of civilisation is the last masterpiece of universal organisation, the highest form of order of which Nature is capable. On the contrary, there are many grounds for seeing in collectivism a form of organisation as much above the *manière d'être* of middle-class nations as their form of order was superior to that of primitive tribes. It would hardly be going too far to say that the transition from economic individualism to the common ownership of the world's productive resources by humanity is a step similar in nature to the transition from lifeless proteins to the living cell, or from primitive savagery to the first community, so clear is the continuity between inorganic, biological, and social order. Thus, on such a view, the future state of social justice is seen to be no fantastic utopia, no desperate hope, but a form of organisation having the whole force of evolution behind it. But the acceptance of this implies a certain revaluation of the idea of progress. The idea of progress as applied to biological and social evolution fell into great discredit as the result of Victorian optimism. It was pointed out that evolution has often been regressive, that parasitism has been a widespread phenomenon in biology, and that before speaking of progress in evolution we should consider 'the hookworm's point of view.' Nevertheless, apart from the fact that the hookworm's nervous system does not entitle it to have a point of view, we cannot seriously bring ourselves to refuse to apply the concepts of higher and lower organisation to the animal world.

Vertebrates *are*, in general, of higher organisation than inver-
tebrates, mammals than other vertebrates, and human beings than
other mammals. Again, in social affairs, the vast miseries caused
by industrialisation and modern warfare were set against the
doubtfully happier conditions of ancient times, and pessimistic
conclusions adverse to the conception of progress were easily
reached. But the time-scale here was insufficient, the exceedingly
short space of time during which human civilisation has existed as
compared with the time taken in biological evolution was forgotten. Post-Victorian pessimism mistook the development of a
certain phase for the whole of progress itself. Of a famous
Edwardian statesman it was said that he approached politics with
the air of one who remembered that there had once been an ice
age and that it was very likely there would be another. He was
unnecessarily chilly. In the light of biology and sociology, those
who remember that there were once autotrophic bacteria and
that there will some day be a co-operative commonwealth of
humanity, are better politicians.

So much for the theme of this disquisition. We shall naturally
have to consider some aspects of Herbert Spencer's own thought
as we develop its variations. But first it may perhaps be of interest
if your lecturer takes leave to run over a few matters of personal
interest, a few points on the intellectual travels which, in one form
or another, it is everyone's fate to take. If one thing is more
fundamental to the world-view outlined above than any other, it
is the importance of the concept of Time.[6] And it was your
lecturer's chance to become convinced of it in more than one
major field of interest.

Time and the Theologians

Perhaps exceptionally among students of science, he came to find
theology, and especially the history of Christian theology, one of
the most fascinating of subjects. The intense persistence of so
many minds, outstanding in their generations, to give rationality
to the irrational and expression to the inexpressible, was an amaz-
ing phenomenon. The quarrels of theologians, orthodox and
heretical alike, over words, letters, or even accents, in their formulations, were understandable enough, once certain premises were
granted. The wonderful poetry of the liturgies carried symbolism
to a point of daring surely hardly reached by any other great
religion. Now it so happened that in the course of time he found

himself influenced successively by two divines, W. R. Inge, the former Dean of St. Paul's, and Conrad Noel, for many years vicar of Thaxted in Essex.[7] It is true they were but vehicles for the teaching of greater than they; Plotinus in the first case, Isaiah in the second. And it was after having experienced a profound attraction for the great tradition of Christian mysticism that he came to feel, in the light of the prophetic and apocalyptic tradition, that the former was almost the evil genius of religion.

For the ancient Mediterranean thinkers, the world, which had neither beginning nor ending, was growing neither better nor worse. It has been powerfully argued (e.g. by Glover[8]) that the major contribution of Christianity, and one of the principal reasons why it vanquished its competitors among the religions of the Roman empire, was precisely that it introduced change and hope into the stagnating sameness of the ancient world. But when asceticism, probably of Indian origin, outbalanced this new belief in the significance of time, the Neo-platonists, whether pagan or Christian, had every reason they needed for turning away from the world and embarking on the ecstasies of the mystical contemplation of the One. 'The intelligible world,' writes Inge,[9] expounding Plotinus, 'is timeless and spaceless, and contains the archetypes of the sensible world. The sensible world is our view of the intelligible world. When we say it does not exist, we mean that we shall not always see it in this form. The "Ideas" are the ultimate form in which things are regarded by Intelligence, or God. *Noûs* is described at once *stasis* and *kinēsis*, that is, it is unchanging itself, but the whole cosmic process, which is ever in flux, is eternally present to it as a process.' A process, but not a progressive process. Where time brings no irreversible change, time is not important. It is strange how close to scientific thought theological thought has often been, for here we are reminded both of the seventeenth-century doctrine of the 'general concourse,' the upholding of the world by divine power without which everything would, it was thought, fly back into chaos again; and of the relations now understood between time and thermodynamic irreversibility. But for Neo-platonic and hence Christian mysticism, just as the sensible world is but a shadow of the intelligible, so action is a shadow of contemplation, suited only to weakminded persons. This leads to what even Inge calls the heartless doctrine that to the wise man public calamities are only stage tragedies. It leads no less to the view that all such calamities are punishments for sin, since any action must be wrong. The medie-val saint and visionary, Angela of Foligno, congratulated herself on the deaths of her mother, husband and children, 'who were great obstacles in the way of God.'

What a profound difference there is between this ascetic Graeco-Indian indifference to time, and the unsophisticated messianism which runs through most of the prophetic writings of the Hebrews, and on into the early Church, forming its other principal current. Here there is an intuition of time's irreversi-bility, the accomplishment of permanent gains, the belief in pro-gressive change. Thus in Isaiah: 'The voice of one that crieth, Prepare ye in the wilderness the way of the Lord, make straight in the desert a high way for our God. Every valley shall be exalted and every mountain and hill shall be made low; and the crooked shall be made straight and the rough places plain; and the glory of the Lord shall be revealed, and all flesh shall see it together: for the mouth of the Lord hath spoken it.'[10] Or again: 'The Lord God will come as a mighty one, and his arm shall rule for him; his reward is with him, and his recompense before him.'[11] Or 'Declare ye the former things, what they be, that we may consider them, and know the latter end of them; or show us things for to come.'[12] Or Jeremiah: 'And they shall come and sing in the height of Sion, and shall flow together unto the goodness of the Lord, for corn and wine and oil, and for the young of the flock and the herd; and their soul shall be as a watered garden, and they shall not sorrow any more at all. Then shall the girls rejoice in the dance, and the young men and the old together; for I will turn their mourning into joy, and will comfort them, and make them rejoice for their sorrow. . . . There is hope for thy latter end, saith the Lord.'[13]

Every word shows clearly a strong sense of the progressive time process. Things have been and shall be; they have been evil, it is promised that they shall be better.

After the period of the Gospels and in the early Church this attitude towards time became associated naturally with the conception of the Kingdom of God, *Regnum Dei*. In the later development of this conception, it came to mean, either the Church itself as a visible organisation, or an invisible company of the faithful, both of the dead and the living.[14] But the more your lecturer considered the history of the concept, the clearer it became that these ideas were later distortions, and that the primitive Christians had held a much more materialist view of the *Regnum*, had thought of it rather as an earthly state of social justice which should, it was true, be brought in by the miraculous second coming of the Lord, but to which meanwhile all their own efforts should be tending. And in conformity with this 'socialist' interpretation of the mind of the primitive church, he noted a number of facts to which as a rule little attention is given. Thus the communism of the Church of Jerusalem is generally, but inadequately, explained away by theological historians. Among the early theological movements, some of which were condemned as heresies or schisms, there are many traces of economic significance to be found, e.g: the *milites agonistici christi* of the North African Donatists, who seem to have been the shock-troops of an agrarian communist rebellion.[15] That there were elements of a hatred of communism in the medieval repressions of the Albigensians and Waldensians is more than probable.[16] All through the late middle ages, the peasant risings against their intolerable conditions were carried out in the name of Christian comradeship, and often had the support of revolutionary clergy, as in the case of our English priest, John Ball. There are strong grounds for suspecting a social revolutionary element in the Lollards and the poor preachers of Wyclif.[17] And when it came to open warfare, the Anabaptists and the Taborites of the sixteenth century[18] and the Levellers of the seventeenth[19] all adopted religious language and modes of thought. It is not to be suggested that any special significance attaches to this fact, for they had no other language or modes of thought at their disposal. But the essential point is that in all the best aspects of Christianity, in those directions in which it has least turned its back upon human life and simple human happiness, the conviction of the reality of progress in time has been present. A time came when the old law gave place to the new. A time came when the people would suffer no longer the oppression of unchristian princes, but actually rose against them, and for a longer or shorter period withstood them. A time would eventually come when the Kingdom of God would be set up on earth, and a new world-order of love and comradeship would come into being.

With such words, we may seem to have travelled far from the cool consideration of biological and social evolution. But in fact we are not far removed from it, for there is a natural affinity between millenniarism and evolutionary naturalism. Such primitive

Christian ideas do justice to time and to progress, and in wandering, as a young man, from one theological realm to another, your lecturer came to see that the reality of time was fundamentally important. When he then returned to take up again the *locus classicus* of Neo-platonic pessimism, the essay of W. R. Inge on progress,[20] it seemed to him, in spite of all its learning, indescribably superficial. All it found to say about the eighteenth-century beliefs in reason and human perfectibility was that in France they 'culminated in the delirium of the Terror.' More than half a century after the beginnings of agricultural chemistry, and oblivious of modern methods of population control, it could still take seriously the views of Malthus. Neither history nor science, it concluded, give us any warrant for believing that humanity has advanced, except by accumulating knowledge and experience and the instruments of living; and the value of this social inheritance is 'not beyond dispute.' Nevertheless he retained sufficient admiration for a great, though perverse,[21] scholar, to continue to regard him as on a totally different level from Cro-Magnon man.

Time and the Biologists

But side by side with these cogitations on the first and last things, your lecturer was occupied in his daily work with biology in general and biochemistry in particular. And since biochemistry is the most borderline of sciences, it was only natural that, like most reflective students of that subject, he should devote a good deal of attention to its philosophical position. That chemistry should indeed be able to cover the realms of both the inanimate and the animate, was in fact quite sufficiently a riddle in itself. The whole history of biochemistry, indeed, has been the scene of a persistent debate between those who have taken the hopeful view that the phenomena of life would one day be fully explicable in physico-chemical terms, and those who have thought themselves able to see in these phenomena evidences of some guiding influence— *spiritus rector, archaeus, vis formativa,* entelechy, or what you will—formally impossible to bring into relation with chemistry. Often enough these 'vitalists,' as they have been called, not content with prognostications of failure, have purported to give proofs of a more or less convincing nature, that the phenomena of life must ever resist scientific explanation.[22] During the first three decades of the present century the majority of working biologists and biochemists were not 'vitalists' but 'mechanists.' About 1928 their position could fairly justly be summed up as follows: 'Mechanists do not say that nothing is true or intelligible unless expressed in physico-chemical terms, they do not say that nothing takes place differently in living matter from what takes place in dead, they do not say that our present physics and chemistry are fully competent to explain the behaviour of living systems. What they do say is that the processes of living matter are subject to the same laws which govern the processes of dead matter, but that the laws operate in a more complicated medium; thus living things differ from dead things in degree and not in kind, and are, as it were, *extrapolations* from the inorganic.'[23]

But the nature of this extrapolation was still obscure. The question entered a new phase, however, some ten years ago, with the publication of J. H. Woodger's remarkable book *Biological Principles*.[24] There it was laid down that the term 'vitalism' should thenceforward be restricted to all propositions of the type 'the living being consists of an X *in addition to* carbon, hydrogen, oxygen, nitrogen, etc. *plus organising relations*.' Recognition of the objectivity and importance of organising relations had always been an empirical necessity, forced upon biologists by the very subject-matter of their science, but the issue was always confused by their inability to distinguish between the *organisation* of the living system and its supposed *anima*. With the abolition of souls and vital forces the genuine organising relations in the organism could become the object of scientific study. Before the contribution of Woodger, 'organicism,' as it had been called, had necessarily been of an obscurantist character,[25] since it was supposed, as, for example, by J. S. Haldane, that the organising relations were themselves the *anima*, and as such inscrutable to scientific analysis.[26] To-day we are perfectly clear (though a few biologists may still fail to appreciate this point) that the organisation of living systems is the problem, not the axiomatic starting point, of biological research. Organising relations exist, but they are not immune from scientific grasp and understanding. On the other hand, their laws are not likely to be reducible[27] to the laws governing the behaviour of molecules at lower levels of complexity. It would be correct to say that the living differs from the dead in degree and not in kind because it is on a higher plane of complexity of organisation, but it would also be correct to say that it differs in kind since the laws of this higher organisation only operate there.

It may be of use to follow a little further the difference between the older dogmatic organicism and the new point of view. Organisation is inscrutable, it was urged, since any inorganic part instantly loses its relational properties on removal from the whole, and no means are available for rendering wholes transparent so that we can observe them while intact. But unfortunately these statements are not true. Woodger[28] has distinguished three main possibilities in the relation of organic part to organic whole: (a) independence, (b) functional dependence, (c) existential dependence. A part of the first sort would pursue its normal activities independently of whether it was in connection with its normal whole or not. A part of the second sort would be disorganised, if so isolated, and a part of the third sort would cease even to be recognisable. Dogmatic organicists, ignoring these distinctions, assumed that all parts are parts of the third sort. Yet this is certainly not the case. Liver cells synthesise glycogen and iris cells melanin in tissue culture as well as in the body. Isolated enzyme systems carry out their multifarious reactions in extracts as well as in the intact cells. Even existential dependence is a difficulty which can be overcome if means exist for making wholes 'transparent,' as by X-ray analysis of membranes or fibres, examination of living cells in polarising microscopes or ultra-violet spectrometers, or by 'marking' in-going molecules by substituting isotope elements in them, such as heavy hydrogen or phosphorus.

It was a striking fact that in other countries other biologists had been coming to similar conclusions. In Russia, under the guidance of an elaborate philosophy at that time almost unknown here, a new organicism had been growing up, but so little were English men of science prepared for it that the very sensible and elaborate communications of the Russian delegation to the International Congress for the History of Science at the Science Museum at South Kensington, London, in 1931, were received with bewilderment.[29] 'The true task of scientific research,' said Zavadovsky,[30] 'is not the violent identification of the biological and the physical, but the discovery of the qualitatively specific controlling principles which characterise the main features of every phenomenon studied. ... It is necessary to renounce both the simplified reduction of some sciences to others and also the sharp demarcations between the physical, biological, and socio-historical sciences.' Again, in a passage which indicates a point of view closely similar to that already outlined, he writes,

'Biological phenomena, historically connected with physical phenomena in inorganic nature, are none the less not only not reducible to physico-chemical or mechanical laws, but within their own limits as biological processes display different[31] and qualitatively distinct laws. But biological laws do not in the least lose thereby their material quality and cognisability, requiring only in each case methods of research appropriate to the phenomena studied.' Or, in other words, biological order is both comprehensible and different from inorganic order. In France, similar views have been put forward, as, for instance, by Marcel Prenant,[32] also in accordance with the indications of materialist dialectics. This philosophy has been called the profoundest theory of natural evolution,[33] the theory of the nature of transformations and the origin of the qualitatively new,[34] indeed the natural methodology of science itself. It was striking to find that its conclusions upon a point of the most fundamental interest to the biochemist, the meaning of the transition from the dead to the living, should coincide with those which he had worked out independently by sincerely following the dictates of scientific common sense.

The question had always been particularly serious for those biochemists who interested themselves in the problems of morphology. The enzymes involved in metabolism may be isolated and studied in relatively simple systems, analyses may be made of the substances entering and leaving the living body, and the blood and tissue fluids may be examined in relation to every conceivable bodily activity, change or disease—but all this avoids the main problem of biology, the origin, nature, and maintenance of specific organic structure. The building of a bridge between biochemical and morphological concepts is perhaps the most important task before biologists at the present time, and it may well be long before it is satisfactorily accomplished. But in the course of the present century several branches of study of great value in this connection have sprung up, particularly in embryology, where the changing organic form is the most obvious variable during development. Experimental and chemical embryology[35] together have made much progress towards the unification of chemical and morphological concepts. But this impressive change of morphological form takes place along the time-axis, and just as we have seen that in the far-away realm of the history of theology, the conviction of the importance of time was brought

home to your lecturer, so also it was inescapable in the realm of
biological science. In the development of the individual organism,
as in that of organisms in general, progression took place from low
to high complexity, from inferior to superior organisation. There
had been a time when a certain level of organisation had not
existed, there would come a time when far higher levels would
appear. Time was the inevitable datum.

Time and Herbert Spencer

We have now to give some consideration to the thought of the
great 'synthetic philosopher' himself. With much of what has so
far been said, he would surely have been in definite agreement,
since for him also the importance of the time-continuum, in
which the irreversible world-process takes place, was cardinal.

'Evolution under its most general aspect,' he wrote, 'is the
integration of matter and the concomitant dissipation of motion;
while Dissolution is the absorption of motion and concomitant
disintegration of matter.'[36] Sometimes the word integration as
used by him seems to mean little more than a mere aggregation of
undifferentiated matter,[37] but as soon as he comes to give
examples of its function in evolution, we see that he means much
what we mean when we speak of successive, and higher, levels of
organisation. Total mass, he says, passes from a more diffused to a
more consolidated state,[36] and the same process happens in every
part that has a distinguishable individuality, and finally there is an
increase of combinations among such parts. Less coherence gives
place to more coherence.[38] As his examples he takes, of course,
the formation of solar systems from nebulae,[39] the development
of the earth from a ball of hot gases,[40] the development of plants
and animals in phylogeny and ontogeny,[41] and the rise of social
relationships from primitive animal gregariousness to human
communities of lower or higher order.[42] Then with perhaps some
weakening of the imagination he goes on to say,[43] 'Of the
European nations, it may be further remarked, that in the
tendency to form alliances, in the restraining influence exercised
by governments over one another, in the system of settling international arrangements by congresses, as well as in the weakening
of commercial barriers and the increasing facilities of communi-
cation, we see the beginnings of a European federation—a still
larger integration than any now established.' So throughout the
range of levels, the same processes are seen—increase in the

degree to which the parts constitute a co-operative assemblage, increase in the co-ordination of parts, increase in combination and juxtaposition and mutual dependence of the parts, and of the parts of the parts.[44]

Side by side with integration goes differentiation; the scission of wholes into parts, and parts into smaller parts.[45] Instances of this growing heterogeneity he finds in sidereal changes, in the changes of the earth's crust, in ontogenetic development (cf. the passage on chemical embryology quoted in ref. 35, pp. 166–7 below) in phylogeny and in sociology. He ends by his celebrated definition of evolution:[46] evolution is a change from a relatively indefinite incoherent homogeneity to a relatively definite coherent heterogeneity, accompanied by integration of matter and concomitant dissipation of motion.[47] We may smile at what we suppose to be the presumption of such a cosmic formula, but we may find ourselves smiling on the wrong side of our faces, if, as is not unlikely, Herbert Spencer had hold of the right end of the stick. We should be foolish to put ourselves in the position of the devil, who was defined by the patristic writer, Hippolytus, as 'he who resists the world-process.' With Spencer's attempt to elucidate the causes of this process, to say why evolution should go on at all (the instability of the homogeneous[48]), we need not here be concerned; the important point is his realisation of its universal scope. In reading his work today, we are likely to feel that he is most right where he emphasises integration and organisation rather than homogeneity and heterogeneity.

In Spencer's biological writings, too, there is much of great interest for the modern biologist who cares to know how ideas familiar today in science had their origin. The definition of life as the continuous adjustment of internal relations to external relations was his,[49] and so too was the conception of increasing dependence of the environment accompanying increasing organisational level.[50] 'One of those lowly gelatinous forms,' he writes, 'so transparent and colourless as to be with difficulty distinguished from the water it floats in, is not more like its medium in chemical, mechanical, optical, and thermal properties, than it is in the passivity with which it submits to all the influences and actions brought to bear upon it; while the mammal does not more widely differ from inanimate things in these properties, than it does in the activity with which it meets surrounding changes by compensating changes in itself.' When in just twenty years' time we celebrate the centenary of Spencer's first formulation of this rule of increasing independence,[51] we shall be able to look back upon a vast structure of knowledge in comparative biochemistry and physiology which in many directions (e.g. osmotic regulation,[52] thermal regulation,[53] constancy of the internal medium,[54] respiratory pigments,[55] laws of nitrogen excretion,[56] etc.) has verified the synthetic philosopher's insight.

Nor was this much less remarkable in matters of embryology. His treatment of animal development as a passage from instability to stability has been profoundly justified in modern experimental embryology, in which the restriction of potentialities which goes on under the influence of the hierarchy of organiser-hormones bears him out.[57] Already before 1898 he had clearly enunciated the process we know now as 'self-differentiation' under the name 'autogenous development.'[58] Even the organisation-centre, with its primary organiser-hormone, not discovered till 1924, he had adumbrated thirty years earlier, in the guise of an analogy with a party of colonists in new country, which forms for itself an organisation of 'butty' or 'boss' and those who work under his directions.[59]

But Spencer's treatment of sociological problems is of most interest for the present analysis. He has the great merit of having been among the first thinkers to apply evolutionary concepts to sociology, and for this we owe him a great debt.[60] Nevertheless we meet continually with the paradox that having spoken so convincingly of the progressive integration of systems into ever higher levels of organisation, he stopped short at nineteenth-century England and found in its individualism Nature's supreme achievement. The common ownership of the means of production, logical though it might be, did not seem to him the necessary next step in organisation, the next integrative level. There is thus a striking contradiction in his evolutionary thought. By what strange arguments was he able to convince himself that the liberal economic individualism of the mid-nineteenth century was the high state of integration to which all cosmic development had been tending? His life, his controversies with others, the internal evidence of his writings, may give us the clue.

A society, he says, is an organism.[61] How must we envisage its integration and differentiation? At once arises the question of the origin of classes and vocations, the division of labour.[62] It is the physiological division of labour, says Spencer, which makes the society, like the animal, a living whole. Complication of structure accompanies increase of mass, as the classes, military, priestly, slave, etc., differentiate—a progress from the general to the special. But he always fails to emphasise the different relationships of these classes to the production of goods or commodities, he always regards them with an exclusively political eye. Instead of seeking the origins of their economic relationships he elaborates, to a degree sometimes almost fantastic, the analogy between animal and social organisms. Thus the superior military class of warriors corresponds to the ectoderm, and the inferior class of cultivators, in close contact with the mechanism of food-supply, to the endoderm.[63] The origin of the State, he thinks, was the necessity of a centralised neural apparatus to co-ordinate the military activities of the organism-society against other societies. The more plausible explanation, that it was required as the instrument of domination of one class over the other, does not occur to him. As the peasants correspond to endoderm, so the king's council corresponds to the brain's medulla.[64]

In spite of this, however, Spencer was well aware of the limitations of the analogy.[65] There was, he said, a cardinal difference between the animal and the social aggregate. 'In the one, consciousness is concentrated in a small part, in the other it is diffused throughout; all the units possess the capacities for happiness and misery, if not in equal degrees, in degrees that approximate.' The society exists for the benefit of its members, not its members for the benefit of the society. But there exists also another cardinal difference not mentioned by Spencer, namely, that once the early determinative processes of morphogenesis have gone on, all further cell-divisions produce like from like. Muscle-cells produce muscle-cells and neurons neurons. In a society every point corresponding to a cell-division means a completely new genetic shuffling of the pack of inheritable characters. Hereditary castes have thus no biological basis. Spencer shows some appreciation of this where he points out that succession by descent favours the maintenance of that which already exists, while succession by fitness favours transformations 'and makes possible something better.'[66]

It is fairly clear today that, if any form of society is most in accord with what we know of the biological basis of human common life, it is a *democracy that produces experts*. Consciousness, and all the higher human qualities, are dispersed pretty

evenly throughout the world's population. But the unclearness of
Spencer on this matter, it is interesting to note, together with a
thoroughly uncritical social outlook, led in the hands of one of the
most distinguished of your lecturer's predecessors, the great biologist William Bateson, to a striking Herbert Spencer lecture.[67] It
well merits a short digression. Beginning badly by urging that
biology must be the supreme guide in human affairs (as though
sociology were not a higher organisational level than biology), it
went on to say that, whereas 'democracy regards class distinction
as evil, we perceive it to be essential. . . . Maintenance of heterogeneity, of differentiation of members, is a condition of progress.
The aim of social reform must be not to abolish class, but to
provide that each individual shall so far as possible get into the
right class and stay there, and usually his children after him.'[68]
By this mischievously misleading use of the term class, Bateson
wholly surrendered the prestige of science into the hands of the
middle-class employer and entrepreneur, assuring him that class-
stratification was biologically sound and that the public-school tie
covered all the best genes. Doubtless Bateson was referring to
vocational differences. He certainly underrated the genetic shuffling in each reproductive act. But to confuse the various vocations
for which individuals should, of course, be as well suited as possible, with the division into classes differing according to their
relation with the material means of production, some controlling
these means, and others having access to them only by the grace
and on the terms of the former, was a tragic mistake, worthy to
stand side by side with the use of the theory of natural selection as
a justification for *laissez-faire* economics.[69]

Now Spencer's main line of distinction in human societies was
between 'Predatory' and 'Industrial.'[70] The former type was one
in which the army and the nation had a common structure, the
army being the active manifestation of the nation. The latter
type, though possessing some defence organisation, was characterised by voluntary co-operation in commercial transactions. It is
clear that Spencer regarded the industrial type as higher than the
predatory type. In describing examples of it (more or less convincing), his sympathies may be discerned; thus he speaks of 'the
amiable Bodo and Dhimals,'[71] 'the industrious and peaceful
Pueblos,'[72] and the development of free institutions in
England.[73] In conformity with his view, already mentioned, on
the good of the State as against that of the individual, he identifies

the predatory organisation with the former and the industrial organisation with the latter. In this way we arrive at the classical position of nineteenth-century optimism, that all things work together for good for them that love profits, and that in an economic system where each man is for himself, the net resultant will always be for the benefit of all.

And now appears the remarkable, almost pathetic, naïveté of the synthetic philosopher. Spencer, approving of English capitalism in its quiet home-transforming phase (the industrial type of society), viewed with horror the rise of British capitalism in its imperialist phase.[74] It was, he said, the retrogression of the ideal form of society to a predatory phase. He abominated 'the recent growth of expenditure for army and navy, the making of fortifications, the formation of the volunteer force, the establishment of permanent camps, the repetition of autumn manoeuvres, and the building of military stations throughout the kingdom.' As his *Autobiography* shows,[75] he was even willing to take active part in the rather ineffective anti-militarist movements of his day. But the nature of his position forced him to fight on two separate fronts at the same time. He did not approve of imperialism, but neither did he approve of socialist, anti-individualist, legislation, favouring the working-class. By an extraordinary extension of the word 'militarism' he was able to include both tendencies in the same condemnation. His individualism carried him to impressive lengths. Thus the compulsory notification of infectious diseases and the unification of examinations for the learned professions were regarded by him as unwarrantable interference with the freedom of the industrial social unit. Municipal housing, nationalised telegraphs, public museums, even universal compulsory sanitary inspection and main drainage, were all put down as 'tyrannical,' 'coercive philanthropy.' 'Not by quick and certain penalty for breach of contract,' he complained bitterly, 'is adulteration to be remedied, but by public analysers.' Deeply ingrained in his sociology was the conception of free competition : 'From the savings of the more worthy shall be taken by the tax gatherer means of supplying the less worthy who have not saved.' Or again, in his autobiography we find a passage[76] in which, while describing one of his early essays, he says, 'Among reasons given for reprobating the policy of guarding imprudent people against the dangers of reckless banking, one was that such a policy interferes with that normal process which brings benefit to the sagacious and disaster to the stupid.' In such considerations men of Spencer's mind never stopped to reflect that the 'less worthy' might also be the 'more generous,' or that 'rapacious' might have been a better word in the sentence just quoted.[77]

We have already said that Spencer saw how succession by inheritance was a principle of social stability, while succession by fitness or efficiency was a principle of social efficiency.[78] Yet in his references to periods of social crisis when the principles of stability are challenged, when the forces tending towards a higher and hence more efficient level of organisation struggle openly with the forces of conservatism, he shows all the typical middle-class fear of supersession. He can even compare such upheavals with a gangrenous disease.[79] Just as in morbid changes, putrefactive dissolution may occur, so in 'social changes of an abnormal kind, the disaffection initiating a political outbreak implies a loosening of the ties by which citizens are bound up into distinct classes and sub-classes. Agitation, growing into revolutionary meetings, fuses ranks that are usually separated. . . . When at last there comes positive insurrection, all magisterial and official powers, all class distinctions, all industrial differences, cease; organised society lapses into an unorganised aggregate of social units.' A revolutionary might have reminded Spencer that not all dissolutions are morbid, that in the metamorphosis of insects, for instance, though there may be a histolysis, it is but the prelude to a new and more beautiful form of organisation.

Spencer and his Contemporaries
The contradictions in Spencer's sociology appear again when we examine a few of the controversies and discussions in which he engaged. One of the most famous was that with the American sociologist Henry George. In Spencer's first book, *Social Statics*,[80] it was contended that the alienation of the land from the people at large had been inequitable, and that there should be a restoration of it to the State (the incorporated community) after compensation made to the existing landowners. 'In later years,' he wrote,[81] 'I concluded that a resumption on such terms would be a losing transaction, and that individual ownership under State-suzerainty ought to continue.' George, who in his *Progress and Poverty*[82] had quite rightly advocated the national-isation of the land, expecting it, however, to solve all social problems, replied with an attack (*A Perplexed Philosopher*)[83] which

Spencer much resented. To George's accusation of consorting with Dukes, Spencer replied that it was only in a body partly founded by himself, the London Ratepayers' Defence League! It was a poor defence. Another controversy was with the Italian penologist Enrico Ferri,[84] who found that Spencer 'stopped half-way in the logical consequences of his doctrine.' In Ferri's view, natural selection and the struggle for existence in human society should not be interpreted as between individuals, but between classes. 'Spencer believes,' wrote Ferri acutely in 1895, 'that universal evolution rules all orders of phenomena with the exception of the organisation of property, which he declares is destined to exist eternally in its individualistic form. Socialists, on the other hand, believe that it will itself undergo a radical transformation ... towards an increasing and complete socialisation of the means of production, which constitute the physical basis of social life and which ought not to, and will not, remain in the hands of a few individuals.' Spencer complained bitterly in a letter to the Italian press.

With Beatrice Potter (later Mrs Sidney Webb), the philosopher had close intellectual contact. While occupied with her long-continued studies on working-class conditions, she came to realise that the sphere of economics should include 'social pathology,' e.g. oppressive labour conditions. In 1886 she wrote to him putting this point as clearly as possible. He replied that on the contrary 'political economy cannot recognise pathological states at all. If these states are due to the traversing of free competition and free contract which political economy assumes, the course of treatment is not the readjustment of the principles of political economy, but the re-establishment as far as possible of free competition and free contract.' In other words, as she points out in her autobiography *My Apprenticeship*,[85] political economy is an account of the normal conditions in industry. But is not the first step to find out just what *are* the normal, or rather, the healthy, conditions in industry? Spencer, however, had made up his mind *a priori* on this subject, and his flat refusal to question the dogma of free competition betrays, indeed, no little unconscious prejudice. The old man and the young woman agreed to go each on their way, and fifty years later the publication of the Webbs' great book on the Soviet Union[86] showed where the search for health in industrial relations had led.

That Spencer's sociology ended in a paradox has already been shown. It can hardly be understood except in the light of the thought of his contemporary, a man at least equally great, Karl Marx. Born within two years of each other and both living in England, they had, so far as we know, no contact of any kind.[87] Yet it is only in the light of the historical concepts of the great revolutionist in thought and action (as the Master of Balliol calls him[88]) that the failure of the great evolutionist to complete his edifice can be understood. Marx, with his friend Engels, was the genius, it has been said,[89] who continued and completed the three chief intellectual currents of the early nineteenth century, classical German philosophy, classical English political economy, and the French revolutionary doctrines which led to French socialism. Here we can only mention his combination of materialism with the dialectics of the Hegelian school, his economic formulations, especially that of surplus value, and his account of the roles of social classes in history. The former led to a philosophy, dialectical materialism, to which we have already had occasion to refer, which based itself upon that very evolutionary progression which Spencer described with so much care. His successive levels of integration are allowed for in the dialectics of Nature, as in hardly any other philosophy. The concept of surplus value, says Dickinson,[90] has very unjustly shared in the logical discredit into which the labour theory of value has fallen. If Marx's theoretical foundation for it is unsatisfactory, some other must be found. But it is an undeniable fact of observation that the labour of men organised in society produces a surplus above the immediate requirements of the producers, and that this surplus may be disposed of in three main ways : (*a*) it may become the material basis of social growth, either absorbed in the support of an additional number of producers, or embodied in the increase and improvement of the means of production, or used to maintain more complex forms of social organisation, (*b*) it may appear as increased leisure or increased supply of consumption goods available for society as a whole, (*c*) it may be appropriated by a dominant class, appearing as rent, royalties, dividends, interest, profit, excessively high salaries, or various minor forms of privileged income. Here is a concept the lack of which one deeply feels in reading Spencer's sociology. Again and again in his descriptions of the origins and nature of classes[91] he comes near to considering their relative economic *privileges*, but never clearly describes the phenomena of class-domination and the class-struggle. Hence he cannot realise the nature of the State; the neuro-muscular apparatus of control developed by the dominating class.

The history of all human society, past and present, wrote Marx and Engels in 1848, is the history of class-struggles.[92] 'Freeman and slave, patrician and plebeian, baron and serf, guild-burgess and journeyman—in a word, oppressor and oppressed—stood in sharp opposition each to the other. They carried on perpetual warfare, sometimes masked, sometimes open and acknowledged; a warfare that invariably ended, either in a revolutionary change in the structure of society, or else in the common ruin of the contending classes.' The history of the European West can only be understood in the light of this empirical fact. In the course of a long process extending over some four centuries, from about 1400 to 1800, the power of the feudal aristocracy gave place to the power of the middle-class. The work of historians, such as Pirenne[93] and Borkenau,[94] gives us an insight into the first embryonic origins of the new form of appropriation of surplus value which was later to be known as capitalism. Far back in the middle ages, the beginnings of long-distance transport, especially by sea, initiated the tradition of free finance and unlimited profit-making which did not come into its own until in seventeenth-century England the City of London, backing Cromwell's military force with all its might, made our country safe for Spencer's 'sagacious' bankers. The process so brilliantly begun came to its fullness a hundred years later in France, when the chains of feudalism were finally broken and Europe's large-scale industries could develop in earnest. It must, of course, be emphasised that in those earlier days the middle-class 'merchant venturers' and industrialists were the really progressive class. By Herbert Spencer's time, this was ceasing to be the case. Spencer stood just at the critical point when the middle-class was hesitating between the old policy of Manchester light industry and the new policy of Birmingham heavy industry. The export of finished goods was about to yield its hegemony to the direct exploitation of colonial countries and peoples, in a word, to imperialism. State expenditure on the army was 14.9 million pounds in 1873–5, 18.1 in 1893–5, and 28.0 in 1911–13. Upon the navy it was 10.4 million pounds in 1873–5, 17.6 in 1893–5, and 45.3 in 1911–13. No wonder Spencer noted a 'retrogression' from the industrial to the predatory State. The sociology for which he stood was that of the early nineteenth-century English middle-class, favouring 'cheap production and cheap government,' i.e. low wages and no social legislation, a small army and navy, and even a moderate republicanism since bureaucracy and royalty might be thought unnecessary expenses. Still in the position of the early mill-owners and ironmasters, he objected equally to the expenses of imperialism and to the pressure towards social legislation exerted by the growing working-class movement. His grand sweep of vision from the nebulae to man truncated itself in the narrow prejudices of the dying class to which he belonged. But it is none the less valuable to us, for we can draw the conclusions he would not, and look forward to the inevitable further onward march of the principle of progressive integration and organisation.

The Giant Vista of Evolution

Let us now take another look at the giant vista which has all along been the background of our thoughts. The stage once prepared by cosmic evolution for the appearance of life, what follows shows an ever-rising level of organisation.[95] The number of parts in the wholes increases, as also the complexity of their structure and their inter-relations, the centralisation and efficiency of the means of control (whether humoral or neural) and the flexibility and versatility of their actions on the external environment. The wholes become, indeed, ever more independent of the external environment; by regulation of exchanges in energy and materials an interior equilibrium is doggedly maintained, and though death destroys it in the individual, it continues in the species. If we run through any biological textbook,[96] we find abundant illustrations of this. Although some of the paracrystals already mentioned show a degree of complexity which seems to approach that of the simplest living organisms, it is the autotrophic bacteria which first exhibit the basic phenomena of the new level, reproduction and metabolism. They were (and are to-day) able to synthesise all the carbon compounds needed for their architecture from the carbon dioxide of the atmosphere by the aid of energy obtained from oxidations of inorganic substances (iron, sulphur, etc.). The many kinds of parasitic bacteria with which most of us are more familiar are to be supposed a regression from these primitive forms. But all was not regression, for by another big step cells grew enormously larger and the protozoa came into being. Some of these developed the photosynthetic mechanism, others did not.

The former, when united together in colonies, became the first plants, the latter, similarly co-operating, became the first animals.[97] Then began that long procession of morphological forms and physiological achievements which the biologists have charted, with all its turning-points, the first coelomic organisation, the first endocrine mechanism, the first osmo-regulatory success, the first vertebral column, the first appearance of consciousness, the first making of a tool. At the point at which social life begins, factors set in so new as to constitute a recognisably higher level. Rational control of the environment now for the first time becomes a possibility.

The view of mind as a phenomenon of high organisational level, a quality of elaborate nervous organisation, is of course opposed by all idealist philosophers and many theologians, but it has wide support among psychologists and scientific philosophers. As examples I would mention a striking passage of the great psycho-pathologist, Henry Maudsley[98]; also the expressions of Samuel Alexander,[99] and the psychologists, R. G. Gordon,[100] C. K. Ogden,[101] E. B. Holt,[102] with many others. It need hardly be said that this view of mind has no connection with that which regards it as an 'epiphenomenon.' Perhaps few realise how well Lucretius stated the view of mind as a quality of high organisational levels in his great poem[103] :

> sed magni referre ea primum quantula constent,
> sensile quae faciunt, et qua sint praedita forma,
> motibus ordinibus posituris denique quae sint.
>
> (. . . but much it matters here
> Firstly, how small the seeds which thus compose
> The feeling thing, then, with what shapes endowed,
> And lastly what *positions* they assume
> What *motions,* what *arrangements.* . . .)

About the first beginnings of social organisation we know rather less than about some of the earlier, biological, stages. It is doubtful how far our consideration of humanity's problems can be assisted by a knowledge of the phenomena of social life in ants and bees (the social hymenoptera), for the anatomical nature of these animals, with its exoskeleton and rather inferior nervous system, is so far removed from our own.[104] The behaviour of the sub-human Primates has much more to tell us, but even that, as Zuckerman points out,[105] does not tell us much. Man's precursors probably lived a social life similar to that of all old-world monkeys and apes and were probably frugivorous. Probably at the beginning of the Pliocene, some twenty million years ago, when forests were reduced and the earth became more arid, a group of Primates with more plastic food-habits than the rest, managed to survive by becoming carnivorous. This transfer from a grazing to a hunting life must have had important social and sexual consequences, for with the change of diet there had to go a sexual division of labour in food-collection. Hence there had to be a repression of the dominant impulses which lead to polygyny in sub-human Primates. 'The price of our emergence as Man,' writes Zuckerman, 'would seem to have been the overt renunciation of a dominant Primate impulse in the field of sex. The price of our continued existence may well be further repressions of dominant impulses, and *further developments*[106] of the co-operative behaviour whose beginnings can be vaguely seen in our transition from a simian to a human level of existence.'

This was precisely Spencer's 'blind spot'. But we must take a closer look at co-operative behaviour, the necessary foundation for a higher order of human society. What has so far been said amounts to this, that evolution is not finished, that organisation has not yet reached its highest level, and that we can see the next stage in the co-operative commonwealth of humanity, the social-isation of the means of production.[107] Among the many evidences of this, there is space only to refer to two or three.

In the first place, the class-stratification such as we know it in all civilised communities, modelled on the pattern of Western Europe, is an ankylosis, a rigidity, a biological petrification, analogous in some ways to the armour-plating in which so many extinct animals spent their efforts. Jennings quite rightly says[108] that biology does not support democracy if democracy is defined as the belief that all human beings are alike or equal. It takes only common sense to see that they are each quite different from the other. But they all have needs and desires which could be satisfied and they all have contributions to make to the executive and productive power of the human collectivity. If democracy is defined as such a constitution of society that any part of the mass can in time supply individuals fitted for all its functions, then biology sanctions democracy. A democracy that produces experts.[109] Now it is painfully clear that in a class-stratified society there are very grave hindrances to this free utilisation of

existing ability. There is no real equality of opportunity. Ninety
per cent of the leaders are drawn from fifteen per cent of the
community. Geniuses and unusual types are likely to be stifled in
childhood. There is a crushing effect on the very birth of initiative
and constructive ability among the masses of the workers 'Not
merely poverty and bad living-conditions, but soul-killing cap-
touching subjection to a master class and the consciousness of
toiling to produce profits for that class, deadens initiative and
rouses hostility and antagonism to the whole industrial
machine.'[110]

But not only does society, in this lower stage of organisation,
fail to draw upon anything like the full force of good gene-
combinations that exist within it; it also fails to create as many of
these as would otherwise exist. The whole rationale of the sexual
reproductive system from its beginning among the lower inverte-
brates upwards, can only be understood as a mechanism for
producing an almost infinite diversity of qualities among the individuals of a species. Gene packs are shuffled anew in every reproductive act. The wider the range of individual differences the
greater the chance of favourable variations. Yet in class-stratified
human societies very severe checks are placed upon the mating-
choices of individuals, a procedure quite irrational sociologically
and ripe for conscious abolition.

The fact that the class-stratification has arisen, as we have said,
from differences in the relations of men to tools and productive
resources, some being owners of these essential things, and others
having access to them on the owners' terms, also brought about a
situation in which the accumulation of personal wealth is the only
recognised sign of success. In Herbert Spencer's own thought we
have had frequent occasion to remark upon it. The 'sagacious,'
the 'more worthy,' the 'prudent' etc., shall prosper, the weak shall
go to the wall. Spencer was perfectly well aware that this psychological valuation might have biological consequences; he hoped it
would. But the puzzle is that he should have been so certain that
the characteristics which lead men to rise economically in a class-
stratified capitalist society were those most desirable from a social
point of view. Where predatory rather than co-operative
behaviour wins the day, the path towards the higher social organisation is closed.[111] It was strange that Spencer could not see that
the very predatoriness which he described in primitive societies of
the 'military' type saturated also even the most highly developed

societies of what he called the 'industrial' type. By a curious and happy irony, however, the effects of this high valuation of socially undesirable qualities have been much less than might have been the case, for the birth-rate of the socially successful groups has for long been far below that of the socially unsuccessful, and hence relatively uneducated, workers. The use of the expression, 'survival of the fittest' for social success has therefore attained a definitely comic level. The only Darwinian meaning the term could have was as applied to those who send the largest number of offspring into the next generation. The successful capitalist, therefore, might be fittest for having a good time, but not for transmitting his genes to posterity.

The foregoing biological arguments have shown that the higher level of integration or organisation of the classless society would be greatly preferable to the class-stratified society. At this point the plain man might well object that a society with two, three, or four classes must surely be a more complex system than a classless one. To this, however, an obvious biological analogy provides the answer. We might as well assert that an annelid with twenty or thirty ganglia down its body is more complex than a mammal with a highly developed single brain. The almost unimaginable complexity of neurons, synapses, commissures, etc. in the human brain, forms a far higher organisational level than that of the annelid ganglia.[112] The human brain, indeed, is the outward and visible sign of the most fundamental of human characteristics, that by virtue of which sociology is a higher level than biology; the possession of consciousness. It follows that the more control consciousness has over human affairs, the more truly human, and hence super-human, man will become. Now the common ownership of the means of production implies the consciously planned control of production. No longer is production to be governed by the self-acting mechanism of profitability; it is to be carried on for communal use. No longer, at a given conjuncture of the world-market, will so many dozen factories automatically go out of action in some far corner of the earth, throwing some thousands of workers into immediate poverty, and diverting the energies of the owners into other channels. No longer will thermodynamic efficiency and geographic common sense alike be turned upside down at the irrational dictates of a profit-making system. By the deliberate decisions of a central planning body the production and distribution of goods will be consciously organised. Spencer might well have welcomed such a body as the real analogue of the higher nervous centres for which he had to seek in contemporary society in vain. Its rationalisation of the irrational in terms of practice will be the precise counterpart of the rationalisation of the irrational in terms of theory which the scientific method carries out in research every day.

But this vast extension of conscious control could not take place without the willing conscious co-operation of the constituent effector persons. In Vaughan's discussion of Rousseau there is a fine passage on the conception of the State.[113] 'It is of the essence of Rousseau's theory,' writes Vaughan, 'that the State is no power which imposes itself from without; that, on the contrary, it is more truly part of the individual than the individual himself. The change he wrought in the conception of the individual involves a corresponding change in the conception of the State. The bureaucratic machinery, which had slowly fastened itself on Europe, is thrown to the winds. Its place is taken by the idea of a free community, each member of which has as large a share in determining the "general will" as his fellows; in which, so far as human frailty allows, the general will takes up into itself the will of all. . . . The only State he recognises as legitimate is the State of which the sovereign is the People.' But it is evident that none of this service which is perfect freedom can be secured without unlimited universal education and the abolition of classes. The matter has been put more shortly : 'Every cook,' said Lenin, 'must learn to rule the State.'

Every transition from the unconscious to the conscious implies a step from bondage to freedom, from lower to higher level of organisation. All early agriculture and storage of food-products necessitated more conscious control than before. Increases in the efficiency of mechanisms of transport from the horse to the aeroplane widened men's conscious horizons. In the realm of the individual, modern psychology provides brilliant examples of the liberating effects of a passage from the unconscious to the conscious, e.g. in the cure of the obsessional neuroses. Up to the present all commercial transactions have been the instruments of a peculiarly subtle form of bondage which was called by Marx the 'fetishism of commodities.'[114] Relations such as those of exchange in the open market between commodities, appear at first sight to be relations between things, but are on the contrary relations between persons, the persons who produced them and the persons who will consume them. To forget this is to be forced to assent to the various 'iron laws' of political economy, which have in reality nothing inescapable about them, once the personal relationship is grasped.[115] In one of the most inspired passages he ever wrote,[116] Engels said that 'the seizure of the means of production by society puts an end to commodity production and hence to the domination of the product over the producer. Anarchy in social production is replaced by conscious organisation on a planned basis. The struggle for individual existence comes to an end. And at this point, in a certain sense, man finally cuts himself off from the animal world, leaves the conditions of animal existence behind him, and enters conditions which are really human. . . . It is humanity's leap from the realm of necessity into the realm of freedom.'

Lastly, it must be emphasised that our present civilisation is manifestly not a state of stable equilibrium. The enormous advances in scientific knowledge and practical technique, due themselves in a large degree to the middle-class economic system of which Spencer was the representative, have made that system an anachronism. Nothing short of the absolute abolition of private ownership of resources and machines, the abolition of national sovereignties, and the government of the world by a power proceeding from the class which must abolish classes, will suit the technical situation of the twentieth century.

After all, within single human lifetimes it has sometimes been possible to discern the advance of human society to ever more complex unities and higher levels of organisation. Towards the end of his noble autobiography,[117] that great American, Henry Adams, noted the two outstanding instances of the victory of the larger unit in his own experience, first, the triumph of the North in the American Civil War, secondly, the failure of the 'trust-busting' period of legislation. 'All one's life one had struggled for unity, and unity had always won.' It may be illuminating to regard the present World War (1942) as a movement of secessionism just as surely as the Civil War which Adams lived through—not indeed from a World State already in being, but from the idea of the World State for which humanity is obviously ready. All dominating racialisms, at this stage of world history, are secessions from this wider idea. And secessionist minorities are bound to fail because, as Seversky[118] has put it, that side 'with the greatest economic strength, industrial capacity, and engineering ingenuity will have the advantage, as always throughout history.' We may agree with the words of a Russian philosopher; 'However strong the forces of armed reaction, in the end progressive mankind has invariably found the strength to win the victory, and to preserve and develop the achievements of the human mind.[119]

Evolution and Inevitability

Now if it has been shown that the organisation of human society is only as yet at the beginning of its triumphs, and that these triumphs are *inevitable*,[120] since they lie along the road traced out hitherto by the entire evolutionary process, is there not some danger lest the effect of such a belief should be to withdraw our own activity from the daily struggle for a better, because better organised, world? If collectivism[121] is inevitable, why not just sit and wait for it? There is here a moral and psychological problem of considerable interest, to which a whole book has been devoted by Brameld.[122] How do real alternatives arise in the world-process, if the result is inevitable? To this question the answer of a representative communist spokesman would be of interest. We have it in a recent paper of R. P. Dutt, arising out of a controversy with the Dutch writer de Leeuw.[123] 'It is the very heart,' he says, 'of the revolutionary marxist understanding of inevitability that it has nothing in common with the mechanical fatalism of which our opponents incorrectly accuse us. This inevitability is realised in practice through living human wills under given social conditions, consciously reacting to those conditions, and consciously choosing their line between alternative possibilities seen by them within the given conditions. "Man makes his own history, but not out of the whole cloth." We are able scientifically to predict the inevitable outcome, because we are able to analyse the social conditions governing the consciousness, and the line of development, of those social conditions. We are able to analyse the growth of contradictions, and the consequent accumulation of forces generating ever greater revolutionary consciousness and will in the exploited majority, till they become strong enough to overcome all obstacles, and conquer. We are able to lay down with scientific precision that every failure, every choice of an incorrect path, can only be temporary, because the outcome can in no way solve the contradictions generating the revolutionary consciousness and will. These contradictions then only lead to renewed and intensified struggle, up to final victory. The process is inevitable. But the human consciousness of the participants in this inevitable process is not the consciousness of automatic cogs in a predetermined mechanism. It is the consciousness of living, active, human beings, revolting against intolerable evils, deliberately with thought and passion choosing a new alternative, doing and daring all to achieve a new world, and ready to give their lives in the fight because of their intense desire to help by such actions to make possible the achievement of the goal. This fighting revolutionary consciousness is by no means a bowing to an inevitable outcome, but is most actively a seeking to tip the balance and make certain by action the victory of one alternative and the defeat of another alternative. Every revolutionary worth his salt acts in every stage of the fight as if the whole future of the revolution depended on his action. And in presenting the issues of the present day to the masses, we present them not as placid inevitabilities to contemplate like the movement of the stars, but as a gigantic issue with the whole future of humanity at stake, calling for the utmost determination, courage, sacrifice, and will to conquer. This is the essence of the revolutionary marxist understanding of inevitability.'

From this passage two principal thoughts emerge. In the first place, the marxist writer speaks of inevitability only because he is confident that he understands the nature of human beings and their reactions to external conditions. Their knowledge of good and evil, pleasure and pain, will have its ultimate effect and that effect is inevitable.

We can take our stand upon the simple, natural, healthy, human desires of the mass of mankind, for love, for children, for socially useful work, for fundamental decency and dignity. This is the meaning of the ancient Confucian advice to rulers, in the *Ta Hsüeh* (Great Learning)—*Min chih so hao, hao chih; min chih so ô, ô chih*; 'Love what the people love, and hate what the people hate.'

If we explore more closely the mechanism of this inevitability we see that it is connected with the contradictions which arise in each successive stage of human history. Thus modern nationalist states must arm their workers in their struggles with foreign imperialisms, yet at the same time this is to arm their destroyers. They must engage in colonial development, but this gives rise to native movements of liberation. In the last resort fascist theory is brought in to save the decaying structure, and this essays to substitute for Reason a fantastic irrational mythology, but on the other hand modern capitalism cannot get on without effective control over Nature, and this necessitates scientific rationality.

Secondly, inevitability once admitted, the time-scale remains only too obscure. It is true that we might envisage a long period of stagnation as the outcome of our present civilisation. China is sometimes thought (without much justice) to present a century-long spectacle of such stagnation. But whereas this might be compatible with an agricultural, bureaucratic, isolated community lacking good communications and so able to sterilise revolutionary movements within itself, it is much more difficult to imagine such a state of affairs existing in a civilisation based on scientific technology. Let us grant, however, that some kind of scientifically stablised stagnant class-stratified totalitarian social organism might succeed our own age. Hence the great significance of the word 'temporary' used in the passage from the writer quoted above. Failures and set-backs and blind alleys there may be in plenty, but though the ultimate victory is not in doubt, it must be remembered what each failure may mean. It may mean the enslavement of whole peoples for many generations, the destruction of culture and learning over a wide part of the world, the stagnation of social progress in such regions, the martyrdom of many thousands of our best and noblest friends. In the ancient phrase : 'the saints under the altar cry, O Lord, how long, how long?' To speak of the inevitability of our higher integrative level is to say nothing of when it will come.[124]

Conclusion

It would be a pity, however, to conclude this lecture upon a note of sadness. Let us return to the year 1838, when Herbert Spencer was a young man of seventeen. The youth of anyone so exsuccous as Spencer was in his old age has always a peculiar charm. This was the year in which Marx was toiling in Berlin at his doctoral dissertation on Democritus and Epicurus, Engels was quietly acquiring a business training at Bremen, and Darwin, just back from the voyage of the *Beagle*, was starting his first Notebook on the Transformations of Species.[125] Spencer, as befitted his later outlook, was in the midst of British industry. Under Mr Robert Stephenson, the chief engineer of the London and

F

Birmingham Railway, young Mr Spencer made measurements of embankments and cuttings, drafted out plans, and sketched minor inventions in his spare time. To every man who much affects his fellows, there comes at one time or another in his life a symbolic event, and some sixty-five years later Spencer described it in language which insists upon quotation.[126]

'Harris and I were sent down one day early in August to make a survey of Wolverton station, and we completed it before evening set in. Wolverton, being then the temporary terminus, between which and Rugby the traffic was carried on by coaches, was the place whence the trains to London started. The last of them was the mail, leaving somewhere about 8. If I remember rightly there were at that time only five trains in the day and none at night. A difficulty arose. The mail did not stop between Watford and London, but I wished to stop at the intermediate station, Harrow, that being the nearest point to Wembley. It turned out that there was at Wolverton no vehicle having a brake to it—nothing available but a coach-truck. Being without alternative, I directed the station-master to attach this to the train. After travelling with my companion in the usual way till we reached Watford, I bade him goodnight, and got into the coach-truck. Away the train went into the gloom of the evening, and for some six or seven miles I travelled unconcernedly, knowing the objects along the line well, and continually identifying my whereabouts. Presently we reached a bridge about a mile and a half to the north of Harrow station. Being quite aware that the line at this point, and for a long distance in advance, falls towards London at the rate of 1 in 330, I expected that the coach-truck, having no brake, would take a long time to stop. A mile and a half would, it seemed, be sufficient allowance, and on coming to the said bridge, I uncoupled the truck and sat down. In a few seconds I got up again to see whether all the couplings were unhooked, for, to my surprise, the truck seemed to be going on with the train. There was no coupling left unhooked, however, and it became clear that I had allowed an insufficient distance for the gradual arrest. Though the incline is quite invisible to the eye, being less than an inch in nine yards, yet its effect was very decided; and the axles being, no doubt, well-greased, the truck maintained its velocity. Far from having stopped when Harrow was reached, I was less than a dozen yards behind the train! My dismay as we rushed through the station at some thirty miles an hour may be well imagined. .... After passing Harrow station the line enters upon a curve, and a loss of velocity necessarily followed. The train now began rapidly to increase its distance, and shortly disappeared into the gloom. Still, though my speed had diminished, I rushed on at a great pace. Presently, seeing at a little distance in front the light of a lantern, held, I concluded, by a foreman of the plate-layers, who was going back to the station after having seen the last train pass, I shouted to him; thinking that if he would run at the top of his speed he might perhaps catch hold of the waggon and gradually arrest it. He, however, stood staring; too much astonished, even if he understood me, and as I learned next day, when he reached Harrow, reported he had met a man in a newly-invented carriage which had run away with him... ! After being carried some two miles beyond Harrow, I began rather to rejoice that the truck was going so far, for I remembered that at no great distance in advance was the Brent siding, into which the truck might easily be pushed instead of back to Harrow. I looked with satisfaction to this prospect, entertaining no doubt that the waggon would come to rest in time. By and by, however, it became clear that the truck would not only reach this siding but pass it; and then came not a little alarm, for a mile or so further along was the level-crossing at Willesden, where I should probably be thrown out and killed. .... However, on reaching Brent bridge, the truck began to slacken speed, and finally came to a stand in the middle of the embankment crossing the Brent valley.'

How Spencer had to seek help to clear the line and finally got home in the early hours of the morning, we need not here relate. But of all the symbolic occurrences which have happened to great men, this is surely one of the most remarkable. Spencer wanted to stop at the intermediate station in evolutionary sociology, but in the progress of organisation to ever higher levels, there is no such opportunity. The class of which he was the intellectual representative wanted to stop at the intermediate station of domestic capitalism, but the inner logic of the process demanded that expansion should go on and the local mill-owner should give place to the trustified imperialist. Moreover, the inevitable industrialisation of the working-class led to demands of diametrically opposite nature, so that Spencer was driven into protesting vainly against both the 'degeneration' into militarism, and the socialist movement which fought against 'free competition.' His wide, and substantially correct, survey of evolution led up only to the anti-climax of middle-class liberal economic individualism, past which, in spite of himself, he was carried on protesting.

But let us celebrate his noble range of vision nevertheless. The onward progress of integration and organisation cannot be arrested. As I write, there rages in one of the most beautiful of European countries a tragic and terrible struggle between the People and their Adversary. The sound of its gunfire penetrates any College court, no matter how peaceful it may seem. Some faith may be needed to assert with boldness that, even if Spanish democracy be overwhelmed, even if the great democracy of the Soviet Union itself were to be overwhelmed, no matter what shattering blows the cause of consciousness may receive, the end is sure. The higher stages of integration and organisation towards which we look have all the authority of evolution behind them. It is no other than Herbert Spencer himself who contributes to this faith, if faith it be. The devil, as Hippolytus said long ago, may resist the cosmic process. But the last victory will not be his.

Notes

1. I am not quite sure when the term 'levels' was first used in this way, perhaps in S. Alexander's *Space, Time and Deity* (London, 1927, vol. ii, p. 52; 1st edn., 1920). This led to an interesting discussion among American authors (H. C. Brown, *Journ. Philos.*, 1926, **23**, 113; G. P. Conger, *Journ. Philos.*, 1925, **22**, 309) which I did not know about when this lecture was first written and printed. Nor did I know of the valuable book of the veteran American biologist, E. G. Conklin, *The Direction of Human Evolution* (New York, 1921), and that of the Manchester anatomist, F. Wood-Jones, *Design and Purpose* (London, 1942), which, broadly speaking, urge the same general viewpoint as that of the present lecture.
2. Something approaching a definition of organisation will be given later, see Cf. also pp. 20, 143, 152.
3. References to Herbert Spencer's own writings will be found in the footnotes as follows:
   > FP, *First Principles* (6th edn., London, 1900).
   > PB, *Principles of Biology* (London, 1898).
   > PS, *Principles of Sociology* (London, 1876).
   > A, *Autobiography* (London, 1904).
4. Though it must be remembered that Roman Catholic writers are still fighting a rearguard action against it, and the devout engineer, R. O. Kapp, has attempted to reintroduce special creation under new terminology in his *Science versus Materialism* (London, 1940).
5. See the papers by N. W. Pirie and others in the Hopkins Presentation Volume, *Perspectives in Biochemistry* (Cambridge, 1937).

6. Cf. Samuel Alexander, *Space, Time and Deity* (London, 1927), vol. i, p. 36 fn.: 'I should say' (in contradistinction to Bertrand Russell) 'that the importance of any particular time is rather practical than theoretical, but to realise the importance of Time as such is the gate of wisdom.'

7. Conrad Noel's books, *Byways of Belief* (London, 1912); *The Battle of the Flags* (London, 1922); *Life of Jesus* (London, 1937); and *Jesus the Heretic* (London, 1939), deserve to be even more widely known than they are, but his influence spread far and wide by the compellingness of his preaching and the exceptional beauty and grace of the Liturgy as celebrated at Thaxted.

8. Glover, T. R., *The Conflict of Religions in the Early Roman Empire* (London, 1919).

9. W. R. Inge, *Christian Mysticism* (London, 1921), p. 95; see also his *Philosophy of Plotinus* (London, 1929).

10. Ch. 40, v. 3 ff.

11. Ch. 40, v. 10.

12. Ch. 41, v. 22.

13. Ch. 31, vv. 2–20.

14. For the historical development of the idea of the Kingdom, see Bp. A. Robertson's *Regnum Dei* (London, 1901).

15. Cf. C. A. Scott, art. 'Donatists' in Hastings' *Encyclopaedia of Religion and Ethics*.

16. R. Pascal, 'Communism in the Middle Ages and the Reformation' in *Christianity and the Social Revolution* (London, 1935).

17. Cf. F. Engels, *The Peasant War in Germany* (New York, 1926).

18. Cf. K. Kautsky, *Communism in Central Europe in the Time of the Reformation* (London, 1897), and R. Pascal, *The Social Basis of the German Reformation* (London, 1933).

19. Cf. E. Bernstein, *Cromwell and Communism* (London, 1930).

20. 'The Idea of Progress' in *Outspoken Essays*, vol. ii (London, 1923). It must with regret be recorded that some ten years afterwards Inge, in his Spencer Lecture for 1934, 'Liberty and Natural Rights,' gave his official blessing to fascism as the best form of human society yet devised. Opposition to the idea of progress is, indeed, a characteristic common to all fascist philosophers. Examples are easy to find. 'The materialist outlook,' wrote Otto Strasser, 'has, as is well known, the idea of progress as one of its motive forces. There is no worse sort of fatalism than this spiritual hallucination that humanity has for millions of years now been marching along a road which leads for ever upward, decorated on the right and left with the milestones of development. How has this fixed idea become possible? Surely everyone knows from his own experience that life is a circle, not a line' (*Wir suchen Deutschland*, p. 165). So also Othmar Spann: 'Darwin and Marx have done terrible harm to our civilisation by their mechanical (*sic*) conception of development. For this conception of development deprives every activity of value since today each one is overcome by tomorrow. And this has given birth to utilitarianism, materialism, and nihilism (*sic*) which are characteristic of our time' (*Kategorienlehre*, 1924, p. 211). And the Russian Orthodox Church adds its mite to the treasury. It has an Inge of its own. 'The Humanism of the Renaissance,' writes Berdyaev, 'has not strengthened man but weakened him; that is the paradoxical *dénouement* of modern history.... European man strode into modern history full of confidence in himself and his creative powers, in this dawn everything seemed to depend upon his own creative powers, to which he put no frontiers or limits; today he leaves it to pass into an unknown epoch, discouraged, his faith in shreds, threatened with the loss for ever of the core of his personality' (*The End of Our Time*, 1933, p. 15). In 1940 Inge returned to his attack on the idea of progress in *The Fall of the Idols* (London).

21. Another essay, *Our Present Discontents* (1919), will long remain a museum

piece of upper middle-class spitefulness, unworthy of a Christian, still less a priest.

22. Such as Hans Driesch in his *Science and Philosophy of the Organism* (London, 1908).

23. SB, p. 247.

24. (London, 1929).

25. 'Obscurantist' organicism was well castigated by N. I. Bukharin in the Marx Memorial Volume of the Moscow Academy of Science, 1933 (Eng. tr. *Marxism and Modern Thought*, p. 26).

26. C. D. Broad in his *The Mind and its Place in Nature* (London, 1925), had argued along lines similar to Woodger's when he rejected both 'substantial vitalism' and 'biological mechanism' in favour of 'emergent vitalism', but his treatment was for various reasons unsatisfactory and did not have much influence among biologists.

27. 'Every new form of moving matter thus has its own special laws. But this enriched form and these new laws are not cut off by a Chinese wall from those historically preceding them. The latter still exist in "sublated form" '; Bukharin, *loc. cit.*, p. 31.

28. *Proc. Aristot. Soc.*, 1932, **32**, 117.

29. English scholars owe a debt to Lancelot Hogben, who was one of the first about this time to try to translate dialectical materialism (more or less successfully) into English idiom; cf. his article in *Psyche*, 1931, **12**, 2. Certain mistakes afterwards pointed out (P. A. Sloan, *Psyche*, 1933, **13**, 178) do not diminish this debt. In the Aristotelian Society's Symposium on Materialism for 1928 there had been no mention of dialectical materialism, and a similar silence had reigned in the French symposium *Le Matérialisme Actuel* (Paris, 1920) to which H. Bergson, H. Poincaré, Ch. Gide, and others had contributed.

30. Art. 'The Physical and the Biological in the Process of Organic Evolution' in *Science at the Cross Roads* (Kniga, London, 1931); [2nd. ed., Cass, London, 1971].

31. In the belief that the sense of the original is better conveyed, the word 'different' is substituted for 'varied' which actually appears in the text.

32. M. Prenant, *Bull. Soc. Philomath.*, Paris, 1933, **116**, 84.

33. V. I. Lenin, 'The Teachings of Karl Marx,' in *Marx, Engels and Marxism* (London, 1931).

34. J. D. Bernal, in *Aspects of Dialectical Materialism* (London, 1934), pp. 90 and 102.

35. It is interesting that Spencer himself had something to say on chemical embryology, in his time an almost uncharted field:

'The clearest, most numerous, and most varied illustrations of the advance in multiformity that accompanies the advance in integration, are furnished by living bodies. . . . The history of every plant and every animal, while it is a history of increasing bulk, is also a history of simultaneously-increasing differences among the parts. This transformation has several aspects. The chemical composition, which is almost uniform throughout the substance of a germ, vegetal or animal, gradually ceases to be uniform. The several compounds, nitrogenous and non-nitrogenous, which were homogeneously mixed, segregate by degrees, become diversely proportioned in diverse places, and produce new compounds by transformation or modification. . . . The yelk, or essential part of an animal-ovum, having components which are at first evenly diffused among one another, chemically transforms itself in like manner. Its protein, its fats, its salts, become dissimilarly proportioned in different localities; and multiplication of isomeric forms leads to further mixtures and combinations that constitute minor distinctions of parts. Here a mass, darkening by accumulation of haematine, presently dissolves into blood. There fatty and albuminous matters uniting, compose nerve-tissue. At this spot the nitrogenous substance takes on the character of cartilage; at that calcareous salts, gathering together in the cartilage, lay the foundation of bone. All these chemical differentiations slowly become more marked and more numerous.' FP, p. 306.

36. FP, p. 261.
37. FP, pp. 258, 259.
38. FP, p. 299.
39. FP, p. 281.
40. FP, p. 282.
41. FP, p. 284.
42. FP, p. 288.
43. FP, p. 290.
44. FP, p. 300.
45. FP, pp. 301–14.
46. FP, pp. 351 and 367.
47. It is important to note that much of Spencer's argumentation depended on assumptions about energy which antedated modern statistical interpretations of the second law of thermodynamics. There is now, therefore, a certain contradiction here. The universe is passing, it is said, from less probable to more probable states, as if a basic shuffling process was continually at work. The word 'organisation' is applied to the initial state of the universe, so that the increase of entropy must imply progressive disorganisation. The irreversibility of time is said to depend on this. We must, therefore, say either that thermodynamical organisation is quite a different thing from crystalline-biological-social organisation, or else that the persistent increase in the latter with time, which cannot be gainsaid, involves a correspondingly greater decrease of organisation somewhere else in the universe. See pp. 173, 184 ff. below.
48. FP, pp. 368 and 372.
49. PB, I. 99.
50. PB, I. 176.
51. It was first formulated in a review 'Transcendental Physiology' in the *Westminster Review* in 1857 (A, I, 503). Whether his contemporary, Claude Bernard, who developed the concept of the *fixité du milieu intérieur* had any hand in it, we do not know.
52. See E. Baldwin, *Comparative Biochemistry* (Cambridge, 1937).
53. See A. S. Pearse & F. G. Hall, *Homoiothermism* (New York, 1928).
54. See J. Barcroft, *The Architecture of Physiological Function* (Cambridge, 1934).
55. See A. C. Redfield, *Quart. Rev. Biol.*, 1933, **8** 31.
56. See J. Needham, *Chemical Embryology* (Cambridge, 1931).
57. FP, pp. 382 ff; see C. H. Waddington, *Organisers and Genes* (Cambridge, 1940).
58. PB, I. 365.
59. PB, I. 367.
60. PS, I. 617.
61. Though full of errors, both in fact and theory, the grandiose world history of O. Spengler, *The Decline of the West*, which since its first uncritical reception, has fallen into undeserved discredit, is strikingly in the Spencerian tradition, for it delineates the rise and fall of quite distinguishable cultural 'organisms,' (see pp. 103 ff, above).
62. PS, I. 468, 470, 491, 495.
63. PS, I. 512.
64. PS, I. 547, 552.
65. PS, I. 479 and 612, A, I. 504.

66. PS, II. 260.
67. The seventh; 'Biological Fact and the Structure of Society' in *Herbert Spencer Lectures, Decennial Issue* (Oxford, 1916). The lecture was given in 1912.
68. Loc. cit., pp. 31 and 32.
69. On this a great deal could be written. Reference may be made to the following discussions as valuable starting-points for investigation:
C. Bouglé, art. 'Darwinism and Sociology' in *Darwin and Modern Science*, ed. A. C. Seward (Cambridge, 1910); D. G. Ritchie, *Darwinism and Politics* (London, 1889); J. G. Haycraft, *Darwinism and Race Progress* (London, 1900); L. Woltmann, *Die Darwinische Theorie u.d. Sozialismus* (Dusseldorf, 1899); O. Hertwig, *Zur Abwehr des ethischen, sozialen, und politischen Darwinismus* (Jena, 1921); J. S. Huxley, *Proc. Brit. Assoc.*, 1936, p. 81.
    We know now that the results of intra-specific competition are by no means necessarily good. As Huxley says, 'they may be neutral, they may be a dangerous balance of useful and harmful, or they may be definitely deleterious.'
70. PS, I. 577, 590.
71. PS, I. 585.
72. PS, I. 585.
73. PS, I. 587.
74. PS, I. 601.
75. A, II. 329 ff., 375 ff. Spencer attributed much of his breakdown in health to his activities in connection with a league for 'anti-militancy' and 'anti-aggression,' which seems to have got little public support.
76. A, II. 5.
77. Spencer's discussion of communism illustrates this point strikingly. 'State administrations,' he says (PS, II. 751), 'worked by taxes falling in more than due proportion upon those whose greater powers have brought them greater means, will give to citizens of smaller powers more benefits than they have earned. And this burdening of the better by the worse, must check the evolution of a higher and more adapted nature.' It is almost incredible that Spencer could have taken business success as his criterion of a high and adapted nature. 'The diffusion,' he says (loc. cit.), 'of political power unaccompanied by the limitation of political functions, issues in communism. For the direct defrauding of the many by the few, it substitutes the indirect defrauding of the few by the many; evil proportionate to the inequity, being the result in the one case as in the other.' An invitation to think out just what this means obviates any other comment.
78. PS, II. 264.
79. FP, p. 335.
80. (London, 1850).
81. A, II. 459.
82. (London, 1881.)
83. (London, 1893.)
84. See E. Ferri's *Socialism and Positive Science* (London, 1906), p. 153.
85. *My Apprenticeship*, by B. Webb (London, 1929), p. 292.
86. *Soviet Communism*, by S. and B. Webb (London, 1935).
87. In Spencer I find no reference to Marx; in the letters of Marx, however, there is one reference to Spencer. Though a little cruel, it is too amusing to omit. Writing to Engels on May 23, 1868, Marx says:
    'Du scheinst mir auf dem Holzweg zu sein, mit Deiner Scheu, so einfache Figuren wie G-W-G etc. den englischen Revue-philister vorzuführen. Umgekehrt. Wenn du, wie ich, gezwungen gewesen wärst, die ökonomischen Artikel der Herren Lalor, H. Spencer, Macleod, etc. im Westminster Review, etc. zu lesen, so würdest Du sehn, dass alle die ökono-

mischen Trivialitäten so zum Hals dick haben—und auch wissen, dass ihre Leser sie dick haben—dass sie durch pseudo-philosophical oder pseudoscientific slang die Schmiere zu würzen suchen. Der Pseudo-charakter macht die Sache (die an sich = O) keineswegs leicht verständlich. Umgekehrt. Die Kunst besteht darin, den Leser so mystifizieren und ihm kopfbrechen so verursachen, damit er schliesslich zu seiner Beruhigung entdeckt, dass diese hard words nur Maskeraden von *loci communes* sind. Kommt hinzu, dass die Leser der Fortnightly wie der Westminster Review, sich smeicheln, die longest heads of England (der übrigen Welt, versteht sich von selbst) zu sein.' Marx-Engels Gesamtausgabe, ed. Riazanov, Abt. III, Bd. 4, p. 58.
   [G-W-G means Geld-Ware-Geld.]

88. In *Karl Marx's Capital* by A. D. Lindsay (Oxford, 1935).

89. By V. I. Lenin in *Marx, Engels and Marxism* (London, 1934), pp. 7 and 50.

90. H. D. Dickinson, *Highway*, 1936, p. 82.

91. e.g. FP, p. 391.

92. *Communist Manifesto*, 1848; first published in England, 1850.

93. H. Pirenne, *Economic and Social History of Medieval Europe* (London, 1936).

94. F. Borkenau, *Der Übergang von feudalen zum bürgerlichen Weltbild; Studien zur Geschichte der Philosophie der Manufakturperiode* (Paris, 1934).

95. This 'preparation of the stage' presents problems of much interest, the classical treatment of which is *The Fitness of the Environment* (New York, 1913) by Lawrence J. Henderson. Consideration of the properties of water, carbon dioxide, ammonia, etc., shows that if anything with properties at all akin to what we know as life was to develop, they must needs have the properties they actually did have. This reciprocal fitness of the environment greatly strengthens our view of the unity and continuity of the evolutionary process.

96. For a student of another subject, an admirably philosophic introduction to biology as a whole can be had in the freshly-written book of H. H. Newman, *Outlines of General Zoology* (New York, 1936). An excellent discussion of progress in evolution is given by J. S. Huxley in his presidential address to the British Association, 1936, pp. 96 ff.

97. The beginnings of social behaviour, if not of social organisation, can be seen already in the aggregations of free-living protozoa (cf. H. S. Jennings, *Behaviour of the Lower Organisms*, New York, 1906; *The Beginnings of Social Behaviour in Unicellular Organisms*, Philadelphia, 1941; and in *Science* 1941, **94**, 447; also W. C. Allee, *Animal Aggregations*, Chicago, 1931; *Biol. Rev.*, 1934, **9**, 1; *The Social Life of Animals*, New York, 1938).

98. *Body and Will* (London, 1883), p. 132.

99. *Space, Time and Deity* (London, 1927), vol. i, p. xiii.

100. *Personality* (London, 1926).

101. *The Meaning of Psychology* (New York, 1926).

102. *The Concept of Consciousness* (London, 1914).

103. *De Rer. Nat.* II, 894.

104. Popular writers such as J. Langdon-Davies in his *Short History of the Future* (London, 1936) go somewhat astray here.

105. S. Zuckerman, article 'The Biological Background of Social Behaviour,' in *Further Papers in the Social Sciences* (London, 1937).

106. Italics mine.

107. For lack of space we pass here over the enormous gulf between the first beginnings of social organisation and the inadequacies of social organisation still existing in our own time. This emphasises the continuity of the factor of co-operation, with all the psychological adjustments that that implies. But

it is essential to realise that within the sociological level there have been separate stages or levels, analogous perhaps to the mesoforms which we find as we pass from true liquids to true crystals. Thus it seems that the first attainment of an efficient agriculture was of enormous significance since it provided a food surplus and led to the formation of classes when this surplus came under partly or wholly private ownership. Similarly the first attainment of efficient machinery for the production of commodities had a profound effect, in the 'industrial revolution' and the appearance of a truly proletarian class. The problems of today pre-suppose the accomplishment of these great changes in human social life; hence it is useless to ask why a classless society or the conscious control of production could not have been introduced centuries ago.

108. H. S. Jennings, *The Biological Basis of Human Nature* (London, 1931), p. 221.

109. Jennings, loc. cit.

110. *Britain without Capitalists* (London, 1936), p. 48.

111. This is the theme of the classical essay of the geneticist H. J. Muller, 'The Dominance of Economics over Eugenics,' *Sci. Monthly*, 1933, **37**, 40.

112. The processes of 'rationalisation' in industry offer another parallel. When the American Railway Association reduces the number of types of axles from 59 to 5 numerical complexity decreases but organisation increases. *Mere* complexity has, of course, nothing to do with organisation—it may mean confusion only—and purposed reduction of complexity at a lower level is in the interest of activities at higher levels. Industrial standardisation is an example which would have appealed greatly to Herbert Spencer, the railway engineer.

113. *The Political Writings of J. J. Rousseau*, edited with introduction and notes by C. E. Vaughan (Cambridge, 1915), p. 112.

114. 'The commodity form and the value relation between the labour products which finds expression in the commodity form, have nothing whatever to do with the physical properties of the commodities or with the material relations that arise out of these physical properties. We are concerned only with a definite social relation between human beings, which in their eyes, has here assumed the semblance of a relation between things. To find an analogy, we must enter the nebulous world of religion. In that world, products of the human mind become independent shapes, endowed with lives of their own, and able to enter into relations with men and women. The products of the human hand do the same thing in the world of commodities. I speak of this as the *fetishistic character* which attaches to the products of labour, as soon as they are produced in the form of commodities. It is inseperable from commodity production.'—K. Marx, *Capital*, tr. E. and C. Paul (London, 1928), p. 45.

115. The realisation of the entry of personal relationships at this point gives us the answer to the perplexity of Frederic Harrison the positivist in his Herbert Spencer lecture of 1905. He said that while according to 'evolutionary philosophy' the unceasing redistribution of matter and motion seemed to be the fundamental law, he himself could be content with nothing which did not include mention of 'progress,' 'order,' 'living for others,' justice, love, etc. But these things are not something superadded to nature, they arise within it and grow out of it. Comradeship is precisely one of the essential conditions for high social organisation, and like all the other highest human qualities a natural product. After Bacon's time, said Marx (in the *Holy Family*) materialism became misanthropic and ascetic. It was rescued by the French and by Marx himself.

116. F. Engels, *Anti-Dühring* (London, n.d.), p. 318.

117. *The Education of Henry Adams* (first published by the Massachusetts Historical Society, 1907, also London, 1928), pp. 398, 402, 500.

118. A. Seversky, *Victory through Air Power* (London, 1940), p. 140.

119. G. Alexandrov, *Soviet War News*, 2nd June, 1942. Cf. also 'It will be convincingly demonstrated that those who invoked force in violation of their obligations to a world order were destroyed by the inherent capacity of the world order to invoke a greater force in its own defence' (2nd Report of Carnegie Organisation of Peace Commission, 1942, p. 163).

120. 'The downfall of the bourgeoisie and the victory of the proletariat are equally *inevitable*.'—Marx and Engels, *Manifesto*, 1848.

'Once you unbridle the forces (of world war) which you will be powerless to cope with, then, however matters go, you will be ruined at the end of the tragedy, and the victory of the proletariat will either have already been won, or will in any case have become inevitable'—Engels, preface to Borkheim's *Erinnerung*, 1887.

With these passages it is interesting to compare a Christian formulation: 'We believe that there is a purpose running throughout the whole universe, a purpose and a plan, and that if there be a purpose there must be a Purposer, whom we call God; and that in spite of the at present inexplicable mystery of pain and cruelty, He is expressing Himself through the everyday virtues of the common people, through the heroic self-sacrifice and service of the saints, and through Jesus, the crown of humankind, God's word and energy who gives meaning and purpose to the age-long process. We believe that . . . he opened the gate of heaven to all believers. This gate is not only a gate into a realm beyond death, but into a realm which descends and is incarnated in a fair, joyful, and equal commonwealth on the arena of this earth.'—Conrad Noel, *Church Militant*, 1937.

121. There exists a misapprehension in the minds of some, that the various forms of fascist government embody collectivism. This, however, has been completely exploded by many students, see e.g. G. Salvemini, *Under the Axe of Fascism* (London, 1936), and R. Pascal, *The Nazi Dictatorship* (London, 1934), or F. L. Schuman, *Hitler and the Nazi Dictatorship* (London, 1936), for Italy and Germany respectively. It is clear that fascism is a screen for the maintenance and stabilisation of existing class-stratification. The barbaric and militaristic tenets of fascism would be menacing indeed if we did not reflect that a relapse into barbarism seems to accompany each great transformation of economic structure. When feudalism was giving place to middle-class capitalism there were the 'wars of religion,' and the witchcraft mania, even before the English civil war and the French revolution. The middle class will not consent to merge itself in the comradeship of mankind without similar catastrophes.

122. T. B. H. Brameld, *Philosophic Approach to Communism* (Chicago, 1933).

123. R. P. Dutt, *Communist International*, 1935, **12**, 604.

124. Cf. the interesting analysis of causality and determinism by H. Levy, *Proc. Aristot. Soc.*, 1937, **37**, p. 89. 'Such a form of analysis,' he concludes, 'will tell us how the causal process operates, and, in terms of the qualities of subsidiary group-isolates, when a dialectical change will occur. It cannot express the prediction in terms of time.' So also the conclusion of an acute student of the history of science: 'Great men are not absolutely essential to the progress of science, but they increase its speed.'—J. G. Crowther, *The Social Relations of Science* (London, 1941), p. 453.

That moving play of Robert Ardrey's, *Thunder Rock* (London, 1940) gave brilliant expression to this (see esp. around p. 117).

125. Comte, with his conviction that philosophy must acquire a social relevance, his appreciation of social evolution before biological evolution was sub-

stantiated and accepted, and his realisation that the classification of the sciences concealed a real problem, deserves a lecture to himself. At this time he was publishing his *Positive Philosophy*, the first volume of which appeared in 1839 and the last in 1842.

126. A, I. 134.

6

Evolution and Thermodynamics

(1941)

The development of modern science has led to a curious divergence of world-views. For the astronomers and the physicists the world is, in popular words, continually 'running down' to a state of dead inertness when heat has been uniformly distributed through it. For the biologists and sociologists, a part of the world, at any rate (and for us a very important part) is undergoing a progressive development in which an upward trend is seen, lower states of organisation being succeeded by higher states. For the ordinary man the contradiction, if such it is, is serious, because many physicists, in expounding the former of these principles, the second law of thermodynamics, employ the word 'organisation' and say it is always decreasing. Is there a real contradiction here? If so, how can it be resolved?[1]

At the outset it must be recognised that there is no question of rejecting the second law of thermodynamics. It is the basis of all our engineering technique which gives mankind power in controlling natural processes. The only question is, what exactly does it mean?

The Meaning of the Second Law of Thermodynamics
In the general language which scientific workers use every day we say simply that free energy, that is, energy capable of doing work, is constantly decreasing, and bound energy (entropy) is correspondingly increasing. This absolutely irreversible process accompanies every natural change, whether physical or chemical. In a series of linked changes, however, there may be local decreases of entropy, provided that over the whole system entropy

increases. The irreversibility of the 'degradation' of energy has been identified by Eddington[2] and many other writers with the basis of our knowledge of the one-way character of time. Only in reversed cinematograph films, but never in Nature, does water flow uphill of itself, or the smoke and gases of an exploding bomb recompress themselves, like the djinn of fable, into the reassembling case with its explosive content.

This description approaches the simple examples which are given by all elementary expositions of statistical mechanics.[3] If a number of atoms are introduced at one corner of a room, they will in a short space of time be found equally distributed within it (assuming that their kinetic energy is great enough to overcome their mutual attractions). In other words, it is impossible for a gas in a vacuum to occupy anything less than the whole of the space available. In the same way, if 'hot' molecules are introduced at one corner of the room, and 'cold' molecules at another, their collisions will soon ensure that all the molecules have the same velocity and that the temperature of the room is uniformly warm.

The significance of the second law of thermodynamics is, therefore, that all particles, when left to themselves, tend to become disarranged with respect to one another. Now such a process is similar to the shuffling of a pack of cards, or the random distribution of a quantity of black and white balls when continuously shaken together. 'Shuffling,' wrote Eddington, 'is the only thing Nature can never undo.' High probability, therefore, is associated with randomness, low probability with the opposite, whatever you like to call it—perhaps arrangement or order. Hence the definition that entropy is the sum of the logarithms of the probabilities of the 'complexions' of the parts of a system. A complexion or micro-state is simply an assembly of particles having the same velocity, rotational energy, rotational axis, etc. The more complexions there are in the system the less disordered it is. The presence of many complexions having very high or very low energies different from those in their vicinity is the condition under which useful work can be obtained from the system. This relatively unusual or improbable state constitutes what the physicist calls 'order' or 'arrangement.' The corresponding 'disorder' is measured by the logarithm of the probability.

Thus in an isolated system the net increase of entropy implies a net decrease of 'order' and a net increase of 'disorder.' In such an isolated system a decrease of entropy can only occur in one part provided it is over-compensated by a simultaneous and greater increase of entropy in another part. The two parts must, of course, be interlinked by some sort of action, e.g. radiation. The essential physical meaning of increase of entropy is a loss of power of spontaneous action. Two bodies at different temperatures automatically tend to come to a common temperature, but having done that they stop doing anything. It is the same with matter at different levels (subject to the law of gravity), electricity at different potentials, and so on. The tendency is always to come to a state of passivity, and whenever such a tendency takes effect, entropy increases. The 'running down' of the world is therefore a drift towards a state of relative quiescence.

From the point of view of other sciences and of the human world-view in general, it is important to note exactly what words the physicist uses to describe his improbable order and his probable disorder. If we turn to the writings of the American mathematical physicist, Willard Gibbs, the first among the great founders of thermodynamics, we find that he only uses one 'ordinary' word to describe high entropic states, namely 'mixed-up-ness.'[4] This does not occur in any of his published writings, but only as the title of a paper which he had intended to write, and which was found among a list of such titles among his papers after his death. The opposite of 'mixed-up-ness' is separatedness.

Later on, however, the practice grew up among physicists and astronomers of using the term 'organisation' for pre-entropic states. Eddington has been a protagonist of this use, as the following passages from his *Nature of the Physical World* show:

'We have to appeal to the one outstanding law, the second law of thermodynamics, to put some sense into the world. It opens up a new province of knowledge, namely, the study of organisation; and it is in connection with organisation that a direction of time-flow and a distinction between doing and undoing appears for the first time.'[5]

Or again;

'Let us now consider in detail how a random element brings the irrevocable into the world. When a stone falls it acquires kinetic energy, and the amount of the energy is just that which would be required to lift the stone back to its original height. By suitable arrangements, the kinetic energy can be made to perform this task; for example, if the stone is tied to a string it can alternately fall and reascend like a pendulum. But if the stone hits an obstacle its kinetic energy is converted into heat-energy. There is still the same quantity of energy, but even if we could scrape it together and put it through an engine we could not lift the stone back with it. What has happened to make the energy no longer serviceable? Looking microscopically at the falling stone we see an enormous multitude of molecules moving downwards with equal and parallel velocities—an organised motion like the march of a regiment. We have to notice two things, the *energy*, and the *organisation* of the energy. To return to its original height the stone must preserve both of them.

'When the stone falls on a sufficiently elastic surface the motion may be reversed without destroying the organisation. Each molecule is turned backwards and the whole array retires in good order to the starting-point.

> The famous Duke of York
> With twenty thousand men,
> He marched them up to the top of the hill
> And marched them down again.

'History is not made that way. But what usually happens at the impact is that the molecules suffer more or less random collisions and rebound in all directions. They no longer conspire to make progress in any one direction; they have lost their organisation. Afterwards they continue to collide with one another and keep changing their direction of motion, but they never again find a common purpose. Organisation cannot be brought about by continued shuffling. And so, although the energy remains quantitatively sufficient (apart from unavoidable leakage which we suppose made good), it cannot lift the stone back. To restore the stone we must supply extraneous energy which has the required amount of organisation.'[6]

A similar use of the term 'organisation' occurs at many other places in Eddington's writings.[7] In the above example, it seems to mean no more than a group of uniformly directed motions, and such an order might conceivably be regarded as the most primitive form of organisation. But to the biologist there is a sharp contradiction between this use of the term, and hence the view that the organisation in the universe is perpetually decreasing; and his own use of it which is associated with the evolutionary process. Here, in a part of the universe, at any rate, organisation is always increasing.

The matter is brought to a head when we find a physical chemist[8] describing the laws of probability and the second law of thermodynamics as the 'law of morpholysis.' This is well calculated to astonish the evolutionary morphologist, and makes imperative the effort to clarify the terminological situation.

The Meaning of the Law of Evolution

Modern biology is nothing if not evolutionary. There are now no reasonable grounds for doubt that during successive ages after the first appearance of life upon the earth it took up a succession of new forms, each more highly organised than the last. This is not gainsaid in any way by the existence of highly adaptive parasitism and retrogression in certain types of plants and animals, nor by the fact that a hundred disadvantageous mutants may have to be produced for every one which is of evolutionary value. It is surprising that the theory of biological organisation is still in such a backward state. Though there are few penetrating accounts of it in the literature, every biologist has a rough working idea of what he means by it.[9] Here one may perhaps say that as we rise in the evolutionary scale from the viruses and protozoa to the social primates, there is

(1) a rise in the number of parts and envelopes[10] of the organism and the complexity of their morphological forms and geometrical relations;

(2) a rise in the effectiveness of the control of their functions by the organism as a whole;

(3) a rise in the degree of independence of the organism from its environment, involving diversification and extension of range of the organism's activities;

(4) a rise in the effectiveness with which the individual organism carries out its purposes of survival and reproduction,[11] including the power of moulding its environment.

There is nothing vitalistic about these criteria. All the levels of biological organisation are higher than the physico-chemical level, hence it is only natural that regularities will be expected to occur in them which cannot be seen at any physico-chemical level. But this is not to say that biochemistry and biophysics are not the fundamental sciences of biology. A living organism is both a 'patterned mixed-up-ness,' and a 'patterned separatedness.' The mere fact of the aggregation of millions of cells together into a functioning metazoon necessitates the provision of efficient means of control of the whole. Hence the mysterious similarity between the view that we see when looking down a microscope at a transparent blood-vessel, and the view of Broadway from the top of a skyscraper. Hence the mysterious similarity between the nerve fibres and the pyloned wire striding across the countryside. The new walls built in and around bombed buildings in London seem like scar tissue growing in an animal's body. A partly built steel-frame building, with its maze of pipes visible, seems like a metal organism in which human beings are parasitic. We speak of the 'saturation' of anti-aircraft defences just as we speak of the saturation of an enzyme by its substrate, and the filtering of tanks through a line of defences resembles diapedesis.[12] Those thinkers who apply biological analogies to human society and its products are as foolish as any who would conversely try to persuade us that there really *are* micro-telephone-operators within the coelentrate nerve-net. The point is that the works of organisation have a certain similarity at all levels of their operation.

Furthermore, it is in general true that the higher the level of biological organisation, the more independent of the environment the organism is. Among the higher types decrease in number of reproductive products and corresponding increase of parental care illustrate this, and vast chapters of comparative physiology and biochemistry are devoted to the origin and development in evolution of body-temperature regulation, desiccation control, adjustment of the composition of the blood and the like. 'The constancy of the internal medium' said Claude Bernard, in an aphorism popularised by Barcroft,[13] is the condition of all free life.' Nor is there in purposiveness anything that lies outside the scientific frame of reference. The Aristotelian theory of causation is irrelevant. Biological purposiveness and adaptation are concepts inseparable from biological facts, and as Donnan[14] has shown, there exist branches of mathematics, such as integro-differential equations, which may be able to cope with systems whose behaviour differs according to their past history. Consciousness is the highest phase of this behaviour and when the organisational level is reached at which psychological phenomena first appear, sociological phenomena appear too. One may say that biological organisation is as much an organisation of processes as of structures.

The point at issue is, then, whether the concepts of organisation as used by physicists and by biologists have anything in common.[15]

The Two Concepts of Organisation

It is curious that this difficulty has not been more widely felt. Some thinkers have, indeed, been acutely troubled by it, for instance Rusk,[16] who spoke of a 'conflict of currents,' the physical world losing organisation and the biological world gaining it; and Ralph Lillie,[17] who opposed in an 'apparent paradox' the 'diversifying tendency' of evolution to the 'dissipative tendency' making for uniformity, of the second law. So also Levy,[18] in his popular exposition of the sciences, remarks :

'The fact is that the second law of thermodynamics, which regards systems as passing from orderly arrangement to disorderly randomness, classifies any future pattern or more complex orderly arrangement that may arise subsequent to the original order, as one of the innumerable accidental situations that have no special significance for man; as if a complex computing machine were indeed a random combination of parts. It may indeed mean that the energy of the original material from which the metal was drawn is now less available in one sense, but as a computing machine, it has now made available a mass of energy that was not previously capable of being tapped. Side by side, therefore, with the second law of thermodynamics, in so far as it may be valid for large-scale systems—if it is so valid—there must exist a law for the evolution of novel forms of aggregated energy and the emergence of new qualities. A generalisation of this nature has not yet been made but that a general rule of this type must exist is evident.'

One wonders why Levy did not allude at this point to the law of biological, psychological and sociological evolution. Long before, Engels, whom nothing escaped, had faced the problem, as we see from the following passage (in his *Ludwig Feuerbach*):

'It is not necessary here to go into the question of whether this mode of outlook [evolutionary dialectical materialism] is thoroughly in accord with the present position of natural science which predicts a possible end for the earth, and for its habitability a fairly certain one; which therefore recognises that for the history of humanity also there is not only an ascending but also a descending curve. At any rate we still find ourselves a considerable distance from the turning point at which the historical course of society becomes one of descent, and we cannot expect Hegelian philosophy to have been concerned with a subject which natural science had at that time not as yet placed upon the agenda.'[19]

By this he would seem to have meant that a time may some day come when the struggle of mankind against the adverse conditions of life on our planet will have become so severe that further social evolution will become impossible. This was a sensible approach, but it was made in 1885, before statistical mechanics was fully developed, before the second law of thermodynamics had attained its present position of canonical importance, and before its interpreters had challenged the biologists by appropriating the term 'organisation.'

One reason why the apparent contradiction between the second law and the process of evolution has not caused more perplexity is that the attention of those few scientific thinkers who try to unify the world-view of science has been largely directed towards the question of the existence of disentropic phases within living matter itself. From the description of the second law already given it must have been quite clear that this generalisation has a statistical basis, and hence that if we had to deal with vessels so small that individual 'complexions' could be separated, the statistical law valid for swarms of them might not in all cases hold good. Disentropic, 'unusual,' fluctuations might then, if amplified (and amplification is a process at which living matter is very efficient), account for such phenomena of high organisational level as 'free will.' Such a point of view has been ably put by Ralph Lillie[20] and discussed by Donnan.[21] It would be related to the standpoint of A. H. Compton,[22] and of G. N. Lewis,[23] who describes living organisms as 'cheats in the game of entropy.'

'They alone,' he wrote, 'seem able to breast the great stream of apparently irreversible processes. These processes tear down, living things build up. While the rest of the world seems to move towards a dead level of uniformity, the living organism is evolving new substances and more and more intricate forms.'[24]

Evidently he grasped the whole of the problem, but there is still one insuperable obstacle to the view that living organisms evade the second law of thermodynamics. It is simply that no evidence of any infringement of the second law on the part of living organisms has ever been forthcoming, and on the contrary a great deal of evidence that they obey it. Their life is always associated with, and depends upon, the processes of metabolism, in which there is always a net loss of free energy, complex organic compounds being broken down to CO_2 and water, and their energy being dispersed as irrecoverable heat. The processes of metabolism, moreover, are invariably very inefficient.[25]

The idea that living organisms might be cheats in the game of entropy originated from the conception of the so-called Clerk-Maxwell demon. Clerk-Maxwell, in his expositions of the second law, found it convenient to picture a vessel divided into two compartments connected by a hole and a trap-door which could be opened and shut at will by a 'being whose faculties are so sharpened that he can follow every molecule in its course.'[26] The demon could thus let through fast molecules but not slow ones, in which case, starting from a uniform temperature, one side would get hot and the other side cold. He could therefore easily, in Kelvin's words,[27] make water run uphill, one end of a poker red-hot and the other ice-cold, and sea water fit to drink. The idea has thus often been put forward that living organisms evade the second law. 'Es gibt seine Dämonen,' cried Driesch,[28] 'wir selbst sind sie.' But as Clark[29] rightly says, what had really been proved was not that the second law was inapplicable to living matter, but that *if* a mind could deal with individual molecules, and *if* it had suitable frictionless apparatus at its disposal, and *if* it was desirous of doing so at the moment when an observer happened to be looking, it *could* decrease entropy. These conditions are never, in practice, fulfilled. So far as we know, living organisms and their minds cannot handle molecules individually. The Maxwellian demon had in fact been endowed in its definition with just the qualities our minds possess of arranging, sorting and ordering. And our minds do not exist 'in a vacuum,' created from nothing; they belong to the highest stage in an evolutionary process continuous back to the most primitive single living cells. But the paradox is that in all this arranging, sorting and ordering which living things perform, there is never any infringement of the second law of thermodynamics.

A Paradox with Social Significance

At this point I wish to pause before pursuing the argument further in order to meet the criticism that the whole question is of purely academic interest. What difference does it make, one may ask, whether the world is thought to be 'running down' or not, or whether the emergence of novelty in evolution is real? The answer is that our ideas on these questions have very marked and sometimes unrealised effects on our social behaviour.

The social significance of the first law of thermodynamics, i.e. the law of the conservation of energy, has long been realised. It was one of the basic pillars required for the development of industrial civilisation, as the physicists of the last century themselves knew very well. Crowther has summarised the matter:

'The discovery of the conservation of energy is connected with the notion of exchange value. Capitalist civilisation cannot be operated without an exact knowledge of the equivalence of different forms of energy.... When coal, electricity, gas and labour are to be sold in exchange, they must be measured and a common currency found for them. That currency is energy.'[30]

And again:

'All matter appeared to be made of electricity; industrial civilisation had at length succeeded in interpreting the universe in terms of one of its own concepts. The cosmos was conceived as made of one universal world material, electricity.'[31]

Thus the thought introduced by the pre-Socratic Ionian philosophers 2500 years before, came to fruition. Thomson[32] has reminded us, in connection with the tyrant Midas and the first invention of gold coinage, that Heraclitus said, 'Fire is the primary substance of which the world is made. Fire is exchanged for all things and all things for fire, just as goods for gold and gold for goods.'

As with the first law, so with the second. Since it involves the time process more profoundly than any other scientific law, it immediately brings up all the 'first and last things' of theology, from the creation to the last judgement. It has been a godsend to theologians filled with pessimism about human affairs, and delighted to find scientific backing for their despite of nature—'the heavens shall perish . . . they shall all wax old as doth a garment.' That arch-reactionary neo-Platonist, W. R. Inge, the former Dean of St Paul's, devoted an entire book to demonstrating that since the universe is steadily approaching a state of thermal equilibrium and immobility, therefore (a) all evolution and human progress is an illusion and (b) men should return to what he calls the *philosophia perennis* of Christianity, the conviction that all man's good lies in another life.[33]

'We have here no continuing city, neither we ourselves nor the species to which we belong. Our citizenship is in heaven, in the eternal world to which even in this life we may ascend in heart and mind.'[34]

'So far as I can see,' he goes on, 'the purposes of God in history are finite, local, temporal, and for the most part individual. They all seem to point beyond themselves to the "intelligible world" beyond the bourne of time and place. . . . In so far as the modern doctrine of the predestined progress of the species is only a spectral residuum of traditional eschatology, I think we must be prepared to surrender it.'[35]

We might leave these stately passages to summarise Inge's position, were it not for another remark elsewhere in the same book which breathes the very spirit of the ecclesiastical department of the bourgeoisie :

'Those who throw all their ideals into the future are as bankrupt as those who lent their money to the Russian or German governments during the war.'[36]

In justice to the theologians, it must be remembered that some have strongly contested Inge's views, notably Rashdall.[37]

Another reason for which theologians or theologically-minded scientists extol the second law is that it is tempting to identify the 'winding-up' process, whatever it was, which started our galaxy off on its course with a maximum of free energy, with the act of creation by a personal deity. This always seems to me extremely premature, for we have no evidence that the universe does not operate in a cyclical way, periods of entropy-increase alternating with the appearance of new free energy. Milne[38] has pointed out that 'the arrow of time' should more properly be regarded as a flight of arrows, since other galaxies are not at the same stage of their development as ours. Moreover, it may be that at the 'edges' of the universe—if this expression means anything—free energy is continually being formed, so that like animals living in a stream or pipe which find the water always going by, we should see our world always 'running down' but never reaching the end of the process. For those who like theological speculation, this might be regarded as a modern form of the doctrine of the 'General Concourse' in which God must ever uphold the universe which he created. But I am unable to see that these speculations do anyone any good except those who are concerned to give ideological justification to ideas associated with backward social tendencies. It would be far better to await the further discoveries of astronomy and astro-physics with an open mind.

Thinkers approach the second law, therefore, with various forms of tacit bias, and these should be taken into account in considering what they say. One welcomes the degradation of energy and the disintegration of the world in the interests of other-worldly theology; another seeks evidence for a creator. I have no reason to suppose that I am without bias myself; in so far as anyone can state his own with any accuracy, I find the background of my thought to be the elucidation of the nature of life and man, the definition of the direction in which evolution has occurred, and the establishment of hope for man's struggles towards the perfect social order. The reason why the contradiction between the two concepts of organisation is so important is because the world-view, and hence the behaviour, of men in general is deeply affected by the 'first and last things' of the world and of life and man within it.

The Two Views of the Contradiction
We may now proceed to consider the two views which may be held about this contradiction. They are as follows:

(1) The concepts of organisation as held by physicists and biologists are the same; but all biological, and hence social, organisation is kept going at the expense of an over-compensating degradation of energy in metabolic upkeep.

(2) The two concepts are quite different and incommensurable. We should distinguish between *Order* and *Organisation*.

First of all, can we find the first of these opinions explicitly stated?

Metabolism and Irreversibility

It is not difficult to do so. The physicist, Schrödinger, refers to the matter in his interesting book *Science and the Human Temperament* :

'We are convinced,' he writes, 'that the second law governs all physical and chemical processes, even if they result in the most intricate and tangled phenomena, such as organic life, the genesis of a complicated world of organisms from primitive beginnings, and the rise and growth of human cultures. In this connection the physicist's belief in a continually increasing disorder seems somewhat paradoxical, and may easily lead to a very pessimistic misunderstanding of a thesis which actually implies nothing more than the specific meaning assigned to it by the physicist. Therefore a word of explanation is necessary.

'We do not wish to assert anything more than that the total balance of disorder in Nature is steadily on the increase. In individual sections of the universe, or in definite material systems, the movement may well be towards a higher degree of order, which is made possible because an adequate compensation occurs in some other systems. Now according to what the physicist calls "order," the heat stored up in the sun represents a fabulous provision for order, in so far as this heat has not yet been distributed equally over the whole universe (though its definite tendency is towards that dispersion) but is for the time being concentrated within a relatively small portion of space. The radiation of heat from the sun, of which a small proportion reaches us, is the compensating process making possible the manifold forms of life and movement on the earth, which frequently present the features of increasing order. A small fraction of this tremendous dissipation suffices to maintain life on the earth by supplying the necessary amount of "order," but of course only so long as the prodigal parent, in its own frantically uneconomic way, is still able to afford the luxury of a planet which is decked out with cloud and wind, rushing rivers and foaming seas, and the gorgeous finery of flora and fauna and the striving millions of mankind.'[39]

Thus in this charming passage we are to visualise biological order as identical with that order which thermodynamically is always disappearing, the local increase being more than compensated for by the decrease due to the cooling of the sun. Eddington, though more uncertainly, adopts a like view, in his *New Path-ways in Science.*

'In using entropy as a signpost for time we must be careful to treat a properly isolated system. Isolation is necessary because a system can gain organisation by draining it from other contiguous systems. Evolution shows us that more highly organised systems develop as time goes on. This may be partly a question of definition, for it does not follow that organisation from the evolution-ary point of view is to be reckoned according to the same measure as organisation from the entropy point of view. But in any case these highly developed systems may obtain their energy by a process of collection, not by creation. A human being as he grows from past to future becomes more and more highly organised—or so he fondly imagines. At first sight this appears to contradict the signpost law that the later instant corresponds to the greater dis-organisation. But to apply the law we must make an isolated system of him. If we prevent him from acquiring organisation from external sources, if we cut off his consumption of food and drink and air, he will before long come to a state which everyone would recognise as a state of extreme "disorganisation".'[40]

Here, then, are statements of the view that there is no essential difference between thermodynamic and biological order. No doubt this is the simpler of the two alternatives.

Among the reflections which have led thinkers to support it is a recognition of the irreversibility which exists both in the second law and in biological evolution. The pioneer work of the palaeont-ologist Dollo[41] led to the generalisation which has since been called by his name. An organ which has been reduced in the course of evolutionary development never again reaches its original importance, and an organ which has altogether dis-appeared never again appears. Further, if in connection with adaptation to a new environment (such as aquatic, terrestrial, or aerial life) an organ is lost which was valuable in the pre-vious environment, and if, as often happens, a secondary return to the previous environment occurs, this organ will not re-appear. In its place some other organ will form a substitute. In a word, evolution is reversible in the sense that structures which have been gained can be lost, but it is irreversible in the sense that, once lost, these structures can never be regained. Since Dollo's time it has been shown that his generalisations hold good,

not only for the morphological body structures which he elucidated, but also for numerous physiological and biochemical
adaptations.[42]

In explanation, Dollo himself did not go much further than a
vague appeal to the 'indestructibility of the past.' 'In the last
analysis,' he wrote, 'it is, like other natural laws, a question of
probability. Evolution is a summation of determined individual
variations in a determined order. For it to be reversible, there
would have to be as many causes, acting in the inverse sense, as
those which brought about the individual variations [mutations,
as we should say to-day] which were the source of the prior
transformations and their fixation. Such circumstances are too
complex for us to suppose that they ever exist.' This idea has
something in common with the second law of thermodynamics.
The universe is always passing from less probable to more probable states.

The position was further elaborated in the brilliant and unique
book of Lotka, who defined evolution as the history of any system
undergoing irreversible changes, and practically identified it with
the second law. But although his discussion is one of the three or
four greatest contributions to biological thought of the present
century, he never really faces the problem that the second law
involves a decrease, and the law of evolution an increase, of order.
His pleasure at being able to unite all forms of irreversibility
under one law leads him to an undue denigration of the genuine
rise in level of organisation which evolution shows. Evolution, he
rightly maintains, is not a mere changeful sequence. Mere unlikeness of two days does not tell us which preceded the other. It is
necessary to know something of the character of this unlikeness.

'In a vague way,' he goes on, 'this character is indicated by the
term "progress," which is associated in popular conception with
evolution. And the more rigorous scientific disciplines of biology,
too, leave us with a not very clearly defined idea of "progression"
as one of the fundamental characteristics of those changes which
are embraced by the term evolution. Such phrases as the "passage
from lower to higher forms," which are often used to describe the
direction of evolution, are vague, and undoubtedly contain an
anthropomorphic element. At best they give every opportunity
for divergence of opinion as to what constitutes a "higher" form.
If, on the other hand, it is stated that evolution proceeds from

simpler to more complex forms, or from less specialised to more specialised forms, then the direction is but poorly defined, for the rule is at best one with many exceptions.'[43]

And to this he adds in a footnote the remark of Bertrand Russell : 'A process which led from amoeba to man appeared to the philosophers to be obviously a progress—though whether the amoeba would agree with this opinion is not known.' After which he proceeds to take irreversibility as the principal character of the evolutionary process.

But this will not do. Denial of the rise in organisational level during evolution (and social evolution too) is not, and cannot be, acceptable to biologists. Definitions of what this means have been attempted above. Russell's wit is empty. It is mere verbiage (though it might in some circumstances be poetry) to talk about the opinions of molecules, or in that favourite phrase, 'the hookworm's point of view' when its nervous system does not entitle it to have a point of view. Philosophers, on the contrary, are so entitled.

Here Max Planck has a relevant passage :

'The second law of thermodynamics has frequently been applied outside physics. For example, attempts have been made to apply the principle that all physical events develop in one direction only, to biological evolution; a singularly unhappy attempt so long as the term evolution is associated with the idea of progress, perfection, or improvement. The principle of entropy is such that it can only deal with probabilities, and all that it really says is that a state improbable in itself is followed on the average by a more probable state. Biologically interpreted, this principle points towards degeneration rather than improvement. The chaotic, the ordinary, and the common, is always more probable than the harmonious, the excellent, or the rare'.[44]

And yet, in spite of these difficulties, and the general trend towards probable disorder, the rise in level of organisation during evolution has in fact occurred.

Patterns in the non-living world

We come now to certain reflections which seem to suggest rather strongly that the thermodynamic principle of order is indeed fundamentally different from the biological principle of organisation. Biological organisation depends universally upon aggregations of particles, of high complexity. The molecule of protein, to say nothing of the paracrystalline protein micelle, is an entity so complex that though our analysis of it has begun, we are not as yet in sight of a clear understanding of it. Now although biological organisation, as we have seen, depends everywhere on a continuing metabolic upkeep, energy entering the plant as light or the animal as chemical energy in the foodstuffs, and being degraded in combustions and dissipated as heat; biological organisation is only the extrapolation of patterns already to be found in the non-living world. We cannot make any sharp line of distinction between the living and the non-living. At the level of the submicroscopic viruses, they overlap. Some particles show some of the properties of life but not others. Some 'dead' protein molecules are much bigger than the particles of some 'living' viruses. Particles which show the properties of life can be had in paracrystalline, and even in crystalline form. There are many similarities between the morphology and behaviour of crystals and living organisms.[45]

Among the patterns found in the non-living world, crystalline arrangement, and above all the arrangement of the more complex liquid crystals, is doubtless the most highly ordered and organised. But below the crystalline level there is the molecular level, and below that again the level of the atoms, some of which have a much more complex 'solar system' of elementary physical particles than others. When crystals form spontaneously they do so in processes which involve decreases in free energy.[46] The physicist must therefore say that disorder has increased, but the biologist, as a student of patterns, cannot but say that there is more order and organisation in the well-arranged crystal than in its homogeneous mother-liquor or corresponding gas.[47]

So also in the development of our world. In its earliest stages, we are told, there were nothing but the elementary physical particles, and conditions were such that the atoms of the elements we know could not exist. But as the temperature of the earth grew colder, the atoms of the elements became stable and at last even the heaviest ones, with their dozens of revolving electrons, were able to persist.[48] Here, from the biologist's point of view, pattern and organisation had increased, but certainly from the physicist's point of view, order had decreased. The chaos which ensues upon the degradation of energy cannot therefore be the same chaos which existed at the beginning of the world before the atoms of the elements were stable. For that chaos coincided with a maximum of free energy, and the former accompanies its successive minima.

The point is, therefore, (a) that we cannot refuse to extend the concept of organisation downwards to include non-living patterned aggregations,[49] and (b) that since these require no continuing metabolic upkeep for their persistence, the 'metabolic' theory which asserts that biological order and thermodynamic order are identical, but that the former is over-compensated, should be rejected in favour of a wider generalisation. We are led, in fact, to the second hypothesis mentioned above, namely that thermo-dynamic order and biological organisation are entirely different things.[50] Only we should now perhaps have to call the latter by some such term as 'holistic' in order to indicate that pattern is not the biologist's perquisite, but occurs also at non-living levels.

As David Watson has well put it :

'The suggestion I wish to make is that all material organisation, whether living or lifeless, has its roots in the same facts, and that the symmetry and beauty of the products of the synthetic chemist, of geological formations, of trees, of flowers, and of young girls, are in essence traceable to the same kinds of designing agents.'

Let us now return to the fundamental definition of Willard Gibbs—entropy is 'mixed-up-ness.' The opposite of mixed-up-ness is separatedness, not organisation. From this point of view, one can see that in the early stages of our world's development all the elementary particles of physics were in fact separated from one another, and free energy was then at its maximum. But as time went on, the temperature fell, and mixed-up-ness increased —or perhaps we ought to say that time went on because mixed-up-ness increased. The basic misconception we have unearthed comes to light here, namely that mixed-up-ness necessarily means chaotic mixed-up-ness; on the contrary there may also be patterned mixed-up-ness. Indeed it is hard to see how the most complex patterns could ever have been formed if there were not a number of different elements from which they could be formed. The world of life is a painting in full colours, not a monochrome. If this is accepted, we must make a sharp distinction between thermodynamic order or separatedness, and biological organis-ation or patterned mixed-up-ness. And the general upshot would be that the world has been moving steadily from a condition of universal separatedness (order) to one of general chaotic mixed-up-ness (thermodynamic disorder) plus local organisation (patterned mixed-up-ness).

The point could perhaps be illustrated by a homely analogy. Inside the nursery cupboard there are certain large boxes of bricks, each box containing bricks of identical colour and shape. When they are all tumbled out in confusion on the nursery floor we have the highly probable universe of the thermodynamician. But when in one corner of the room the bricks are assembled into a factory or a railway station, we have an analogy for the organising activities of life. There are two kinds of mixed-up-ness, indistinguishable for the physicist, but clearly visible to the biologist who is on the look-out for patterns.

The only thinker who seems to have arrived at somewhere approaching this position is the late J. S. Haldane.[51] He clearly expressed the idea that though with the passage of time thermodynamic mixed-up-ness constantly increases, this mixture does not necessarily give rise to chaotic states but on the contrary involves much pattern and organisation. Indeed, we may find the first traces of pattern even in those 'fortuitous concourses' of particles which gases and homogeneous liquids were formerly thought to be, for it is now thought that temporary associations of particles exist in these systems, though they are of a duration so transient that they can only be observed by special methods. Such organisation would be around the molecular level.

Thermodynamic order and Biological organisation essentially different

We have arrived, then, at the conclusion that thermodynamic order and biological organisation are two quite different things. But this is not to say that there are no connections between them. What Haldane said illustrates some of the connections. And there is another very simple way of showing how pattern may arise where there was none before, through the operation of the law of entropy. If we return to the example given earlier of two vessels filled with gas at different temperatures, and isolated from all other environment, we know, of course, that with the passage of time they will come to exact thermal equilibrium. When this point is reached it will certainly not be possible to get any further work out of the system, but a pattern has now appeared where it was not before. The system has passed from asymmetry to symmetry.[52]

It is, of course, a far cry from this simplest possible case of symmetry to the extraordinarily complex patterns of symmetry produced by living things, but it may be that this apparently jejune idea hides a profound truth. Every stage in the thermodynamic primrose path to the everlasting (but tepid) bonfire, has its own criteria of stability. In the earliest stages when free energy was maximal, even the atoms of the elements were not stable. Later on the minerals of which the earth's geography was built were stable for a long time before any living protoplasm was stable. The fibrous proteins (essential for the construction and maintenance of the higher forms of life)[53] can be regarded as 'degenerated' linear polymers of the globular proteins, which themselves, as the work of the ultra-centrifuge school has shown, are polymers of a small and relatively simple unit. Polymerisation, too, is a notable feature of the carbohydrate group. Now polymerisation is a process which goes on with a decrease of free energy, just as crystallisation does, and since the most complex morphological forms require the most highly polymerised substances, Bernal[54] has pointed out that this fact helps to explain for us the contradiction between thermodynamic order and biological organisation.

From this point of view, life could be regarded as the characteristic stable form of the proteins.[55] 'Life,' wrote Engels[56] in a famous definition, 'is the mode of motion of the albuminous substances.' So also in earlier essays I was always deeply impressed by a fact so obvious that it never seemed to have occurred to many biological philosophers, namely, that proteins, carbohydrates and fats are never found in colloidal combination or even alone anywhere outside living organisms.[57] It was therefore irrelevant to demand of biologists that they should show the existence of similar phenomena in the inorganic world before applying the methods of physics and chemistry, as far as they would go, to the phenomena of life.

Goethe had faced this problem:

> Wer will was Lebendigs erkennen und beschreiben
> Sucht erst den Geist herauszutreiben,
> Dann hat er die Teile in seiner Hand,
> Fehlt leider! nur das geistige Band.
> *Encheiresin Naturae* nennt's die Chemie,
> Spottet ihrer selbst, und weiss nicht wie.

Which we might translate: 'He who wishes to understand and describe living organisms first drives their spirit out of them, and then in his hands he finds nothing but the dead parts; the spiritual bond which united them has disappeared. Chemistry calls this the "Manipulation of Nature," insulting herself by so doing, and not even realising she does so.' The investigation of this 'spiritual bond' by the methods of natural science is the task of biology, and we have known too many victories in the past to fall a prey now to the pessimism of Mephistopheles.

It would be quite erroneous to say, therefore, that because thermodynamic order and biological organisation are two quite different things, there is any conflict between them. Only as the time-process goes on, only as the cosmic mixing proceeds, only as the temperature of the world cools; do the higher forms of aggregation, the higher patterns and levels of organisation, become possible and stable. The probability of their occurrence increases. The law of evolution is a kind of converse of the second law of thermodynamics, equally irreversible but contrary in tendency. We are reminded of the two components of Empedocles' world, *philia*, friendship, union, attraction; and *neikos,* strife, dispersion, repulsion.

There remain one or two final points. First, we have not answered the question why a metabolic upkeep becomes necessary about the level of the beginnings of life. Basal metabolism, as it is called, that continuous slow rate of combustion which goes on all the time when the living organism is as much at rest as it can possibly be, is classically described as the energy turnover required to 'keep the organism in being as a physical system,' to maintain separation of phases, do work at membranes, etc., etc. It is fair to say that basal metabolism only appears slowly as we ascend the taxonomic scale. We hardly know as yet whether it is a concept which can be applied to bacteria, and there is much evidence that some forms of life, such as viruses, bacterial spores, and even some animal eggs, can remain for long periods of time in an inert state, consuming none of their stores and apparently as much without metabolism as any crystal. Presumably the higher living patterns do demand a good deal of additional energy to keep them going.

Secondly, there is the question of measurement. The nature of holistic organisation is certainly not susceptible of the same kind of measurement as thermodynamic mixed-up-ness, but we have no reason whatever for supposing that its measurement is impossible.

When such a measurement has been achieved, it would be feasible to apply it also to human social evolution. I see no reason for doubting the possibility of this.

Thermodynamics and Social Evolution

Mention of social evolution brings up a few reflections which inescapably present themselves. If the general principles here enunciated are sound, the most highly organised social communities should be the most stable, perhaps the most long-lasting. Here the social insects bear a testimony, for the forms of their different castes have been identified embedded in amber many thousands of years old, but they differ so severely from the primates in their morphology that they have less to teach us than is often supposed. The most highly organised social communities should also be the least wasteful. Hence it is significant that much of the criticism directed against our existing social order by those who wish to see a more highly organised state of society is precisely on the ground that our present arrangements are wasteful. Wasteful of human effort, when infinite care is devoted to the growing of a crop of coffee, only for it to be shovelled into locomotive fireboxes. Wasteful of energy, when heavy goods, the transport of which is not urgent, are transported by air or rail, while for purely financial reasons canals lie unused or derelict. Is there not a thermodynamic interpretation of justice? Is not injustice wasteful? Is not the failure to utilise to the maximum the available talent and genius of men a wasteful thing? As has been acutely said; 'Those fundamental human rights which have so often been regarded as absolute postulates—liberty, equality, fraternity—turn out to be necessary conditions for a truly efficient productive mechanism and for the provision of sound social environment.' That great aggregation of mankind to which we all look forward, the kingdom of heaven on earth, will be nothing if not efficient. There was a false contradiction in Richard Baxter's immortal remark: 'I had rather go to heaven disorderly, than be damned in due order.' The more truly orderly order is the more it approximates to the heavenly, and this process is our own social evolution itself, our own history, in which it is our duty to participate. But we must always beware of mistaking the lesser forms of order for the greater, and, as Auden reminds us, we must be modest in our claims.

> Great sedentary Caesars who
> Have pacified some dread tabu,
> Whose wits were able to withdraw
> The numen from some local law,
> And with a single concept brought
> Some ancient rubbish heap of thought
> To rational diversity;
> You are betrayed unless we see
> No Codex Gentium we make
> Is difficult for Truth to break.
> The Lex Abscondita evades
> The vigilantes in the glades;
> Now here, now there, one leaps and cries,
> 'I've got her and I claim the prize,'
> But when the rest catch up, he stands
> With just a torn blouse in his hands.

There is only one thing more to say. The increasing mixed-up-ness in the world gives the direction of time's arrow. Perhaps when it is possible to measure biological organisation the increasing patternedness will be found to lead to the same result. In the meantime it might be thought that what has happened to the world is that what was one single original pattern has split up into millions of subsidiary patterns—all were born from

> The universe of pure extension where
> Only the universe itself was lonely. . . .

The extraordinary thing is that Richard Baxter's contemporary, Thomas Browne, said it all in a flash of intuition in his pious seventeenth-century way three hundred years ago, as if foreshadowing what we are thinking now:

'All things began in order, so shall they end, and so shall they begin again, according to the ordainer of order, and the mystical mathematicks of the city of heaven.'

Notes

1. In thinking over these problems I have had the invaluable help and counsel of a number of friends: Professor Bernal, Dr. R. E. D. Clark, Dr. Danielli, Professor Dingle, Professor Donnan, Sir Arthur Eddington, Dr. Guggenheim, Dr. Robin Hill, Dr. Neuberger, Professor Polanyi, Dr. Shen Shih-Chang, Dr. Waddington, and Mr. Lancelot Whyte. Should this survey chance to fall

under their eye, they will recognise points which they themselves have emphasised, but the whole responsibility for the general line and conclusions must necessarily be borne by me.

2. E.g. in *The Nature of the Physical World* (Cambridge, 1928).

3. E.g. *A System of Physical Chemistry* by W. C. McC. Lewis, 3 vols., vol. iii (London, 1919).

4. *Collected Scientific Papers of J. Willard Gibbs* (London, 1906), p. 418.

5. *The Nature of the Physical World*, p. 67.

6. *The Nature of the Physical World*, p. 70.

7. E.g. *The Nature of the Physical World*, p. 104.

8. R. E. D. Clark in *Evangelical Quarterly*, 1937, **9**, 128, and in *School Science Review*, 1939, **21**, 831; 1940, **21**, 1117; see also his book *The Universe and God* (London, 1939).

9. Attention may be drawn to R. W. Gerard's thoughtful discussion 'Organism, Society and Science' in *Sci. Monthly*, 1940, **50**, 340, 403 and 530; and to a paper of A. H. Kamiat, *Internat. Journ. Ethics*, 1933, **43**, 395.

10. [This term refers to the enveloping of components at a lower organisational level by a unit immediately above it.]

11. There is a sense, of course, in which an amoeba is as organised as a man in that it carries out all the functions of assimilation, metabolism, reproduction, etc., but the difference lies in the variety of conditions under which it can do so, and the kind of limitations on the type of life which it can lead. There is also a sense in which all those species of plants and animals which have succeeded in persisting through evolutionary change are equally successful. But this is not the only criterion of success. Merely to persist is certainly the *sine qua non*, but we have also to consider under what variety of changed circumstances this persistence can occur, and also what the organism does with its persistence. One of the main objects in defining biological organisation and its rise during evolution is to get rid of as much subjectivism as possible in our outlook on other living things.

12. C. M. Beadnell, *Literary Guide*, 1942, **57**, 79 ['Diapedesis': the passage of white blood cells through the unruptured walls of the capillaries into the tissues.]

13. 'La Fixité du Milieu Intérieur est la Condition de la Vie libre,' by J. Barcroft, *Biol. Rev.*, 1932, **7**, 24; and later as part of his book *Features in the Architecture of Physiological Function* (Cambridge, 1934).

14. F. G. Donnan in *Acta Biotheoretica*, 1936, **2**, 1.

15. We consider mainly in this survey the rise in level of organisation during phylogenesis (evolution). But embryologists also see a rise in level of organisation during ontogenesis (the growth and differentiation of the individual). So far as we know, nothing that happens during embryonic development infringes the second law, and apart from the energy turnover in metabolic upkeep during development, there is little or no energy associated with the highly complex finished structure. For further information on this difficult subject see the section on energetics in *Chemical Embryology* by J. Needham, (Cambridge, 1931) and the review of O. Meyerhof (*Handbuch d. Physik*, 1926, **11**, 243).

16. R. D. Rusk, *Atoms, Man and Stars* (New York, 1937), p. 273.

17. R. S. Lillie, *Amer. Nat.*, 1934, **68**, 318; *Philos. of Sci.*, 1934, **1**, 297.

18. H. Levy, *Modern Science; a Study of Physical Science in the World Today* (London, 1939), p. 203.

19. F. Engels, *Ludwig Feuerbach and the outcome of Classical German Philosophy* (London, n.d.), p. 22.

20. R. S. Lillie, *Science*, 1927, **66**, 139; *Journ. Philos.*, 1930, **27**, 421; 1931, **28**, 561; 1932, **29**, 477; *Amer. Naturalist*, 1934, **68**, 304; *Philos. of Sci.*, 1934, **1**, 296; 1937, **4**, 202.

21. F. G. Donnan, *Journ. Gen. Physiol.*, 1927, **8**, 685.
22. A. H. Compton, *The Freedom of Man* (Yale, 1935).
23. G. N. Lewis, *The Anatomy of Science* (Yale, 1926), chs. vi and viii.
24. *The Anatomy of Science*, p. 178.
25. See J. Needham, 'Recent Developments in the Philosophy of Biology,' *Quart. Rev. Biol.*, 1928, **3**, 77.
26. J. Clerk-Maxwell, *Theory of Heat* 4th ed. (Cambridge, 1875), p. 328 ff.
27. Kelvin, *Proc. Roy. Inst.*, 1879, **9**, 113.
28. Driesch, H., *Science and Philosophy of the Organism* (London, 1912), vol. ii, p. 202.
29. Clark, R. E. D., *School Sci. Rev.*, 1940, **21**, 1125.
30. J. G. Crowther, *The Social Relations of Science* (London, 1941), p. 409.
31. Loc. cit., p. 455.
32. G. Thomson, *Aeschylus and Athens* (London, 1941), p. 85.
33. *God and the Astronomers* (London, 1933). Cf. also *The Fall of the Idols* (London, 1940). I confess that the general level of the argument in these books, though not its trend, reminds me of the well-known story in which a lecturer was giving a popular talk on the subject of the second law of thermodynamics and its implications. As soon as the meeting was thrown open for discussion, a member of the audience rose and said, 'How long, sir, did you say it would be before the universe ran completely down?' The lecturer replied that he had said seven hundred million years. His questioner heaved a deep sigh of relief and said, 'Thank God. I thought you had said seventy million years.'
34. Ibid., p. 137.
35. Ibid., p. 172.
36. Ibid., p. 28.
37. *Ideas and Ideals* (Oxford, 1928), by H. Rashdall.
38. E. A. Milne, *Relativity, Gravitation and World Structure* (Oxford, 1935), p. 286.
39. E. Schrödinger, *Science and the Human Temperament* (London, 1935), p. 39.
40. A. S. Eddington, *New Pathways in Science* (Cambridge, 1935), p. 56; see also *Nature*, 1931, **127**, 448.
41. L. Dollo, numerous papers, some of the more important of which are referred to in *Biol. Rev.*, 1938, **13**, 225.
42. By J. Needham, 'Contributions of Chemical Physiology to the Problem of Reversibility in Evolution,' *Biol. Rev.*, 1938, **13**, 225.
43. A. J. Lotka, *Elements of Physical Biology* (Baltimore, 1925), p. 22.
44. M. Planck, *The Philosophy of Physics* (London, 1936), p. 101.
45. Cf. such books as H. Przibram, *Die Anorganische Grenzgebiete d. Biologie* (Berlin, 1926), and F. Rinne, *Grenz fragen des Lebens* (Leipzig, 1931).
46. Cf. G. N. Lewis & M. Randall, *Thermodynamics*, p. 122.
47. Certain writers dispute this, e.g. R. O. Kapp (*Science versus Materialism*, London, 1940). They see in inorganic nature nothing but particles of different sorts 'flying about' and 'shaking down'; life alone introduces a plan or pattern. But may not life be the way the proteins shake down when in conjunction with lipoids, carbohydrates and certain other constituents?
48. F. Wood-Jones (*Design and Purpose*, London, 1942), p. 55, has related how he, as a student, was struck by the similarity between Mendeléev's table of the elements and Huxley's table of biological types. Both have the status of evolutionary sequences. For an account of where Mendeléev's table of the elements stands to-day, see F. A. Paneth, *Nature*, 1942, **149**, 565.
49. It should be noted that this conclusion is also that of certain philosophies; the emergent evolutionism of Lloyd-Morgan and others, the organic mechanism of Whitehead, and the dialectical materialism of Marx and Engels. It has also been finely expressed by the eminent physiologist Otto Meyerhof, in a review which is the best account of thermodynamics and life from the physiological point of view (*Handbuch d. Physik*, 1926, **11**, 238). 'In unseren Augen,' he says,

'stellen die Lebewesen eine höhere Organisationsform der unbelebten Materie dar, die sich etwa zur Organisation der Moleküle (oder Atome) so verhält, wie diese sich zu den Elektronen und Protonen, aus denen sie aufgebaut sind. Auch das Molekül und Atom stellt nur eine Struktur- und Funktionseinheit dar, von relativer Stabilität, von annähernd, aber nicht vollständig bestimmter Form, wechselndem Energiegehalt und numerisch bestimmten, aber individuell unbestimmten, d.h. austauschbaren, Elementarbestandteilen. Ja, darüber hinaus differieren sogar die Atome eines Elements unter sich unter gleichen Umständen, wie die Statistik des radioaktiven Zerfalls beweist, haben verschiedene Lebensdauer und besitzen demnach eine Individualität.' Meyerhof, however, does not consider the problem of evolutionary rise in organisation as opposed to thermodynamic increase of disorder.

50. This is also the standpoint of David L. Watson in an important paper (*Quart. Rev. Biol.*, 1931, **6**, 143). Probability, he says, with Lotka, is essentially a matter of classification. An improbable event is one that is a member of a small class, and whether it is so or not depends on our system of classification. A classification based on morphological form and efficiency of function (means to ends) would give a different picture from that of statistical mechanics.

51. See especially J. S. Haldane, *Realist*, 1930, **3**, 10, and *The Philosophy of a Biologist*, (Oxford, 1936), p. 25.

52. So also—as showing the different possible definitions of order—an equalitarian view might claim that when all the molecules had the same velocity the system had attained greatest order.

53. Cf. W. T. Astbury, *Fundamentals of Fibre Structure* (Oxford, 1933), and J. Needham, *Order and Life* (Yale and Cambridge, 1936).

54. J. D. Bernal, in a paper to the Theoretical Biology Club, 1937.

55. Stable, of course, only in a wide sense, including within itself a vast range of intermediate levels of stability. O. Meyerhof (*Handbuch d. Physik*, 1926, **11**, 240) gives an excellent description of the fundamental bases of life phenomena: 'Ebenso wie die Atomkerne durch Einfangen von Elektronen Eigenschaften gewinnen, die die Elementarbestandteile noch nicht besitzen, die sich aber aus deren Eigenschaften herleiten, so würden die verschiedenen Lebensäusserungen—Wachstumsfähigkeit, Reizbarkeit, Stoffwechsel, Regeneration, usw.—aus der höheren Organisation der organischen Molekülen entspringen, aber diese Moleküle selbst schon Eigenschaften enthalten, aus denen jene im Fall der Organisierung abzuleiten sind. Der Bauplan der Lebewelt wäre daher schon in der unbelebten Natur vorgezeichnet. Neben der Eignung der Umwelt nach Temperatur, Feuchtigkeitsgrad, Kohlensäuregehalt, usw., ist vor allen die Elektron-neutralität des Kohlenstoffs wesentlich, die die Bildung der homoiopolaren Verbindungen, das Aneinanderlagern langer und beliebig verzweigter Ketten von Radikalen veranlasst, womit die unendliche Mannigfaltigkeit der organischen Stoffe gegeben ist. So entstehen Moleküle von bedeutender Grösse und hinreichender Stabilität. Ihre kolloidalen Eigenschaften veranlassen widerum den gelatinösen Zustand der Zellen, der einen mittleren Grad des Diffusionsaustausche im Inneren ermöglicht; hiermit ist ein wichtiger Faktor der Reaktionsgeschwindigkeit der biologischen Umsetzungen gegeben, usw.'

Cf. also R. S. Lillie's remark, 'It seems clear that the concept of form and the concept of stability are closely allied. No form would be possible in chaos' (*Philos. of Sci.*, 1937, **4**, 220). Successive states of form in embryonic development are now treated from the point of view of stability levels (see my *Biochemistry and Morphogenesis*, pp. 112 ff.). Consider also an animal in a vessel isolated from any environment. If the energy present throughout the vessel were suddenly to be concentrated in the animal its temperature would rise to, say, 10,000° and it would die. Thermodynamic order would have increased and biological organisation would have decreased.

56. F. Engels, *Anti-Dühring*, p. 94.
57. J. Needham, *The Sceptical Biologist* (London, 1929), pp. 207 ff.

7

Aspects of the World Mind
in Time and Space

(1941)

The view of the world which modern science has disclosed to us embodies what at first sight seems a curious contradiction. The collective work of physicists and chemists, of astronomers and engineers over more than two centuries has given us, among certain other fundamental natural laws, the great generalisation known as the law of entropy. The universe, or at any rate the parts nearest to us, are continually passing from more improbable to more probable states, free energy is constantly decreasing and entropy (or bound energy) increasing, and it would seem that we are slowly approaching a condition of thermal equilibrium in which no further utilisation of energy can occur. They expound this as meaning that the order in the universe is continually decreasing and the disorder continually increasing. Thinkers with theological axes to grind have embraced this doctrine with enthusiasm, some because the prospect of the 'heavens waxing old as doth a garment' seems to them to justify an appeal to Neoplatonic other-worldly mysticism, others because the apparent original winding-up of the universe seems to restore a Creator to the necessities of thought. The ever-present possibilities of cyclical trends, however, or a continuous flow of energy through the universe, render their enthusiasm premature.

Side by side with the law of entropy, however, the chemists, geologists, biologists and sociologists, had been laying the foundations of the law of evolution. For us, the inheritors of the work of the great popular exponents of the Victorian period, the knowledge of the evolutionary development of the world is the permanent background of our thinking. We know that the original chaos of physical particles gradually gave place to the chemical elements as we see them today, including those with highly complex atomic structures; we know how these slowly aggregated into molecules and these in turn into the very well-ordered crystals and paracrystals. We recognise that in this milieu when the stage of complexity of protein molecules was reached, life appeared, and from then on, through the simplest living cells to the most complicated and organised beings such as ourselves, the line runs clear. Nor can we exempt from this process the development of human societies, themselves in a social evolution attaining ever greater and greater complexity, passing through primitive tribalism, civilised forms of economic association such as feudalism and capitalism, and pointing forward to the world socialism of the future. The only guiding thread we have is the increase and development of organisation.

There is no reason for thinking that this organisation may not be measurable, just as entropy is. Embryologists have long needed a measure of differentiation during development of the individual. If we could have such a measure of increasing organisation during evolution, we might be able to assess the progress of human societies in concrete terms.

Here there is no opportunity to discuss how this seeming contradiction between physics and death on the one hand, psychology and life on the other, may be resolved. It is probable that the physicist's concept of order means only separatedness. Mixed-up-ness may be patterned as well as chaotic. It may be best to say that the world is passing from universal order to general disorder plus local, though ever higher, states of organisation. Of these we ourselves form part. The order regnant when free energy was at its maximum might thus almost be considered as the necessary precursor of biological order, and the world-process as a vast metamorphosis, for which we might find a metaphor in the changes undergone by developing animals such as sea-urchin plutei and butterfly larvae.

For man as a social being, however, the essential thing is that he stands at the growing point of a vast evolutionary process, the characteristics of which we can see pretty well. The march of living organisation, the progress of the world mind, will not stand still where it is today. For us at this middle point of time, the first duty is to appraise the social forces at work around us to see in what direction they are leading. Which of them make for higher social organisation, greater human unity, community and solidarity; which of them seek to perpetuate lower stages of evolution, of the horde, of the tribe, of primitive man or even of animal life? The answer is not in doubt; fascist philosophers stand self-condemned. This is the point of view from which we should approach traditional systems of morality. Morality needs no supernatural sanctions; its function is to state the means whereby human beings may live in harmony together, pooling their talents for the general good and collectively relieving their shortcomings. Since human beings are themselves, as units, the most highly organised living organisms known to us, they cannot be treated as if they were machines or as if they were animals, and any social philosophy which attempts to do so is ultimately doomed, even if, for a while, it should flourish like the green bay tree.

The social significance of science is indeed inescapable. It fundamentally rests on the checking and rechecking of observations of external Nature made by countless human investigators. Their race, colour, religion or nationality is irrelevant to this function. Moreover, science alone, because of the ever-increasing precision and factual content of her language, has discovered how to attain substantially complete communicability between observers. This essentially social structure of science mirrors the oneness of humanity in other affairs, in artistic and religious experience (where communicability is far less) and in the production and exchange of commodities. Science is already a 'communitas,' a 'commune'; it will never be free to exert its full power in the benefaction of mankind until the social structure of mankind is also a 'commune.' Who has better recognised this than our chairman, H. G. Wells? It was the basic assumption of all his 'utopias.'

The founders of 'scientific socialism' called it so because they recognised the rising tide of organisation in the age-old evolutionary process, and they thought that that was a better foundation for a faith in coming human community than the deepest religious aspirations. But there is a further significance in the phrase. Freedom and Authority is an ancient antinomy indeed; social philosophers have ever wrestled with it and theologians have filled a multitude of books with discussions of it. But science is perhaps the only form of human activity in which the clue to its resolution has been found. The scientific view of the world forms a structure on the knowledge of which we have to act, but it is always open to anyone to upset as much of it as he possibly can, and no scientific training is any good unless it encourages the young scientist to question the fundamentals and to believe that the facts may force him to demand their radical modification.[1] Practical authority exists well enough, therefore, but the possibility of a Harvey or an Einstein has always to be taken into consideration, and freedom therefore exists too. It is true that recognition of the ideas of an unorthodox questioner may not come in his own lifetime, but that is a small matter where saecular trends are concerned.

If society, therefore, were to be so based on principles of reason and of ascertained social fact; if the exploitation of men were replaced by the administration of things, it would always be open for improvers to demand radical modification if they could show just cause. No ruling class in history has ever yet dared to face social criticism. Since its material interests are involved, it reacts with police measures, until at length when criticism has become too overwhelming it resorts to civil war and itself passes into the museum of history. But in the classless state, towards which, as the profoundest analysis of social evolution shows us, we must look, the scientific administrators of government should be in the same position as the scientific investigators of nature. Here is a structure, examine it through and through, investigate and assemble your facts, make your proposals for improvement, *if you can*.[2] To have attained this state of social rationality would be to have passed from the necessities of social conflict into the freedom of a realm where man could plan his own destiny.

At what is, in some sense, an international gathering, it is fitting that we should take some account of contributions made to human thought by civilisations other than our own. So far we have been considering the time-process; what of other spatial regions of our world? The very words 'social rationality' call to mind a civilisation, far older than that of these Western islands, which has contributed far more than is often supposed to philosophical and scientific thought. For present purposes we may roughly divide the types of civilisation (excluding abortive Aztec and African upsurges) into the Semitic-Occidental, to which we ourselves belong, the Indian, and the Chinese. It has been said that whenever modern man climbs to the top of some newly-conquered mountain of intellectual achievement, he finds that the Greeks had shot an arrow there two thousand years before.[3]

Those of us who are acquainted with Chinese culture would add that when he looks again he finds a Chinese arrow too. I cannot claim to have anything of value to say on ancient Indian contributions, but I know that a progressive study of the course of Chinese philosophical thought filled me step by step with amazement and delight that in that ancient system, perhaps the only one comparable with the occidental system in richness and variety, so many ideas had found another expression, as if in a symphony on the same themes by another composer. Writing to Lorenzo de Medici in 1515 from China, Andreas Corsalis described the Chinese as 'di nostra qualità,' of the same stuff as ourselves. It was a compliment to us.

In the first place, China's greatest ethical philosopher, K'ung-fu-tzu (Confucius) was a moralist without supernaturalism. Long ages before anyone could have expected to see, as we do today, how ethics could arise as a social product within a natural evolutionary process when social man had arisen, he put human relationships first and supernatural religion a poor second. What are we to do, his disciples were always asking him, about the gods and spirits? 'Respect them from a distance,' was his answer, 'but have as little to do with them as possible. First study how you may live with your fellow-men in peace, justice and love, then, when you have discovered that, you may ask me again concerning the gods and spirits.' When irresponsible ascetics taunted him with his mundane interests he said, 'I cannot live with animals. If I am not to live with my fellow-men, whom am I to live with? If society were as it ought to be, I should not be wanting to change it.' When asked what he would do first for the people, he replied, 'Feed and enrich them'; what next, he replied, 'Educate them.' Confucian naturalist ethics, scientific in spirit long before science, reached Europe in the eighteenth century; they produced a deep impression on the scholars of the time. In Chinese culture the romantic and the rational have always been successfully blended. Its fight today against an imperialist and irrational mysticism is identical with ours.

The greatest disciple of Confucius, Mêng-tzu (Mencius), was extremely important on account of his view that man's nature is fundamentally good. Unlike the West, where Augustine was orthodox and Pelagius heretical, in China Mencius was orthodox and Hsün-tzu unorthodox. This belief too reached Europe in the eighteenth century, and we know that it profoundly influenced the thinkers of the Encyclopaedia movement, who laid the theoretical foundations of the French Revolution and of all subsequent progressive naturalist thinking.

Later Confucian thought became petrified into something of a scholasticism, and it was against this that Taoism reacted. Taoism represented to some degree the desire of the human mind to return from the ordering of human society to the contemplation of Nature. Lao-tzu's diatribes against 'knowledge' were directed rather against Confucian scholasticism; and the Taoists, like the mystical theologians of our own Renaissance, believed in the efficacy of manual operative arts. Many historians of science find that alchemy had its origin in Taoist magic; the search for the pill of immortality. A similar but more theoretical tendency is seen in the clear statement of relativity by the philosopher Chuang-tzu. Particularly interesting is the fundamental Taoist concept of *chêng ching* (serenity of mind) because it bears a close resemblance to the Epicurean ataraxy (*ataraxia*). This peace of mind, which comes from an intellectual contemplation of the works of Nature, and a resignation to, because an appreciation of, the manifold kaleidoscope of change, is still today a factor in the scientific world-view. By denuding the unknown of its terrors, it paves the way for the investigation of the unknown, and eventually the control of the known.

Lastly, the statement has often been heard that Chinese culture has been essentially stagnant, that it contained, unlike Greek thought, no germ of the understanding of evolution. This statement is wrong. In the 'Great Appendix' to the *I Ching,* one of the Chinese classics, dating from the fifth century BC, there is an extremely clear account of three phases of human social evolution. The first phase is described in detail as primitive barbarism; the second (the period of the 'Lesser Tranquility'; *hsiao an*) is an era of private property, coercive government, social cataclysms and war. The third (the period of 'Great Togetherness'; *ta thung*) is no more and no less than the communal ownership of the means of production. Unfortunately we are still at the second stage today. I do not know of any parallel account of social evolution in Greek philosophy. It is true that Aeschylus, Hippocrates, Epicurus and Moschion did envisage the origin of human society from primitive barbarism, but they had little to say of the future, and most of the Greeks were dominated by the idea of cyclical recurrence or even of degeneration from a Golden Age.

As for the causes which prevented the appearance of systematically organised science in China; that is a subject demanding
much research and probably not to be solved without a corresponding understanding of how Chinese differs from occidental
economic history.

Summing up this contribution, then, we have seen that
although physical order is everwhere decreasing, biological and
social organisation is everywhere increasing. The human social
organisation into which we were born has yet far to go towards its
ultimate triumphs. The whole enterprise of science is a manifestation of this social organisation, itself the product of evolution
and the guarantee of further evolution. Our business is to find out
how we may best make ourselves efficacious instruments of the
cosmic process as it manifests itself in evolving human society, not
caring if we perish in this cause, a holy and living sacrifice, seeing
how much we ourselves have benefited from the acts of the
martyrs and ancestors from the beginning of the world. And not
only is this cloud of witnesses about us in the time-process but
also, as has been shown, there come from the other side of the
world ancient men, men of another colour, but our brothers and
kinsmen, witnessing to the truth of human solidarity and the
unity of the world mind.

Final revision
Chungking, Szechuan
July, 1944

Notes

1. The modesty and humility of older scientists worth their salt towards the young
   is charmingly depicted in a botanist's autobiography, 'A Naturalist in the
   City,' by D. C. Peattie, *Atlantic Monthly*, 1941, **167**, 498.
2. This thought found expression as far back as the seventeenth century. J. A.
   Komensky (Comenius), the illustrious Czech educationalist and pioneer of the
   organisation of science, dedicated a book, *Via Lucis*, to the newly formed Royal
   Society in 1668, from Amsterdam, though parts of it had been written many
   years earlier, when he was in London in 1641 on that visit which had stimulated
   the Royal Society's foundation.
   'Let your researches into natural objects,' he said, 'be so well established
   that if a man desires not merely to contemplate your work but even to try
   its accuracy with the most exacting tests of his own device, he shall be
   certain to find that the facts are precisely what you have shown them to
   be. This will be an admirable precedent, and will encourage those who
   are at the helm of human society in the State, or of men's consciences in
   the Church, to act in the same way, following indeed the example of the

Apostles who did not fear to submit all their doctrines to the scrutiny and judgement of the world.' (*Via Lucis*, English translation by E. T. Campagnac, Liverpool, 1938.) Cf. *The Teacher of Nations*, essays in honour of Comenius, Cambridge, 1942.

3. St. L. Strachey, *The River of Life* (London, *c.* 1924), p. 298.

IV

PROCESS AND UNDERSTANDING

8

Metamorphoses of Scepticism

(1941)

He says goodbye
To much, but not to love. For loving now shall be
The close handclasp of the waters about his trusting keel,
Buoyant they make his home, and lift his heart high,
Among their marching multitude he never shall feel lonely.
Love for him no longer a soft and garden sigh
Ruffling at evening the petalled composure of the senses;
But a wind all hours and everywhere he no wise can deny.

(Chorus from *Noah and the Waters*, C. Day Lewis)

This book[1] is the third of a series of collections of essays and addresses; the first, *The Sceptical Biologist*, appeared in 1929,[2] the second, *The Great Amphibium*, was published in 1931.[3] Even today there are many professional scientists who look askance at the action of a colleague who dares to speak out from time to time on general topics. In his spare time, they feel, he should occupy himself with some innocent and health-giving occupation such as golf or fishing, rather than with dubious studies in the history of science or philosophy, the development of economic structures, the ramifications of folk-lore or the language of the Aztecs and the literature of Cathay. The overt rationalisation of this feeling is that a scientific worker can hardly be thought to have sufficient intellectual energy for his scientific work unless he is careful to use none outside it—apart from the fact that general inquiries have a strangely irritating quality for those who quite honestly do prefer golf or bridge. But the real meaning of this feeling is that to enquire too curiously into the structure of the world and society and the history of society is potentially a menace to the stability of society. The innocent scientist who harbours no 'dangerous thoughts' is a far more wholesome member of the community (from the point of view of its *de facto* rulers) than the scientist who prefers to prowl. Like the various departments of some great industrial plant, into which one must not penetrate without a special pass, History and Philosophy would be presented as closed doors, if it were possible, to the scientific investigator in the pay of the bourgeoisie.

I am glad to confess that, like T. H. Huxley, du Bois Reymond, Ernst Haeckel, and many another better man, I have always been a prowler, an explorer, among ideas. The *Sceptical Biologist* and the *Great Amphibium*[4] represented a fairly systematic position in the philosophy of science, but as would be expected in a prowler among ideas, this position has during the past ten years undergone a considerable reconstruction. The first necessity in introducing the present book is to indicate how it links on with the two former ones.

The Differentiation of the Forms of Experience

The task with which I was mainly occupied in SB and GA was the distinctification and differentiation of the great forms of human experience; science, philosophy, religion, history and art. During the previous ten years I had often been nauseated at the confusion of them all together which is so common among superficial thinkers in pulpits and elsewhere, and I tried therefore to show how different each of them was from the others. Each seemed to lead to a characteristic world-view, incompatible with and sometimes frankly contradictory to those of the others. The proper appreciation of the world by man could not arise, I believed, from the pursuit of any one of these forms of experience by itself, but rather by the experience of all of them, though there was little or no hope of uniting them into any kind of *philosophia prima* or coherent view of the universe. The use of the word 'scepticism' in a title implied, therefore, two things; first that I was sceptical of any one of the forms of experience claiming to be a royal road to our appreciation of the world in which we live, and secondly that I was sceptical of the construction of any coherent world-view which would reconcile the conflicting claims of the forms of experience together. In this sense I deliberately use the word 'appreciation' instead of understanding or comprehension, for the purely intellectual would at once cut out the contributions of religion and art, forms of experience which have something in common with being in love. A man who had never been in love might give us a proposal for a world-view, but if we knew this fact about him, we should be right to think twice before accepting it. And the saying of Sir Thomas Browne, 'Thus is Man that great and true Amphibium, whose nature is disposed to live, not only like other creatures in diverse elements, but in divided and distinguished worlds' again emphasised my scepticism as to the possibility of a coherent world-view. I am still a sceptic, but certain processes of metamorphosis have taken place.

We may pause for a moment to note the delineation of the forms of experience. Science (as I then saw it) is abstract, dealing with statistics and avoiding the individual, aiming at the establishment of natural regularities ('scientific truth'), and quantitative, metrical, mathematical and deterministic. It is essentially classificatory, mechanical, analytical and orderly, generalising and impersonal. It has ethical and aesthetic neutrality. It fights mystery and teleology, and it gives a characteristic peace of mind, the Epicurean *ataraxia,* akin to the early Taoist conception of *chêng ching,* 正靜. It is both rational and empirical. Religion, on the other hand, is concrete and individual, based on the sense of the holy, with which are connected the sentiments of reverence and awe. It is qualitative in feeling, opposed to measurement and analysis, 'cornucopial' instead of orderly, personal rather than impersonal, and essentially irrational and alogical in spite of the cloak of rational thought based on uncertain premises which rational theologians, such as the scholastics, have sometimes succeeded in throwing about it. It naturally insists on 'free-will' as against determinism. As for Philosophy, it partakes of the abstraction typical of science, but it is also interested in the individual, the qualitative, and the teleological. Unlike science, it claims to be normative, and it is not so vigorously opposed to mysteries and paradoxes. History again partakes of many of the attributes of science, but its criteria of evidence are not quite the same, and since, like philosophy, it is debarred from the performance of any experiments, its conclusions can never be tested in that way. Predictions are rather in the province of science. Artistic experience finally approximates to the religious domain, in that it is sharply separated from the rational and the expressible, but its importance to man is as great as any of the others, and there is some connection between the appreciation of beauty and the divination of the holy. Such contrasts will be found at length in SB and GA.[5]

Looking back at my efforts ten or fifteen years ago to disentangle the forms of experience, I think now that the description of science was rather too narrow, and the description of religion certainly much too Neo-platonic, idealistic, pietistic and otherworldly. In my anxiety to see the forms of human experience in sharpest antithesis to one another, I almost welcomed characteristics which added to their irreconcilability. I was determined to be a 'divider,' and if indeed the work of previous 'uniters' was insufficiently well-founded, this was no mistake. 'Dividing' and 'uniting' may be looked upon as dialectical opposites, like continuity and discontinuity, which run through the whole history of philosophical and scientific thought, imperfect unions being always doomed to destruction by later 'dividing' critics.

But much the most significant thing about my point of view at that time, as I remember it, was that I was always uncomfortable about the position of ethics. It was the sole department of thought which I could never allot to one or other of the forms of experience. It seemed sometimes to belong to religion, but yet it was obviously profoundly affected by science, and in some situations in time and space, such as early Chinese Confucianism, it existed without any connections with supernaturalism. Nor was it remote from aesthetic experience, since good actions had something beautiful about them; nor could it be considered apart from history, since systems of ethics had changed with changing social conditions.

The explanation of this difficulty was at hand, however.

The Breaking in of Ethics and Politics

During the past twenty years, the one form of experience which in SB and GA was never taken into account,[6] came and forced itself more and more upon my attention, namely politics. Ethics and politics both belong to the realm of man's social life, and my fundamental limitation had been to envisage the experiencing human being as a solitary unit, subject to the diverse forms of experience which I had been classifying. Ethics are the rules whereby men may live together in society with the utmost harmony and the best opportunities for the development of their talents in the common good. Politics are nothing but the attempt to objectify the most advanced ethics in the structure of society, to enmesh the ideal ethical relations in the real world. Hence the class struggles in every age since the origin of private property, which, though at many stages a fundamentally progressive force, at other stages radically hinders the attainment of the next step in social relations. Now so far as my thinking was concerned, ethics and politics proved to be the cement necessary for the unification of the divergent forms of experience. The dividing process was succeeded by a uniting one, and an integrated world-view emerged from the differentiated dissected analysed system which I had made. It was bound to follow the lead of the philosophy which most consistently allows for the social background of our thought and being, and explains what is happening, and has for centuries been happening, to human society as the continuation of all biological evolution.

Perhaps it will not be a digression if at this point I lighten the way by a few autobiographical notes. I tried to keep to my own field, but politics would keep breaking in. I grew up in an extremely bourgeois household, my father a physician (before my time, an anatomist and pioneer in pathological histology) in private practice but later to be a specialist in anaesthesia; my mother a musician and composer. My father was, I believe, an extremely kind man in his practice, among which there were many working-class people, but the atmosphere of my home was saturated with every kind of bourgeois prejudice. I remember with affection, however, an incident which was the first to make me realise the community of flesh and blood which I had with working-class people, who otherwise one might have been tempted to suppose were an entirely different species of living organism. It was at the little French town of Eu, where I (then about thirteen) was travelling with my father on holiday, and as there was no 'correspondance' of trains, we had to stay the night. The hotel was full, so we were accommodated in a neighbouring railwayman's cottage, the simple homely welcome of whose family I never forgot. Such little incidents have untold consequences, and about 1917 in walks with my father I would always argue in favour of socialism against his incurably pessimistic views of human nature, so well suited to the retention of power and privilege by the class which at any given time possesses it.

I remember, too, the first mention I ever heard of bolshevism. I was on my bicycle, while my best school friend, F—. C—. (later

Professor of Architecture at McGill University)[7] walked along beside me. It was the summer of 1918. We had roving minds; he did a good deal of sculpture, and we corresponded in a variety of codes, in Leonardo's mirror-writing, and so on. He was saying, 'The point about bolshevism is, that so far, every ruling class has oppressed everybody else, so now the idea is to take the very dregs of the population and make them the ruling class, so that they can take a turn at oppressing everybody else.' I remember saying I thought it a very *peculiar* theory. I still smile at this, but it was something to be discussing it at all; I believe most of the boys with whom I was at school did not begin to think about it till many years afterwards, if ever.

Later on, as an undergraduate, my interests were largely philosophical and theological, and I was so unpolitical that I never joined the Union Society, on account of a disinclination to be drawn into political debates. But in so far as I was anything, I was vaguely progressive, and remember supporting with great enthusiasm (and owing to my upbringing no small inside knowledge) the proposal for a State Medical Service at a debate at the Junior Acton Club, a social body which united mostly Caius and Emmanuel men but now long since defunct. An influence of considerable importance, after my marriage, was that of our friend the biochemist L—. R—.,[8] whose Eastern and Central European outlook on political questions revolutionised ours. We had got to know him during a period of work at the Roscoff Marine Biological Station, and I remember discussions on the roof, in 1925, while the sun sank over the Ile de Batz, and again in our house in Cambridge later, which were very formative for us.

The process of socialisation of my outlook, however, really began with the General Strike in 1926 and was completed by the rise to power of Hitlerite fascism in 1933. In the general strike I was on the wrong side, and helped in the running of the railway as a volunteer, explaining my action to socialist friends as a straightforward support of constitutionally elected government, a government which I had certainly voted against in the preceeding elections. I so far acted up to my beliefs in this way that at the conclusion of the strike, when the railway company wanted us to remain at our posts in order that their officials could conduct a victimisation process against the returning railwaymen, I spoke against this at a meeting of the volunteers, pointing out that we had no quarrel with the railwaymen, and so helped to ensure that most of the volunteers left without delay. There can be no doubt that these events supplied the most powerful stimulus I had ever had towards reading along sociological and political lines. I carried a little old torn copy of the *Tale of Two Cities* on the footplate, but in the evenings and afterwards I read Shaw's *Guide to Capitalism and Socialism* and went on from that to heavier material. In this way I came to the belief I now hold, that in a sense, in any doubtful case, 'the people are *never* wrong'; through all the ages of oppression since the first beginnings of private property men have been struggling for political freedom, and everything which assists this struggle is right. The later years of work of my wife and myself in the Labour movement, including a long membership of the Cambridge Trades Council, all originated from this time.

By 1933 the general movement among all kinds of intellectual workers in England towards political activity was becoming widespread. In the Universities it was evident in the much increased interest of the undergraduate in political thought, and the concomitant decline in organised large-scale jokes and similar amusing, if childish, exhibitions. A certain loss of lightheartedness was unavoidable. Even in the world of science, our witty periodical *Brighter Biochemistry*, which in its day had had a wide reputation and had been very worth while, died after some seven years of life about this time. The situation was, in fact, getting beyond a joke, and the shadow of the Second World War was upon us.

The Creativeness of Contradictions

I must now turn to sketch the general world-view at which I arrived after I began to realise man as a social being, and in which the various forms of experience which I had so carefully distinguished found their place. Essentially what I had unearthed from these sharp antitheses was a series of contradictions.[9] Now contradictions and deadlocks are far from being a calamity in practical thought; they are only so in formal logic. In practice they find themselves overcome by syntheses at higher levels. And the idea that 'the principle of contradiction is only valid for our reason' is an ancient one; it is found in the mystical writer Dionysius the Areopagite, and again when the middle ages were giving place to the modern era, in Nicholas of Cusa, and in Giordano Bruno.[10] For example, in Master Eckhardt we find

the following, easily decipherable through its archaic German.[11]
'Waz ist widersatzunge? Lieb unde leit, wiz unde swarz, daz hat
widersatzunge, unde die enblibet in wesenne niht. Swenne diu
Seele kumt in daz lieht der Vernünfteekeit, so weiz si niht
widersatzunge.'

All these thinkers placed the reconciliation of contradictions,
however, in the realm of the divine, and did not consider it as
attainable by man in his earthly state. This was the position I too
adopted in my earlier thinking,[12] quoting Robert Boyle : 'When
we die God will enlarge our faculties so as to enable us to gaze
without being dazzled upon those sublime and radiant truths
whose *harmony* as well as splendour we shall then be qualified to
discover, and consequently with transports to admire.' It was a
thought not infrequently met with in the seventeenth century;
thus Sir Thomas Browne said, 'There is yet another conceit that
hath made me sometimes shut my books, which tells me it is a
vanity to waste our days in the blind pursuit of knowledge; it is
but attending a little longer, and we shall enjoy that by instinct
and infusion, which we endeavour at here by labour and inquisition. It is better to sit down in a modest ignorance, and rest
contented with the natural blessing of our own reasons, than buy
the uncertain knowledge of this life with sweat and vexation
which Death gives every fool gratis, and is an accessory of our
glorification.'[13]

But it was left to Karl Marx and Frederick Engels in the last
century, building on the dialectic process of the idealist philosopher Hegel, but profoundly influenced through Darwin[14] by
the new understanding of evolution which was then dawning on
men, to take the revolutionary step of placing the resolution of
contradictions within the historical and pre-historical process
itself. Contradictions are not resolved only in heaven; they are
resolved right here, some in the past, some now, and some in time
to come. This is the dialectical materialist way of expounding
cosmic development, biological evolution, and social evolution,
including all history.

However fascists may laugh, there is something divine about a
committee.[15] One member makes a proposal, another points out
that for some reason or another it will not do; there are further
proposals and counter-proposals, and out of this strife of theses
and antitheses, the synthesis, or final decision, is born, only to
become itself in due time another thesis, again unsatisfactory, and

to be subsumed in further higher syntheses by later meetings or higher committees. This is the dialectical process.[16] Marx and Engels were bold enough to assert that it happens actually in evolving Nature itself, and that the undoubted fact that it happens in our thought about Nature is because we and our thought are a part of Nature. We cannot consider Nature otherwise than as a series of levels of organisation, a series of dialectical syntheses. From ultimate physical particle to atom, from atom to molecule, from molecule to colloidal aggregate, from aggregate to living cell, from cell to organ, from organ to body, from animal body to social association, the series of organisational levels is complete. Nothing but energy (as we now call matter and motion) and the levels of organisation (or the stabilised dialectical syntheses) at different levels have been required for the building of our world. The consequences of this point of view are boundless. Social evolution is continuous with biological evolution, and the higher stages of social organisation, embodied in advanced ethics and in socialism, are not a pious hope based on optimistic ideas about human nature, but the necessary consequence of all foregoing evolution. We are in the midst of the dialectical process, which is not likely to stop at the bidding of those who sit, like Canute, with their feet in the water forbidding the flood of the tide.

I shall not emphasise these consequences here, since in the other essays in this book they are further dealt with. I shall only point out that they fundamentally affect our attitude to time. Hence the title of the present book. As Auden says :[17]

And the poor in their fireless lodgings, dropping the sheets
Of the evening paper; 'Our day is our loss, O show us
    History the operator, the
Organiser, Time the refreshing river !

Sir Thomas Browne was wrong; 'the great Mutations of the world' are not all yet acted, and time will not be too short for the development of human society that is to come. Contrary presentations, of course, spring to the mind :

Time, like an ever-rolling stream
Bears all its sons away,
They fly forgotten, as a dream
Dies at the opening day

as we used to sing as children. But now we have no further

interest in this over-individualistic type of Christianity; those who are prepared to 'work illegally, and be anonymous' that the Kingdom may come, find that this attitude has no meaning for them. Nor will they be depressed by the cultured hopelessness of T. S. Eliot in 'East Coker':

> And so each venture
> Is a new beginning, a raid on the inarticulate
> With shabby equipment always deteriorating
> In the general mess of imprecision of feeling,
> Undisciplined squads of emotion. And what there is to conquer
> By strength and submission, has already been discovered
> Once or twice, or several times, by men whom one cannot hope
> To emulate—but there is no competition—
> There is only the fight to recover what has been lost
> And found and lost again and again: and now, under conditions
> That seem unpropitious. But perhaps neither gain nor loss.
> For us, there is only the trying. The rest is not our business.

Again, this is too individualist. Time is for all men a refreshing river; not merely a perpetual recurrence of opportunities for individual souls to scale the heights of mystical experience or to produce great artistic achievement or to break free from the wheel of things or to attain perfect non-activity, or whatever metaphor of individual perfection you happen to like. The historical process is the organiser of the City of God, and those who work at its building are (in the ancient language) the ministers of the Most High. Of course there have been setbacks innumerable, but the curve of the development of human society pursues its way across the graph of history with statistical certainty, heeding neither the many points which fall beneath it, nor those many more hopeful ones which lie above its average sweep.[18]

Instances of dialectical development in scientific knowledge are so numerous that a few moments' thought provides an embarrassingly large selection. All science progresses by new hypotheses which combine in a synthetic way, not by mere compromise, the truest points in the preceding hypotheses. Deadlocks are thus overcome. Thus in embryology we know now that both egg and sperm are essential contributions to generation from the two parents, but in the eighteenth century and well into the nineteenth this was not understood. The Ovists believed that mammals developed from the egg alone, and that the spermatozoa were adventitious worm-like organisms, perhaps parasites, as the termination '-zoa' of their modern name still indicates to-day. The Animalculists, on the other hand, believed that the animal originated from the spermatozoon only, and that the egg was if anything only a kind of box in which it could develop. The phenomena of inheritance alone should have sufficed to indicate that this deadlock was an absurdity, but it took nearly two centuries before the functions of egg and spermatozoon were understood, and the contradiction was resolved. In the later history of embryology we find a similar contradiction. When the study of the fate of parts of the egg began, it was at first believed that all development is mosaic, i.e. that any injury to the egg at the beginning of development is reflected in a corresponding injury in the finished embryo. Then came the discovery that in some eggs, at any rate, regulative development can occur, i.e. that from a half-egg, or even a quarter-egg, a normal embryo, though small, can be formed. These facts were made the basis of vitalist theories, but the sharp contradiction was at length resolved by the finding that the eggs of some species are mosaic and that those of others are regulative, the only difference between them being the exact time at which the determination of the fates of the various parts occurs.

The same syntheses of contradictions are going on in biochemistry. Some thirty years ago lactic acid was thought to be the causative agent in the contraction of muscle. After the discovery of phosphagen, this substance in turn was regarded as the most important. We know now that neither of these substances is connected with the final process whereby energy is transferred from chemical processes to the muscle fibre but another substance altogether, adenyl-pyrophosphate. Phosphagen is one of the substances involved in the cycles of phosphorylation by which energy is transferred, while the lactic acid is simply the waste-product of the breakdown of glycogen whereby the chemical energy is provided. Or again, adrenalin has long been known to contract blood vessels and also raise the blood-sugar by mobilising liver glycogen. This latter action was thought to be due to the constriction of the liver's small blood-vessels, with consequent anoxaemia and asphyxia. But it was then found that even in well-oxygenated liver cells, adrenalin causes a breakdown of glycogen. This contradiction was subsequently resolved by the further finding that adrenalin intervenes in the oxidative synthesis of glycogen in the cell.

A particularly neat example of the resolution of a dialectical contradiction is that of nucleic acid synthesis by developing eggs. It was first found that during the development of sea-urchin eggs, a large quantity of histologically recognisable nuclein is formed for the increasing number of nuclei. But it was then found that there was no change whatever in the nuclein phosphorus or the nucleic acid nitrogen during development. Here was a flat contradiction, but it was resolved by workers who showed that there are two kinds of nucleic acid, and that during development one of them, situated in the cytoplasm, is transformed into the other kind situated in the new nuclei.

In the field of wider ideas, there is a convincing sense in which one may say that the long-debated controversy between biological mechanists and vitalists (much discussed in SB and GA) was a dialectical deadlock which a judicious organicism has resolved.[19] The mechanists, enamoured of over-simplified physico-chemical explanations of biological processes, which they regarded, quite rightly, as heuristically valuable, maintained that all biological processes were fully explicable in terms appropriate to the sciences of physics and chemistry. The vitalists, always eager to safeguard objective complexity (and at the same time to keep the world safe for animism), maintained that vital phenomena would always escape physico-chemical analysis. This deadlock, which in various forms had run through the whole history of human thought, was overcome when it was realised that every level of organisation has its own regularities and principles, not reducible to those appropriate to lower levels of organisation, nor applicable to higher levels, but at the same time in no way inscrutable or immune from scientific analysis and comprehension. Thus the rules which are followed in experimental morphology or genetics are perfectly valid in their own right, but comprehension will never be complete until what is going on at the other levels, both above and below, is analysed and compared with the level in question.[20] Biological organisation is the basic problem of biology; it is not an axiom from which biology must start.

So in the same way, we may perhaps consider dialectical materialism itself as the synthesis of the age-old contradiction between metaphysical idealism and materialism.[21] Idealism did justice to the highest manifestations of human social activity, but was absolutely incapable of doing justice to that real objective world on which science must insist. Materialism provided a world congruent with scientific activity, but since it lacked the second-ary qualities, a world so 'grey and cimmerian' (in Goethe's phrase) that only the stoutest-hearted or the thickest-headed could accept it as an account of the real world in which some place had to be found for human values. By their fight against both classical idealism and mechanical materialism, and by their insistence on the successive dialectical levels in nature, the highest of them including all man's highest experiences, Marx and Engels overcame this contradiction for the first time in history. Engels pointed out three limitations in former mechanical materialism; first that it was mechanical 'in the sense that it believed in the exclusive application of the standards of mechanics to processes of a chemical and organic nature'; second, that it was anti-dialecti-cal, i.e. that it did not allow for the ever-shifting boundaries in Nature; and third, that it admitted of the preservation of idealism 'up above' in the realm of the social sciences.[22]

In historical events the dialectical process is readily seen.[23] The English civil war in the seventeenth century provides a par-ticularly striking example. The whole feudal system of ideas, represented by the King, the aristocracy and the Anglican bishops came into sharp opposition against the rising middle class led by the smaller country gentry, the merchants and the City of London. Feudal royalism found its antithesis in the radical puritan republicanism of the Commonwealth period. But the time was not ripe for the ideas of the Levellers and Independents, and the Restoration was a dialectical synthesis in which a consti-tutional monarchy, or one which was bound to end as such, combined with a triumphant Parliament controlled by the middle class whose interests the civil war had made secure. The Protest-ant *coup d'état* of 1688 and the Reform Act of 1832 simply completed the process. The French Revolution shows a very simi-lar development. The feudal monarchy was opposed by the revolutionary Jacobins, but the eventual outcome was the rule of the post-Napoleonic bourgeoisie. This dialectical process is the explanation of the feature so characteristic of revolutions, that they move (in common parlance), two steps forward and one step back.[24]

A Reconsideration of Beliefs

In the light of what has now been said, it may be of interest to reconsider some of the points of view in my two previous books of essays. In the first place the attack on vitalism in all its forms[25] was abundantly justified; there is no place whatever in biology for traces of animism, but we must seek to understand the biological level side by side with the physico-chemical level and the psychological level. In saying that living things differ from dead things in degree and not in kind, and are, as it were, extrapolations from the inorganic,[26] I was explicitly adumbrating the scheme of successive levels of complexity and organisation. The essay 'Lucretius Redivivus'[27] was sound in that it emphasised a coming connection between chemical science and mental science, and I look back with pleasure on my enthusiasm for Epicurus and Lucretius, from which I have never seen any reason to depart, and which has since been publicly shared by others in some extremely valuable books.[28] My dislike of fixed boundary-lines in Nature[29] was, I found, in agreement with what Engels says on the question in that great but unfortunately named work the *Anti-Dühring*.[30] At that time, much influenced by Lotze, whom I still consider a remarkable thinker, I emphasised that mechanism was to be considered applicable everywhere, but final nowhere.[31] This was an inadequate way of saying that the scientific method is applicable at all levels but that mechanical explanations are inadequate to deal with the phenomena of organisms. There was a similar confusion between 'scientific naturalism' and 'mechanical materialism'; I often wrote the former when, as I think now, I should have written the latter.[32] But this was because I could at that time see no way of including the highest phases of organisation within the realm of Nature without subjecting them to the distortion which mechanical materialism put upon them, a distortion which involved the characteristic denial I could never bring myself to make, the denial of the validity of one or other of the forms of human experience. Religion and art, for instance, are perfectly valid forms, though they certainly do not mean what their interpreters and experiencers have often thought they meant. Mechanism, then, according to my view, was applicable everywhere but final nowhere, and in biology this led to a position of methodological mechanism for which, in opposition to the neo-vitalists, I used the term neo-mechanism.[33] This was a way of acknowledging the complexity of the high organic levels without giving up the scientific method. It was also a way of acknowledging the imperfection and relativity of the scientific formulations so far attained. It went with, though it did not necessitate, the idea that the other forms of experience, such as religion, philosophy, history and art, were alternative, also imperfect, ways of apprehending the world in which we live. Owing to my ignorance of any form of naturalism other than mechanical materialism, my discussion of biological organicism was somewhat vitiated. While sympathetic to organicism, I assumed that biological organisation could not be investigated scientifically, and must therefore remain a concept of purely philosophical order.[34] Later I was able to revise this view thoroughly, and to show that on the contrary, organising relations *are* open to investigation.[35] It is precisely the organisation of the various levels that constitutes their special quality and gives rise to their special forms of behaviour.

It think it is fair to say that my presentation of the main metaphysical issue was never idealist.[36] But I was much influenced by the trend of thought originating with Ernst Mach, and agreed that the procedures of science do not give us a picture of the external world as it really *is*. While maintaining the real existence of the world (of matter) prior to ourselves, I described many features of the scientific method which suggest that our knowledge of it comes to us in distorted form. However much one may think this distortion amounts to, as long as one admits a knowable objective basis of our experience, one remains a materialist. My ideas on this subject were not cleared up until I read Lenin's book on the Machians, *Materialism and Empirio-Criticism*. Lenin showed that the Machians were really disguised philosophical idealists, not merely affirming the existence of some distortion in our apprehension of the external world, but tending to deny its very existence or to make all science the purely subjective study of an unknowable noumenon. He elucidated the confusion which the Machians had introduced between the objective-subjective antithesis on the one hand, and the absolute-relative antithesis on the other. Scientific truth is certainly relative, since all formulations are imperfect, though approaching, perhaps asymptotically, to the truest possible account of the regularities of external nature; but it is equally certainly objective, in that it deals with real external events, even through the 'optic glasses' of our human limitations.[37] Relativity of scientific truth is taken care of in dialectical materialism, since it is constantly

H

approximating dialectically to truth; but subjectivism, if it be pure, is nothing else than metaphysical idealism in disguise.

The seemingly endless process of the improvement of human knowledge was very much in my mind when the essays of SB and GA were written.[38] Because of my doubt whether any *philosophia prima* could ever be found to reconcile the different forms of human experience, I emphasised all the more the practice of the activities themselves, never doubting that each was undergoing progressive advance and refinement. Hence the quotation from the Nicomachean Ethics of Aristotle with which SB was headed : 'The greatest good which man can know is the active exercise of the spirit in conformity with virtue.' There is a parallel to this in the seemingly endless process of the improvement of human society. Those whose conscious or unconscious interest it is to minimise the achievements of social evolution generally choose one of two ways of attack; saying either that the art and thought of the ancients has had no equal since, or that no matter what changes the further development of human society may bring, it will never approach that perfection which has long been imaginable. The first point of view is the product of a distorted time-scale. The second is the most superficial of all pessimisms. Whether or not human suffering will always exist, it is always our duty to work to decrease it, and the course of social evolution hitherto gives us every confidence for the future. Social, as well as scientific, ethos is summed up in the words of G. E. Lessing (a favourite passage of the great physicist, Max Planck) : 'Not the possession of truth, but the effort in struggling to attain it, brings joy to the searcher.'

The Individualist Fallacy

All the worst deficiencies of SB and GA, as I now see it, were due to thinking of man solely as an individual, with various different facets, or windows, out of which, as in some observatory or conning-tower, he could look. Immediately one begins to consider man under his social aspect, the germs of a unified world-view appear.[39] As I have said, the position of ethics was, for this very reason, always obscure to me. Ethics are the rules whereby man may live in social harmony; Confucius discussed *li* 禮 and *jen* 仁 and *i* 義 in this sense and without any supernaturalism thousands of years ago. They are being discussed to-day in the same spirit.[40] Such rules perhaps correspond to the valency bonds and other forces which hold particles together at the molecular and sub-molecular levels. Politics is only practical mass ethics, some men seeking to perpetuate private possession of the goods of life, others seeking to distribute them as widely as may be; some men seeking for reasons why nothing should ever change, others seeking for true knowledge of the nature of man and how the natural needs can be satisfied. Hence for civilised man, in whom the numinous, the sense of the holy, is irrevocably attached to ethical ideas, religion too becomes a bond playing its part in the coherence of high social organisation. When Society itself has been sanctified by the full incorporation in it of the principles of justice, love and comradeship, religion is destined to pass without loss into social emotion as such. When oppression has been removed, religion as the cry of the oppressed creature will cease to exist, but the sense of the holy, one of man's most fundamental forms of experience, will never disappear. We can already see a similar transformation taking place in poetry, where the most moving implications can be conveyed by the poets in the simplest common words. The religious mysticism of a Donne or a Crashaw; the cosmic pantheism of a Wordsworth; have given place to the social emotion of such poets as Auden, Spender, Day Lewis, and such prose writers as Warner and Upward.

There is a story by that subtlest of writers, V. S. Pritchett, which well exemplifies this.[41] It is a love story and it concerns a commercial traveller and an undertaker's daughter, but the plain ordinariness of the conversation masks the deepest feeling and the most devastatingly subtle irony. This mingling of profound emotion with surface banality strikes an authentic note of what must come to be in future socialist society.[42] Auden has supplied a perfect allegory of it in his poem :

> To settle in this village of the heart,
> My darling, can you bear it ? True, the hall
> With its yews and famous dovecots is still there
> Just as in childhood, but the grand old couple
> Who loved us all so equally are dead;
> And now it is a licensed house for tourists,
> None too particular. One of the new
> Trunk roads passes the very door already,
> And the thin cafés spring up overnight.
> The sham ornamentation, the strident swimming pool,

The identical and townee smartness,
Will you really see as home, and not depend
For comfort on the chance, the sly encounter
With the irresponsible beauty of the stranger?
O can you see precisely in our gaucheness
The neighbour's strongest wish, to serve and love?

Pritchett and Auden and all our best writers are warning us not to be put off by what we may feel are the vulgar externals of modern life; not to retire into fantasies and escape-holes; the reality of human comradeship is as powerful as ever. The lorry-drivers on those roads have T.U. cards in their pockets and their talk in the thin cafés is far from fantastic. Those young men and women in the strident swimming pool are members, perhaps, of L.L.Y. or Y.C.L.[43] The beauty of these people is not strange, not irresponsible, but pregnant with the beauty of the new world-view.[44]

Perhaps a word about modern English poetry might be interjected here. The writings collected in the present book go to show how a scientist deeply responded to the work of poets contemporary with him during the period between the two world wars. He could not refrain from quoting them because they embodied all the elements of his own world-view, the evolutionary background, the materialist view of human history, the task of Eros in social progress, the revolutionary belief in the future world of justice and comradeship. W.B. Yeats,[45] when discussing the achievements of the 'New Country' School and their successors, remarked that certain technical factors such as assonance and sprung rhythm had permitted at last the inclusion of necessary scientific words into poetry. Scientific socialism could then bring science and poetry together.

It is essential, therefore, to view all the forms of human experience in a social context. But I was profoundly sceptical of the right of any one of the forms of experience to have the last word about the world in which we live. To-day I feel more confirmed in this scepticism than ever. A concentration on scientific experience alone gives you the individualistic researcher, inapt for teamwork and bent on priority, the easy prey of all the reactionary social forces tending to make scientists the passive instruments of class domination. In looking round among one's colleagues it has been consistently evident that those with the narrowest specialist interests tend to be politically the most reactionary.

Without history, the scientist will know nothing of social evolution, of the origin and progress of human society, of the laws of change and of the direction in which further progress is likely to take place. Without philosophy he can have no basic world-view, and may fall into all kinds of fantasies—for successful scientific work is compatible with anything from Roman Catholicism, as in the life of Pasteur, to Sandemanism as in the life of Faraday. It would be presumptuous in the case of such men to think that their scientific work would have been better if they had had better philosophies, but the majority of scientists are not of their calibre, and for these it is surely true that the better their philosophy the better their scientific work is likely to be. Without religion, the scientist will know little of comradeship with the mass of men, he will remain isolated from them in intellectual pride, and incapable of that humility which made Huxley give of his best to working-class audiences in 'Mechanics' Institutes' or Timiriazev and Sechenov lecture illegally to Russian working men. Only by recognising where the numinous really lies will he be able to take his part in the great Labour movement. As for the absence of aesthetic appreciation, one need not describe the kind of person he will be without that. All the forms of experience are necessary and no one of them has the last word.

It would be tedious to apply the same arguments to other sorts of men. Thus the historian without science will become a donnish 'period-prisoner,' and without philosophy a pedantic purveyor of meaningless facts. The religious man, without political understanding, will reduce ethics to relations between individuals and will sink into the false and vicious religion of other-worldly pietism. But even should he avoid this, he would become, without some admixture of science and philosophy, a pure social revolutionary, a Utopian lacking all solid background for his faith. Everyone can apply these principles to their own cases. As old Comenius said :

'Can any man be a good Naturalist, that is not seene in the Metaphysicks? Or a good Moralist, who is not a Naturalist? Or a Logician, who is ignorant of reall Sciences? Or a Divine, a Lawyer, or a Physician, that is no Philosopher? Or an Oratour or Poet, who is not accomplished with them all?'

(*A Reformation of Schools,* 1642)

And so I am a sceptic still. It was not by any means a useless task to distinguish with all possible exactness the forms of experience from one another. But the conclusion now is, not as before, that a man should exercise his soul (in Aristotle's phrase) in conformity with virtue, without the hope of unifying in any way the products of its exercises.[46] It is, to view the world as a whole and the place and course of man and of humanity in it, and to know 'what he must *do* while still in his compounded body.' The consideration of man and his experiences as an individual led in the end to contemplation; the consideration of social man and his experiences leads to action. No more shall we take Gautama and Plato for our guide, but rather those determined men who from Confucius to Marx were vehicles of the evolutionary process, working through them to implement the Promise occluded in the very beginning of our world.

Notes

1. [*Time: The Refreshing River* (London, 1943, hereinafter referred to as TRR.]
2. (Chatto & Windus, London, 1929: Norton, New York, 1930.)
3. (S.C.M. Press, London, 1931.)
4. Hereinafter referred to as SB and GA respectively.
5. This kind of treatment, done far better than I, as a working scientist, could ever have hoped to do it, was given in R. G. Collingwood's *Speculum Mentis* (Oxford, 1924); and it is interesting that the subsequent development of this philosopher, as his *Autobiography* (Oxford, 1939) shows, has paralleled my own.
6. There were indications of it in GA, however, cf. p. 43, [and pp. 65, 175, above].
7. [Frank Chambers].
8. [Louis Rapkine].
9. Cf. p. 120.
10. See 'The Cosmology of Giordano Bruno' by Dorothea W. Singer, *Isis*, 1941, **33**, 187, and her forthcoming book on this remarkable man.
11. See *Nicholas of Cusa* by H. Bett (London, 1932), p. 127.
12. Cf. SB, p. 225.
13. *Religio Medici*, I. 9.
14. Marx wanted to dedicate part of *Capital* to Darwin (cf. *Psyche*, 1931, **12**, 7).
15. This is why I like that famous dictum of Conrad Noel's that the universe itself is ruled by a committee. The Christian doctrine of the Trinity, 'neither afore nor after other,' 'without any difference or inequality,' upheld by Athanasius, would thus have been a democratic doctrine as against the totalitarian monotheism of the imperial and Arian party. The same thought occurs in Feuerbach's *Essence of Christianity* (London, 1854), pp. 66 and 288. 'The mystery of the Trinity,' he says, 'is the mystery of participated, social, life, the mystery of I and You,' and he gives patristic sources in support of it.
16. The best introduction to dialectical materialist philosophy known to me is that of R. Maublanc; *La Philosophie du Marxisme* (Paris, 1935); it is a pity there is no English translation. M. J. Adler in his *Dialectic* (London, 1927) p. 10, makes the interesting point that dialectical thinking is essentially social thinking within the one mind, since it involves a conflict of opposites, which

deduction and induction do not. See also the article of A. M. Dunham on the concept of 'tension' in psychology and logic (*Psychiatry*, 1938, **1**, 79).

17. [From 'Spain 1937'. See W. H. Auden: *Collected Shorter Poems*, 1930–1944 (London, 1950), p. 190.]

18. [Cf. Essay 4, above, pp. 101, 105.]

19. This idea was put forward in a paper of mine in 1928, *Quart. Rev. Biol.*, **3**, 80.

20. M. J. Adler, *Dialectic* (London, 1927), p. 164 ff., suggests that the natural connection between dialectical and organicistic thought is simply that entities in opposition are likely to be parts (on one level) of which the whole, the synthesis, occupies the next higher level.

21. Cf. Lenin, 'On Dialectics' in *Works*, **11**, p. 84. Or one might say that Thomas Aquinas made a dialectical synthesis of the points of view represented in earlier scholastic thought by Abelard and William of Champeaux; M. J. Adler, *Dialectics*, (London, 1927), p. 72. Clement of Alexandria actually did say, in the *Stromata*, that Christianity was the synthesis of Greek and Jew.

22. Cf. Lenin's 'Materialism and Empirio-Criticism' in *Works*, **11**, p. 297.

23. As for example by the non-marxist historian H. Butterfield in his interesting book *The Whig Interpretation of History* (London, 1931), where he combats the moralising attitude to historical conflicts, showing that each side stood for some elements which were embodied in the subsequent synthesis.

24. The examples given above show the dialectical process at work in the history of human society and of scientific thought. But it is embodied also in non-human evolution, see TRR, p. 190.

25. SB, pp. 89 ff.; GA, pp. 95 ff.

26. SB, p. 247.

27. SB, p. 133.

28. Such as B. Farrington's *Science and Politics in the Ancient World* (London, 1939).

29. SB, p. 16.

30. Also in *Dialectics of Nature* (Gesamtausgabe edition, Moscow, 1935, p. 629).

31. SB, pp. 28, 136.

32. SB, p. 242; GA, p. 101.

33. SB, p. 38.

34. SB, pp. 83, 84.

35. In my book *Order and Life* (Yale and Cambridge, 1936); [repr. Cambridge, Mass, 1968].

36. SB, p. 26.

37. Cf. Lenin, *Materialism and Empirio-Criticism*, pp. 185, 199, 363.

38. SB, pp. 7, 33 ff.

39. Long before, Feuerbach had passed through precisely the same intellectual process (*Works*, pp. 343, 344). And cf. Bukharin's words, which I read long afterwards, 'The philosophical "subject" is not an isolated human atom, but "social" man.' (Marx Memorial Volume, Academy of Sciences, Moscow, 1933, Eng. tr. *Marxism and Modern Thought*, London, 1936, p. 13.) But there is no need to go so far afield; no one appreciated these things better than the great English psychologist, Henry Maudsley (cf. his *Body and Will*, London, 1883, pp. 44 and 157).

40. See the discussion which followed a paper of C. H. Waddington's in *Nature*, 1941, **148**, p. 270 ff. with contributions by E. W. Barnes, W. R. Matthews, W. G. de Burgh, A. D. Ritchie, Julian Huxley and others; see also *Proc. Aristot. Soc.* 1942, and *Science and Ethics* (London, 1942).

41. 'Sense of Humour' in *New Writing*, 1936, **2**, 16, and in *You make your own Life* (London, 1938).

42. Was this not the meaning of that great saying of Yeats—'Think the thoughts of a wise man, but speak the common language of the people.'

43. [League of Labour Youth; and Young Communist League.]

44. Compare with this a notable passage from George Orwell:
    'The place to look for the germs of the future England is in the light-industry areas and along the arterial roads. In Slough, Dagenham, Barnet, Letchworth, Hayes—everywhere indeed on the outskirts of great towns—the old pattern is gradually changing into something new. In those vast new wildernesses of glass and brick the sharp distinctions of the older kind of town, with its slums and mansions, or the country, with its manor houses and squalid cottages, no longer exist. There are wide gradations of income, but it is the same kind of life that is being lived at different levels, in labour-saving flats or council houses, along the concrete roads, and in the naked democracy of the swimming pools. It is rather a restless, cultureless life, centering round tinned food, *Picture Post*, the radio and the internal combustion engine. It is a civilisation in which children grow up with an intimate knowledge of magnetos and in complete ignorance of the Bible. To that civilisation belong the people who are most at home in, and most definitely of, the modern world; the technicians and the higher-paid skilled workers, the airmen and their mechanics, the radio experts, film producers, popular journalists and industrial chemists. They are the indeterminate stratum at which the older class distinctions are beginning to break down.' (*The Lion and the Unicorn*, London, 1941, p. 54.)
       We are reminded of a great scholar venturing to stand up against one of Inge's diatribes against modern life—'I do not regard it as absurd,' said Rashdall, 'to contend that there is value even in the life of East and West Ham' (*Ideas & Ideals*, 1928, p. 85).
45. In his introduction to the *Oxford Book of Modern English Poetry*.
46. When writing this introductory essay, I happened to be reading that great work of scholarship, George Thomson's *Aeschylus and Athens* (London, 1941), in which he describes the anthropological origins of Greek civilisation and folklore, and the rise of Greek literature and culture from them. From a discussion of Ionian science, especially in Anaximander (p. 83), and Orphic mystical theology (p. 156), he suggests that 'the tendency of aristocratic thought is to divide, to keep things apart' while 'the tendency of popular thought is to unite.' In Orphism, Love implied the reunion of what had been sundered. It would be interesting to investigate the social significance of philosophical 'dividers' and 'uniters' in different historical times; certainly in my own development, Thomson's correlation has been strikingly substantiated. I was unable to find any unified world-view until I took man's social life into account, a thing no aristocratic thinker would ever desire to do, unless as a reaction against democratic thinkers for specifically polemical purposes.

9

Science, Religion and Socialism

(1935)*

The problem of the relationship between the traditional religion of the European West and the coming new world-order, as yet in its details uncertain, seems at first sight to have little to do with the preoccupations of the scientist. Whether the old forms of theology and liturgy disappear, whether the new social order is, or is not, more just than that which is breaking up, whether he has to live and work in the corporate or in the classless State, might seem to be matters of indifference to him. Nevertheless such a view would be superficial. The moment a scientific worker begins to reflect upon the nature and methods of his science, he will find himself involved in its history and philosophy, and hence its relations to historical, economic and intellectual factors, from which religious ideas certainly cannot be excluded. The moment he begins to reflect upon the ends to which others are putting the results of his work, he will find himself involved in the current political discussion of his time. Even some hypothetical scientist who aimed at the most complete neutrality with respect to the world in which he lived could not long escape the ultimate argument of economic forces, and would be induced to think over his relation to his fellows when he found himself unemployed after some sudden restriction of scientific effort.

The beginnings of the scientific movement in the seventeenth century are discussed elsewhere in this book.[1] Acquisition of personal wealth, the fundamental motive of capitalist enterprise, acted then, and for a long time afterwards, as the most powerful

* [The author revised this essay in 1941–42, before its publication in *Time: The Refreshing River* (London, 1943); it is the revised version that appears here.]

stimulus and support for scientific research. But the indiscriminate application of the scientific method to natural things bursts
in the end these limitations. It shows us not only how to make
textiles and cheese, but also how, if we will, a high degree of
universal physical and mental well-being may be achieved. In so
doing, it goes beyond the facts which any single group of men can
lay hold of with the object of acquiring private riches. And it
dictates to the scientific worker a new allegiance, a separation
from his allies (or masters) of three centuries' standing.

The Position of the Scientific Worker

The position of the scientific worker in the world of today is
indeed a very difficult one. Owing to the gradual permeation of
our entire civilisation by the practical results of scientific thought
and invention, the scientific worker has in some measure
succeeded to the semi-oracular tripod previously occupied by the
religious thinker, whether enthusiastic saint or prudent ecclesiastic. That ancient separation of life into secular and sacred,
which arose out of the acquiescence of the early Christians in their
failure to transform the human society of their time into God's
Kingdom on earth, still reigns in our civilisation. Owing to the
increasing intellectual difficulties which the ordinary man of our
time feels with respect to the theology of the traditional form of
Western European religion, he turns more and more to the scientific worker, expecting to hear from *him* a sound doctrine about
the beginning of the world, the duty of man, and the four last
things. The scientific 'ascetic' in the laboratory is the monk of
today, and is tacitly regarded as such by the ordinary man.[2]
Conversely, the secular power, the medieval *imperium*, has been
succeeded by the power of the owner—the owner of factories, the
owner of newspapers and propaganda agencies, the owner of
land, the owner of finance capital.

In a new guise, then, the sacred and the secular are still at war.
We may study their antagonism best by observing the fate of the
concept of *Regnum Dei*, the Kingdom of God—always the surest
indication of the relative power of priest and king. Roughly
speaking, there have been, in the history of the Christian Church,
three separate doctrines about the Kingdom of God, three separate interpretations of the Kingdom-passages in the Gospels.[3]
First, there was the identification of the Kingdom with a purely
spiritual mystical realm of beatitude, either to be reached after

death by the faithful, or attainable here and now through the methods of prayer and ascetic technique, or existing in the future in Heaven after the last judgment. This has been perhaps the commonest theory. It has flourished whenever the secular was strong, since it discountenanced any attempt to improve the conditions of life on earth. As an instance, one could mention the mystical theology of Lutheranism, whose founder held the world to be utterly bad and irredeemable, a realm of Satan, from which the only escape was by means of religious exercises within the organised body of Christians.[4] But secondly, in every age there have been those who have interpreted the Kingdom as a state of divine justice in the future and in the world, to be attained by unceasing effort on the part of men and women. This struggle was the outcome of their thirst for social justice, and gave meaning to all martyrdoms since the beginning of the world.

In ages when ecclesiastical organisation was powerful, the visible Church itself, sharing the world with the temporal emperor in a condominium, could be identified with the Kingdom of God. This was a third interpretation. With the Reformation and the splitting of the universal church into a thousand sects it lost its force.

But if the scientific worker is the modern representative of the medieval cleric, he finds himself in a relatively much worse position. Science in our time is not able to dictate its terms to capitalist 'captains of industry' and the governing class in general; on the contrary, it is in utter bondage, dependent upon their fitful and grudging support, itself divided by dangerous national boundaries and sovereignties. In such a case we should expect that many scientists would interpret the concept of the Kingdom (though none of them, of course, would dream of referring to it under that name) as something spiritual, something harmless, something incapable of any affront to a capitalist world.

This is exactly what we find. Nothing could better illustrate the point than the Huxley Memorial Lecture of A. V. Hill, in 1933, and his subsequent controversy with J. B. S. Haldane—two of England's most distinguished biologists.[5] The discoveries of science, said Hill, whatever mistakes may be made, do gradually build up a structure which is approved by all sane men; in the last three hundred years, the experimental method, which is universal, has produced results beyond all previous human achievements. This universality of its method and results gives science a unique place among the interests of mankind. But 'if scientific people are to be accorded the privileges of immunity and tolerance by civilised societies, they must observe the rules.' 'Not meddling with morals or politics; such, I would urge,' he went on, 'is the normal condition of tolerance and immunity for scientific pursuits in a civilised state.' Nothing would be worse than that science should become involved with emotion, propaganda, or particular social and economic theories. In other words—'My kingdom is not of this world,' must be taken as meaning not *in* this world either. Let unemployment, repression, class justice, national and imperial wars, poverty in the midst of plenty, etc., etc., continue and increase; nothing is relevant to the scientific worker, provided only his immunity is granted—immunity to pursue his abstract investigations in peace and quiet. Here we substitute for the kingdom-concept of mysticism a kingdom-concept of mathematics, equally sterile with respect to human welfare, equally satisfactory to the powers of this world.

'The best intellects and characters, not the worst,' continued Hill, 'are wanted for the moral teachers and political governors of mankind, but science should remain aloof and detached, not from any sense of superiority, nor from any indifference to the common welfare, but as a condition of complete intellectual honesty.' Haldane was not slow to point out that Hill's sterilisation of the scientific worker as a social unit arose from the facile ascription to him of no loyalties save those of his work. In so far as he is a citizen as well as a scientist, he *must* meddle with morals and politics. But Hill's point of view can be attacked more severely from a deeper standpoint. Science does not exist in a vacuum; scientific discoveries are not made by an inexplicable succession of demiurges sent to us by Heaven; science is, *de facto,* involved with 'particular social and economic theories,' since it exists and has grown up in a particular social and economic structure. Here there is no space even to outline the marks which theoretical and applied science bears revealing its historical position. I merely wish to point out that it is not altogether surprising that the ordinary man expects some lead from the scientific worker in his capacity of citizen. In the Middle Ages, life was ruled by theology, hence the socio-political influence of the theologian; today it is ruled by science, hence the socio-political importance of the scientific worker.

The Treason of the Scholars

Hill's conception of the Kingdom as a realm of truth and exact knowledge far removed from the affairs of human life has been most clearly formulated in our time by Julien Benda, in his book, *La Trahison des Clercs.*[6] The betrayal of our generation by the clerks, that is to say, by the scientists and scholars which it has produced, he conceives to consist in the fact that whereas the medieval clerk was wholly devoted to the working out of the implications of a transcendent truth, the modern clerk has no similar task, and therefore engages without hesitation in the political struggles of the time. 'Our century,' says Benda, 'will be called the century of the intellectual organisation of political hatreds. That will be one of its great claims to fame in the history of human ethics.' But does not Benda misread the attitude of the medieval clerk? Preoccupied by transcendent truths he might certainly be, but he was also very much concerned about economic relationships, and by virtue of that fact alone, he *was* politically minded in the modern sense of the words. For modern politics bear no relation to the politics of the medieval world. A thirteenth-century theologian might well leave on one side the quarrels of petty princes about territorial jurisdiction or feudal honours, but he, on his own assumptions, could not, and did not, leave on one side the detailed economics of the commerce and finance of the time. Benda fails to realise that in our days there is no longer any distinction between politics and economics. What are the ferocious modern nationalisms which he describes with such force but devices engineered and operated by economic interests which do not wish co-operation and friendship between the common peoples of the world? What is jingo imperialist patriotism but an instrument designed to drown the call to union of the *Communist Manifesto*?

The medieval scene was supremely characterised by its subordination of other interests to religion. We may call it a period of religious genius, when all poetry, literature, learning, and music was co-opted into the service of this primary preoccupation of men. And since this was the case, no human interests could be regarded as outside the sphere of theology, least of all the interests of the market-place, where every economic transaction was a possible opportunity for the snares of the devil, or, alternatively, could, by right arrangement, be turned into an exercise of spiritual profit. The life of man on earth was regarded not as an end in itself, but as the preparation for a fuller life in Heaven, a fuller life which could not be entered into without the passport of justice, temperance, and piety. It was the province of theology, therefore, to regulate public economic affairs just as much as those of individual devotion. The most important means by which this was done were first, the principle of the just price, and secondly, the prohibition of usury. Every commodity had its just price, based on the cost of its production, and allowing to its producer a margin of profit sufficient for him to live in that degree of comfort which was considered appropriate to his station. It was un-christian to force prices up in a time of scarcity, and thus to take advantage of the necessity of others; un-christian to allow prices to fall in time of glut, and so defraud honest merchants. Usury was prohibited alike by civil and canon law.[7] And the names of many other long obsolete misdemeanours, such as regrating, forestalling and engrossing, remain to show how the theologian systematised medieval economic transactions.[8]

What would happen to our present social structure, we might ask, if by some miracle the medieval Church were to have full power again, and all usury were prohibited, the principle of the just price exacted, and the restriction of profits renewed? We should, of course, observe a very spectacular collapse. The Middle Ages had, in fact, their own conception of collectivism, but it was fundamentally non-equalitarian. Each group, ecclesiastical, military, or commercial, held a distinct place in a system of social orders possessing different degrees of wealth and social prestige. And although it was true that each order had definite duties towards the other orders, not excluding even the peasant basis, it was equally true that these obligations were frequently unfulfilled. Still, medieval society was organic, rather than individualistic and atomic. As Chaucer's Parson said :

'I wot well there is degree above degree, as reason is, and skill it is that men do their devoir thereas it is due, but certes extortions and despite of your underlings is damnable.'

'The clerk can only be strong,' says Benda, 'if he is fully conscious of his nature and his function, and if he shows us that he is conscious of it, that is to say, if he declares to us that his kingdom is not of this world. This absence of practical value is precisely what gives greatness to his teaching. As for the prosperity of the kingdoms of this world, that belongs to the ethic of Caesar, and not to his ethic. And with this position the clerk is crucified, but he has won the respect of men and they are haunted by his words.' Yet if one of Julien Benda's medieval clerks were placed in our modern world, would he not denounce the fantastic system of economics under which we live; would he not criticise the laws which cause food to be destroyed because people are too poor to buy it? It is well that Benda castigates the modern clerk for lending the weapons of his intellect to nationalism, but there are other forces than nationalism at work in the political world today. He can, of course, remain inactive, adopting the position of absolute neutrality laid down by Benda, and urged, as we have seen, by distinguished representatives of science, refusing to take part in the political and social struggle, and finally perishing, like an Archimedes, at his laboratory bench during a war. But what differentiates the position of the modern from the medieval clerk is that, if he was to be active, the latter had no choice in his allegiance, while the former has a choice, and must make it. Thus there are two ways open to the scientific worker at the present time. All the backward pull of respectability and tradition urges him to throw in his lot with the existing capitalist order, with its corollaries of nationalism, imperialism, militarism, and, ultimately, fascism. On the other hand, he can adopt the ideals of social justice and of the classless State; he can recognise that his own best interests lie with the triumph of the working class, the only class pledged to abolish classes; in a word, he can think of the Kingdom *literally* and can work for its realisation. A Kingdom not of this world, but to be in this world.

The transcendent truth of the medieval Church was bound up with a definite economic order, feudalism; and it was capitalism, of course, as it gradually developed, which upset this economic order, and science which superseded this transcendent truth. The geographical discoveries, which made the European home begin to seem a prison; the astronomical discoveries, which made the earth as a whole, previously the scene of the drama of redemption, shrink to one among a vast number of celestial bodies; the mechanical discoveries which opened up the possibility of industrialism; all undermined the strength of the old-fashioned system until hardly anything was left of it. Moreover, there were discoveries in the spiritual world, too; there was the important Protestant discovery that material riches, far from being a presumptive sign of ill dealings, were an outward and visible sign of the inward approval and blessing of God. And most interesting of all, there was the rise of the concept of scientific law, often conceived of in a crude mechanical way, as was only natural at its first beginnings. Who would connect with this the decline in the cult of the Blessed Virgin? Yet there was a certain connection. 'The Virgin,' wrote Henry Adams,[9] 'embarrassed the Trinity. Perhaps this was the reason why men loved and adored her with a passion such as no other deity has ever inspired. Mary concentrated in herself the whole rebellion of man against fate; the whole protest against divine law; the whole contempt of man for human law as its outcome; the whole unutterable fury of human nature beating itself against the walls of its prison-house, and suddenly seized by a hope that in the Virgin there was a door of escape. She was above law; she took a feminine pleasure in turning hell into an ornament, as witness the west window at Chartres; she delighted in trampling on every social distinction in this world and in the next. She knew that the universe was as unintelligible to her, on any theory of morals, as it was to her worshippers, and she felt, like them, no sure conviction that it was any more intelligible to the creator of it. To her, every suppliant was a universe in himself, to be judged apart, on his own merits, by his love for her—by no means on his orthodoxy or his conventional standing in the Church, or his correctness in defining the nature of the Trinity.' What a collapse it was when men came to feel that this way of escape was no longer open to them. As canon law decayed, as confidence in the absoluteness and divine authority of civil law disappeared, so scientific law arose like the growing light of day. The medieval worship of Mary, so charming, so naïve, was a phenomenon of childhood. She could perhaps save a suppliant from a ruling, a decretal, or a codex, but not from the laws of gravitation or thermodynamics. Mankind was now to take up again the guidance of old Epicurus—

> Hunc igitur terrorem animi tenebrasque necessest
> non radii solis, neque lucida tela diei
> discutiant, sed naturae species ratioque.[10]
>
> (These terrors then, this darkness of the mind,
> Not sunrise with its flaring spokes of light,
> Nor glittering arrows of morning can disperse,
> But only Nature's aspect and her law.)

The path lay open now towards a surer freedom, if first necessity could be understood. Amid such vast changes of intellectual climate, it is not surprising that the function of the clerk should both change and yet remain the same.

The Concept of the Kingdom

The concept of the Kingdom is of such importance for every aspect of the relations between Christianity and communism that I must amplify a little what I said above about the forms which it has taken in Christian thought. We may divide the logical possibilities into four. The Kingdom of God has been thought to exist:

(1) Here and now;
(2) Here but not yet;
(3) Not here but now already;
(4) Not here and not yet.

Clearly the most fundamental distinction lies between those who have looked for the Kingdom on earth, whether now or in the future, and those who have interpreted it as meaning an essentially invisible and other-worldly state. The extremest division lies between the second and third alternatives.

The early Church, which for this purpose must be taken as meaning to the end of the third century in the east and the end of the fourth in the west, was almost wholly devoted to the second of these interpretations. It was believed that the second coming of the Lord, which was thought to be imminent, would inaugurate a visible reign of complete righteousness, in which the saints would administer, until the last judgment, a society based on love and justice. This doctrine, known to theologians as millenniarism, chiliasm, or 'realistic eschatology,' found its canonical authority largely in the Apocalypse of John, and its intellectual defenders in such men as Cyprian, Justin, Irenaeus and Tertullian. It was attacked, as time went on, by three principal factors. First, there was the necessity of adapting the prophetic vision of a world made new to a world in which the expected leader did not return. Secondly, there was the influence of Hellenistic mysticism and allegorisation, which in the hands of Origen and other more thorough-going Neo-platonists, tended to emphasise the third interpretation, i.e. that the Kingdom was a purely mystical idea, existing now but elsewhere, wholly in the world of the spirit. Thirdly, there was the increasing organisation of the Church, and the acceptance of this by the secular power in the time of Constantine; this invited men to diminish their ideals of love and justice, and to identify the Kingdom with an actually existing society. This led to the first interpretation. The Kingdom was 'here and now,' either in the form of the Eastern Empire or the Latin Church, which after Augustine claimed, and still claims officially to this day, to be itself the Kingdom. Lastly in all the ages of Christianity there have been supporters of the fourth and most utterly remote interpretation, namely that the Kingdom means only the reign of God after the last judgment.

The millenniarist viewpoint was essentially a continuation of the great strain of Hebrew prophecy, with which all the actors in the drama of the Gospels, whether known or unknown to us, had certainly been familiar. In this the reality of the time process was quite central. Take, for example, the following passage from Amos:[11]

'Hear this, O ye that would swallow up the needy and cause the poor of the land to fail, saying, When will the New Moon be gone that we can sell corn? and the Sabbath, that we may set forth wheat? making the measure small and the payment great, and dealing falsely with balances of deceit; that we may buy the poor for silver and the needy for a pair of shoes. . . . The Lord hath sworn by the excellency of Jacob, Surely I will never forget any of their works. . . . I will slay the last of them with the sword; there shall not one of them flee away. Though they dig into hell, thence shall mine hand take them; and though they climb up into heaven, thence will I bring them down. . . . But in that day I will raise up the tabernacle of David that is fallen, and close up the breaches thereof; and I will raise up his ruins and build it as in the days of old. Behold, the days come, saith the Lord, that the ploughman shall overtake the reaper, and the treader of grapes him that soweth seed; and the mountains shall drop sweet wine, and all the hills shall melt.' It is extremely interesting to contrast the apocalyptic Hebrew conviction that in the future evil will be overthrown and the earth become a common and bountiful treasury for a right-loving people, with the characteristically Hellenistic belief in a former Golden Age from which humanity has for ever fallen away. The only other ancient literature which has resemblances to that of the Hebrews in this respect is the Chinese, where remarkable descriptions of social evolution occur in the *I Ching*, the 'Book of Changes' (fourth or fifth century BC). Hesiod, on the other hand, says that if it had not been for the act of Prometheus, who stormed heaven by force, brought thence the gift of fire, and provoked the gods to withhold from men an easy way of life, 'you would have been able to do easily in a day enough work to keep you for a year, to hang up your rudder in the chimney corner, and let your fields run to waste.'

Thus have decayed the first bright hopes and visions of the Christians. In a most interesting passage, Bishop Robertson reveals the class character of the opposition to millenniarism. 'Intense as was the Christian instinct to which millenniarism gave articulate form, it was in some respects in latent antipathy to the ecclesiastical spirit, and waned as that spirit gathered strength. Its rejection by rational theology, and by the trained theologians who filled the more important places in the Greek Churches in the third and fourth centuries, had practically the effect of ranging the clergy in opposition to it. In fact, millenniarism, by virtue of its direct appeal to minds of crass simplicity, was a creed for the lay-folk and the simpler sort. When religious interest was concentrated upon it, it would indirectly undermine the interest felt in doctrines requiring a skilled class to interpret them. The apocalyptic spirit is in fact closely akin to the spirit of unregulated prophesying, and the alliance has been apparent, not only in the second century, but in medieval and modern times as well.' Crass simplicity—might we not almost say inferior economic position? A skilled class—perhaps a privileged one too?

Of the hopes of the 'simpler sort' we get a glimpse in that very interesting fragment of Papias, preserved by Irenaeus[12] and believed to be an authentic saying of Christ himself,[13] 'The days will come when vines shall grow, each having ten thousand branches, and on each branch ten thousand twigs, and on each twig ten thousand shoots, and on each one of the shoots ten thousand clusters, and on every cluster ten thousand grapes, and every grape when pressed will give twenty-five firkins of wine. And when any one of the saints shall lay hold upon a cluster, another shall cry out, "I am a better cluster; take me; bless the Lord through me." And in like manner, that a grain of wheat will produce ten thousand stalks, and each stalk ten thousand ears, . . .' and so forth.[14] It has often been said that the communism of the early Christians was purely one of distribution, not of production. Here, however, we have, as it were, a dream of the abundance of natural wealth latent in the world's productive forces, and to be unloosed by science so many centuries later.[15] But the inevitable answering note is struck. Asceticism comes to the aid of the possessing classes, and when we turn to Augustine we find : 'The opinion that the saints are to rise again would at least be tolerable if it were understood that they would enjoy spiritual delights from the presence of the Lord. We ourselves were formerly of this opinion. But when they say that those who then arise will spend their time in immoderate carnal feastings—in which the quantity of food and drink exceeds the bounds not only of all moderation, but of all credibility—such things cannot possibly be believed except by carnal persons.'

Whatever happened in later centuries, then, it is certain that the Christians of the primitive church put their Kingdom on the earth and in the future. To this belief of 'crass simplicity' let us return. We reach the paradox that Marx and Engels would have been more acceptable to the martyrs and the Fathers than the comfortable nineteenth-century theologians contemporary with them, seeking to excuse and support the phenomena of class oppression. For the kingdom of Marx was not of this world, but to be in this world.

Yet Benda goes on : 'I regard as being able to say "my kingdom is not of this world" all those whose activities do not pursue practical ends, the artist, the metaphysician, the scientist in so far as he finds satisfaction in the exercise of his science and not in its results. Many will tell me that these are the true clerks, much more than the Christian, who only embraces the ideas of justice and love in order to win salvation.' Here he adopts, as I think, a quite unjustifiable separation of these activities from practical affairs. In science, at any rate, the closest relations exist between practical technology and pure research. Biology would be in an etiolated condition if it were not bound up at every point with stockbreeding, agriculture, medicine, the fisheries, and sociology. With physics and chemistry the case is even more obvious. 'Historically, the sciences grow out of practice, the production of ideas arises out of the production of things.'[16] It is true that in science we must not set out, in general, to solve problems *because* the answer will afford some new invention, but it is often the technical practice which suggests the problem. The great difference which we must recognise between medieval theology and modern science, is that an economic structure was directly and logically derivable from the former, and no clear system in such matters has as yet arisen from the latter. The former incorporated a system of ethics, in the form of moral theology. The latter has not as yet produced one.

Where, then, is the moral theology of today? The only possible answer is that communism provides the moral theology appropriate for our time.[17] The fact that a doctrine of God is apparently absent from it is unimportant in this connection; what it does is to lay down the ideal rules for the relations between man and man, to affirm that the exploitation of one class by another is immoral, that national wars for markets are immoral, that the oppression of subject and colonial races is immoral, that the unequal distribution of goods, education, and leisure is immoral, that the private ownership of the means of production is immoral. It dares to take the 'love of our neighbour' literally; to ensure that by the abolition of privilege each single citizen shall have the fullest opportunities to live the good life in a community of free and equal colleagues. It continues and extends the historic work of Christianity for woman, setting her on a complete equality with man. Its concept of leadership is leadership from within, not from above.

Only because Christian theology three centuries ago gave up the attempt to apply a very similar ethic to human affairs has this state of things come about. The essential weakness of the modern clerk resides in the fact that vast progress in art or science appears at first sight to be theoretically equally compatible with national capitalism or with international communism. The economic doctrines which he must adopt are not at first sight a direct consequence of his own fundamental axioms, but embody themselves in a social theory external to his own sphere. Hence the dual character of the scientific worker, as scientist and as citizen. Hence the temptation for him to shirk his public responsibilities and as 'pure clerk' to be silent except when he gives the results of his own exact researches.

We may remember the bitter words said to have been prefixed by the mathematician, G. H. Hardy, to a book on pure mathematics: 'This subject has no practical value, that is to say, it cannot be used to accentuate the present inequalities in the distribution of wealth or to promote directly the destruction of human life.'

Perhaps the most important task before scientific thinkers today is to show in detail how the ethics of collectivism do in fact emerge from what we know of the world and the evolutionary process that has taken place in it. Scientific socialism (I believe) is the only form of socialism which has the future before it; its theoreticians must therefore show not only that high levels of human social organisation have arisen and will arise by a continuation of the natural process, but what are the ethics appropriate to them. Scientific ethics should be to communist society what Catholic ethics were to feudal society and Protestant ethics to capitalist society.

Theology and the Modern Man

In the preceding section I said that a doctrine of God was apparently absent from communist thought. I used the word 'apparently' because (a) dialectical materialism might be logically compatible with a Spinozistic theology;[18] (b) the immanence of the Christian Godhead as Love is better provided for in communism than in any other order of human relationships. Future communist Clements of Alexandria will have the task of codifying the *praeparatio evangelica* of the Christian centuries.

Today we are all Taoists and Epicureans. For the Taoists, the Way of Nature was *tzu-jan*; it came *of itself*. So also in Lucretius' great poem[19]:

> ... natura videtur
> libera continuo dominis privata superbis
> ipsa sua per se sponte omnia dis agere expers.

> (Nature, delivered from every haughty Lord
> And forthwith free, is seen to do all things
> Herself, and through herself of her own accord,
> Free of all Gods.)

On the one hand there is the cosmic force which is 'responsible' for the vast evolutionary process wherein we form a part, if anything is responsible for it. The modern mind finds the ancient scholastic arguments for the existence of this force or 'prime mover' in no way convincing, still less that it partakes of the nature of what we call 'mind' or 'personality,' and even less still that its essence is good. The good seems to arise out of the evolutionary process rather than to have been in it from the beginning. But the good is an immediate datum, and the holiness of good actions is an immediate datum. These are the occasions of modern religion.

From this point of view, the bonds of love and comradeship in human society are analogous to the various forces which hold particles together at the colloidal, crystalline, molecular, and even sub-atomic levels of organisation. The evolutionary process itself supplies us with a criterion of the good. The good is that which contributes most to the social solidarity of organisms having the high degree of organisation which human beings do in fact have. The original sin which prevents us from living as Confucius and Jesus enjoined[20] is recognisable as the remnants in us of features suitable to lower levels of social organisation; anti-social now. If such an idea is accepted, the insistence that we must have some extra-natural criterion of ethical values ceases to have any point. The kind of behaviour which has furthered man's social evolution in the past can be seen very well by viewing human history; and the great ethical teachers, from Confucius onwards, have shown us, in general terms, how men may live together in harmony, employing their several talents to the general good. Perfect social order, the reign of justice and love, the *Regnum Dei* of the theologians, the 'Magnetic Mountain' of the poets, is a long way in the future yet, but we know by now the main ethical principles which will help us to get there, and we can dimly see how these have originated during social and biological evolution. There is no need for perplexity as to whether we ought to call evolution morally admirable or morally offensive; it is surely neither. The good is a category which does not emerge until the human level is reached.[21]

The difficulty about religion is that it cannot be considered apart from organised religion as embodied in institutions.[22] In practice, its effects throughout the world are, in the present social context, largely harmful. How far religion can be transformed without the disappearance of the old vessels is a very disputable matter. The detailed beliefs of the past—verbal inspiration, eternal damnation, magical efficacy of prayer for 'particular mercies' (in the old phrase), *ex opere operato* rites, miraculous intervention, ascription of psychological states to God, and so on, *are* of course irrevocably of the past, not of the present or the future. None of them is relevant to true religion. Religion is seen not as a divine revelation, but as a function of human nature, in Julian Huxley's words, as a 'peculiar and complicated function, sometimes noble, sometimes hateful, sometimes intensely valuable, sometimes a bar to individual or social progress, but no more and no less a function of human nature than fighting or falling in love, than law or literature.'[23] Theology, indeed, comes off badly in our modern survey. In so far as it is a codification of the experiences of religious mysticism it is an attempt to reduce to order what cannot be so reduced. In so far as it is a description of such experiences, it is engaged on the fruitless task of describing the indescribable. And in so far as it is occupied with cosmology, anthropology, and history, it is trespassing on legitimate fields of scientific activity.

Many students of these problems at the present time see that the essence of religion is the sense of the holy (Julian Huxley, J. M. Murry,[24] Canon J. M. Wilson and others). Religion thus becomes no more and no less than the reaction of the human spirit to the facts of human destiny and the forces by which it is influenced; and natural piety, or a divination of sacredness in heroic goodness, becomes the primary religious activity. Consider also the following words of one of our most judicious philosophers:—'The identification of this-worldly with material values, other-worldly values alone being recognised as spiritual, is what I am concerned to deny. I maintain that spiritual good and evil are to be found in the daily intercourse of men with one another in this world, independently of any relation of man to God; further, that the significance of spiritual value does not depend on God or upon the continuance of human beings after the death of the body.'[25]

These opinions are not indeed very different from those of many modernist and liberal theologians. The difficulty about religion within the framework of organised Christianity is that the 'plain statements in Bible and Prayer-Book stand uncorrected and unannotated,' so that for simple people they mean what they say. For liberal intellectuals, this may be myth, that may be symbol, this may be a valiant attempt to express the inexpressible, that may be an unfortunate inexactitude due to historical causes—but for the majority of people, everything must be taken literally or not at all. Critics, then, have no alternative but to stand outside the traditional Church and give it advice from a distance, so that their remarks acquire a remote and impractical character. But an acquaintance with the life of religion from the inside convinces one that the sense of the holy cannot be ordered about at will, unhooked from one thing and hooked on to something else, or simply detached from ancient traditions and poured into the cold

vacuum of our modern mechanical world. The poetic words of
the Liturgy, for instance, philosophically meaningless though they
may be, cannot be separated from the numinous feeling which
has grown up with them. Though built upon the basis of a world-
view which we can no longer accept today, they retain, for some
of us, enough symbolism of what we *do* believe, to make them of
overwhelming poetic value.[26]

The upshot of the matter is, therefore, that in practice those
who can successfully combine traditional religious life with the
life of social and political action appropriate to our time, will be
relatively few. It is no good being in a hurry to descry and to
welcome the new forms of social emotion; they will emerge in
their own good time and perhaps we shall not live to see them.
But meanwhile, like the last Pontifex Maximus in Rome,[27] we
shall continue those ancient rites which still have meaning for us,
while nevertheless being on the best of terms with the clergy and
people of the New Dispensation.

Few would wish to maintain today that the organised religion
of Christianity has any gift of temporal immortality, and that it
will not find its end just as the religions of ancient Egypt, or of
Mexico, found theirs. But some would certainly wish to maintain
that religion, as a natural department of the human spirit, has
survived these changes and will always survive them. It could also
be held that no historic religious system has failed to contribute
some element of advance to man's social consciousness. The hope
of making religion philosophically respectable is probably quite
vain, and the sense of the holy in its ancient form cannot flourish
in pure isolation away from its ancient trellis. But will not
Christian feeling be succeeded by another form of numinous feeling; a new development of social emotions? Even to ask this
question is to ask where it could come from. We may be certain
that it will not come from the lecture-rooms of academic philosophy, still less from the armchairs of literary critics or the speculations of scientific workers interested in religion from the outside.
Will it not come from the factory? Obviously not the factory as
we know it today, but the factory of the future, the factory of co-
operating producers, when the whole system of commercial
exploitation has been completely destroyed, and the means of production have been taken over in communal ownership. The most
appalling struggles may well be involved in the death-throes of
the present system, and we may perhaps expect that the numinous

feeling of the future will take its origin from the consequent stress and strain. Is not Mayakovsky's poetry, are not the 'Twelve' of Alexander Blok, the symbols of this? But meanwhile, Religion is still resident in her traditional house, and those who would seek her successfully must seek her there as well as in the leaflet distribution and the Trade Union Hall. Auden's words express what is going on :—

> Love, loth to enter
> The suffering winter,
> Still willing to rejoice
> With the unbroken voice
> At the precocious charm
> Blithe in the dream
> Afraid to wake, afraid
> To doubt one term
> Of summer's perfect fraud,
> Enter and suffer
> Within the quarrel
> Be most at home,
> Among the sterile, prove
> Your vigours, love.

Those of us who have loved the habitation of God's house and the place where his honour dwells, would be well content if the traditional forms of rite and liturgy could survive the coming storm.[28] We would like to fill the old bottles of Catholic doctrine with new wine. The words of the Fathers on equality and social righteousness seem more likely to be fulfilled than we had hoped. But if this revivification of the ancient faith cannot be accomplished, then we shall accept the judgement with a *Nunc dimittis*; those who love both the spirit and the letter will not complain if the spirit be taken and the letter left. [. . . .]

Enemies of Human Experience
There is a kind of fundamental validity attaching to the five great realms of human experience, philosophy, history, science, art, and religion. Each of these has its enemies—those who go about to deny their validity, or their right to exist, or their right to play the part which they do play in our civilisation or our individual lives. Let us consider some of these factors in relation to our main theme.

Against Philosophy come many opponents. Particularly, the mathematical logicians point out to us, that there are few, perhaps no, metaphysical propositions which can be translated into the exact language of mathematical logic. Philosophy on this view is an art, a sort of music gone wrong. Among these opponents, however, marxist ethics and orthodox theology cannot be numbered. They, at least, cannot be accused of undervaluing philosophy.

Against Science come many influences, some of which are equally opposed to philosophy. The whole anti-intellectualist movement, so protean in its manifestations in our time, acts in this direction. From the mystical point of view represented by D. H. Lawrence and his followers at one end to the folky-brutal atmosphere of Nazism at the other, we have a thoroughly anti-scientific front. For these minds, if so they can be called, scientific internationalism is an illusion, racial factors dominate human actions, and true patriots must think with their blood. Nothing could be more valuable for the armament manufacturers than these views; nothing could be more in line with the feudal vestiges which have for centuries lingered on in the army-officer class. We are witnessing at the present day a wholesale frustration of science.[29] To the capitalist, scientific research is useful, but only relatively in comparison with other and perhaps even cheaper ways of obtaining profits. It is only when these fail that the capitalist now needs the scientist. Again, the conditions of profit-making forbid the introduction of safety measures and the application of labour-saving devices which could greatly increase world-production, while at the same time equalising leisure in the form of a five-hour day under a planned socialist system. Or improved technical methods may be used for actually destroying a part of the produced material, such as coffee or rubber. Or the area of land sown may be compulsorily restricted. Worst of all, perhaps, is the continuing and increasing use of science in war preparations; the development and application of the most diverse scientific researches to rendering the killing of individuals more effective, cheaper, and possible on a still larger scale than ever before. 'It does not need much economic knowledge,' writes Bernal,[30] 'to see that a system of which the essential basis is production for profit, leads by its own impetus into the present highly unstable and dangerous economic and political situation, where plenty and poverty, the desire for peace and the preparation for war, exist side by side; but it does require far more knowledge to see how an alternative system could be built up. And yet, unless scientists are prepared to study this they must accept the present state of affairs and see the results of their own work inadequately utilised today and dangerously abused in the near future.' Thus the figures of the annual government grants speak for themselves. In 1933, for example, the Medical Research Council received £139,000 and the Department for Scientific and Industrial Research £443,838, while the research grants for the Army, Navy, and Air Force together were £2,759,000, i.e. five times as much as the whole total for civil research.[31]

Another of the influences working in our time against science is the outcome of modern psychology.[32] An argument nowadays need not be answered; it is sufficient to trace it back to the previous psychological history, and hence the prejudices, of the person who propounds it. A misunderstanding of marxism, with its insistence upon the class basis of science, has exposed it to this accusation, but it is perfectly legitimate to apply the class theory of history to the history of science, and the results are frequently highly convincing. On the other hand the fascist struggle (especially in Germany) against 'objective science,' based on the racial theory of history, which has no scientific basis of any sort, is the most dangerous form of this kind of attack which exists, though it can only be seriously proclaimed to the masses under conditions where all criticism is silenced by State power. As for Art, it does not pay.[33] No further enemy is needed. And History, as eminent capitalists have assured us, is bunk.[34]

Against Religion come so many forces that it is hard to count them. The general trend from religion to science which took place in the Hellenistic age and the late Roman Empire repeated itself again in our own Western European civilisation from the Renaissance onwards. Religion has had to face the great pretensions of the medieval secular power, the mechanical philosophies of the seventeenth century, the enlightened atheism of the eighteenth century, and the Victorian agnosticism of the last age. Bourgeois agnostics and proletarian atheists have attacked it from all sides. It is surprising that there is anything left of it : and few people seem even to know what it is. Thus an anonymous writer recently began an article on agnosticism with the words : 'The essence of religion is faith, the ability to accept as a truth a hypothesis for which there is no positive evidence.'[35] Or again, in

Moscow Dialogues, Socratov says,[36] 'We are rather at a loss to point to anything of a positive character in religion. If you can suggest anything positive, I shall be glad to hear it'; and the Bishop (very conveniently) replies, 'Well, first of all, the Church has always stood, even in its darkest days, for law and order.' The first of these writers was confusing, as is so common, theology with religion. Theology has to accept hypotheses for which there is no positive evidence, because in a system so unlikely as the universe, of which there is only one, no comparisons can be made by which to test the credibility of anything. This is no argument in favour of theology, which may or may not be a necessary evil, but on the other hand, it does not discredit religion. The second was erecting an episcopal man of straw in order to have the pleasure of hearing the opium-merchant give himself away red-handed. But the statement is not historically true; when Irenaeus, Clement, and Tertullian were alive; when Lilburne, Rainborough, and their 'russet-coated captains' were riding; the Church was not on the side of law and order. Christians were able to imagine a better law and a juster order than the established system of the Roman Empire,[37] or the government of that 'Man of Blood,' King Charles I.

The clearest understanding of religion has been given, in my view, by the work of Rudolf Otto,[38] a German theologian, who described it as the sense of the holy. In primitive communities we see this 'numinous sense' applied to all kinds of worthless objects and rites, and later incorporated in the apparatus of State government, but in the great religions of the world it forms the essential backbone of the experience of their participators. In Christianity, where the ethic of love found its greatest prophets, the numinous sense has become attached to the highest conception of the relations between man and man that we know. The Christian who becomes a communist does so precisely because he sees no other body of people in the world of our time who are concerned to put Christ's commands into literal execution. If for seventeen centuries the Church has tended to put allegorical constructions on the Gospels, we know that the Christians of the first two centuries did not do so.

That religion has been, and largely is, 'the opium of the people' is plainly undeniable. Proletarian misery in this world has been constantly lightened by promises of comfort and blessedness in the world beyond the grave, an exhortation which might come well enough from some ecclesiastical ascetic who did not spare himself, but very ill indeed from the employer of labour or the representative of the propertied classes. But the conclusion usually drawn, namely, that religion could have no place in a socialist State, where no class-distinctions existed, does not seem to follow. Because religion has been often used as a social opiate in the past, there seems no reason why this should be so in the future. 'Religion would continue to exist,' writes A. L. Rowse,[39] 'in the socialist community, but on its own strength. It would not have the bias of the State exerted in its favour, as it has had so strongly in England up to the present, and in greater or lesser degrees in all Western countries.' It may indeed be said that religion is 'the protest of the oppressed creature,'[40] and that therefore when social oppression, in the form of the class-stratified society, is done away with, the private need for religion will vanish as well as the class which profited by it. This, however, is to forget what we could call 'cosmic oppression,' or creatureliness, the unescapable inclusion of man in space-time, subject to pain, sorrow, sadness and death. Shall we substitute for the opium of religion an opium of science? It has always been the tacit conviction of the social reformer and the person occupied with the practical application of scientific knowledge that by man's own efforts, not merely minor evils, but the major evils of existence may be overcome. This is expressed in that great sentence : 'Philosophers have talked about the universe enough; the time has come to change it.[41] But the problem of evil is not capable of so simple a resolution. So long as time continues, so long as change and decay are around us and in us, so long will sorrow and tragedy be with us.[42] 'Life is a sad composition,' as Sir Thomas Browne said, 'we live with death and die not in a moment.' Or, in the words of the *Contakion*, 'For so thou didst ordain when thou createdst us, saying, "Dust thou art, and unto dust shalt thou return"; wherefore all we who go down into the grave make our song unto thee, sighing and saying, Give rest, O Christ, to thy servants with thy saints, where sorrow and sighing are no more, neither pain, but life everlasting.' The whole realm of thought and feeling embodied in these phrases is fundamentally natural and proper to man, and there is little to be gained by trying to replace it by a eupeptic opium, derived from too bright an estimate of the possibilities of scientific knowledge. Driven out, it will return in the end with redoubled force.

Fundamentally natural and proper to man, the sense of the

holy is as appropriate to him as the sense of beauty. As we have seen, the 'moral theology' of communism lacks a doctrine of God, but this does not affect the existence of the sense of the holy. After all, the theology of the Gospels was not very complicated—Jesus did not meet disease and hunger by persuading people that blessedness was already theirs if they would accept a dogmatic intellectual system; but by curing sickness and distributing bread. This was the practical aspect of his teaching about love. In the motives of atheist communists we detect, therefore, that which is worthy of numinous respect, for they are working to bring in the World Co-operative Commonwealth.

Those who deny the importance of the sense of the holy are in an analogous position to those who cannot appreciate music or painting. It is an attitude towards the universe, an attitude almost of respect, for which nothing can be substituted. 'The problem of death,' it has been said,[43] 'is not a "problem" at all, it is due simply to the clash between an idealistic egoistic philosophy and the disappearance of the individual, not in the least to the fact of death.' On this Epicurean view, science reveals facts to us so clearly as to reconcile us to them.[44] But it is not our own death that we are thinking of. We may well be content to live on only in the effects which our living has produced on our generation and those that come after.[45] The point is that no matter how much we know in the classless State about the biology of death, we shall still suffer when someone that we have loved suddenly dies or is killed. The question then reduces itself to a matter of taste; shall we bury him with unloving haste and a callous reference to the unimportance of the individual? Or shall we remember, as we fulfil the rites of a liturgical requiem, that this is the common end of all the sons of men, and so unite ourselves with the blessed company of all faithful people, those who earnestly looked and worked in their generation for the coming of the Kingdom? It is true indeed, as Merejkovsky has said, that whether we believe in Christ or not, we must certainly suffer with him. And, indeed, it is my opinion that if the ancient Christian modes of satisfying this numinous sense are discontinued (Eliot's *vieilles usines désaffectés*), other liturgical forms will be devised to play their part in attempting to express that which cannot be expressed. This we already see in such cases as the tomb of Lenin himself, and the Red Corners. In [. . .] whatever society man arranges himself he must take up some attitude towards the universe, and to the fate of individuals in it, and in this attitude, the sense of the holy will always be an element.

Scientific Opium

Not to be awake to the iniquity of class oppression, then, is religious opium. Scientific opium would mean not being awake to the tragic side of life, to the numinous elements of the world and of human effort in the world, to religious worship. Scientific opium has often been thought an integral part of marxism by its opponents, but for us the question is what break with tradition the contribution of England and the west of Europe to the socialisation of the world must involve. In this connection there are two considerations which seem relevant, but which have not often been discussed. In the first place, it is a historical coincidence that the early marxists adopted the anthropological and psychological arguments against religion which were fashionable at the time. These arguments are insufficient ground for condemning one of the greatest forms of human experience. The anthropological arguments all confuse origin with value, as if primitive barbarism were not in the end responsible for science, art, and literature just as much as for religion. To say that the concept of God is derived from, or modelled on, the relation of primitive exploiting lord to primitive exploited slave is to say nothing about the religious value of the concept in a society where exploitation has been abolished (should it continue to exist there); still less about religion itself as opposed to theology or philosophy. For religion does not know what God is; it only knows him, if he exists, to be worthy of worship—a God comprehended would be no God—and it does not know why the universe is as it is, but only that there is holiness in it. An excess of mystical religion may indeed engender an attitude of inactivity against the external world, but we need it as a salt, not a whole diet. Must we have prohibition in the classless State because some men drink too deeply today? In the end, there is but one end, and communism can overcome the last enemy no more than any other of man's devices. It is difficult, no doubt, to combine scientific 'pride' with religious 'humility,' but the best things often are difficult.

In the second place, the Byzantine nature of eastern Christianity is relevant. From the very beginning the Byzantine Church showed a speculative rather than a practical tendency.[46] The east enacted creeds, the west discipline. The first decree of an eastern council was to determine the relations of the Godhead; the first decree of the Bishop of Rome was to prohibit the marriage of the clergy. Eastern theology was rhetorical in form and based on philosophy; Western theology was logical in form and based on law. The Byzantine divine succeeded to the place of the Greek sophist; the Latin divine to the place of the Roman advocate. The eastern Church, therefore, occupied with philosophy and theology, made little or no pretensions to control of economic affairs, no attempt to subordinate the secular power to itself in the interests of a particular theory as to how the mercantile life should be lived. The Patriarchs, chosen from a monastic order remarkable for its detachment from secular business, left all economic questions to the chamberlains and officials who thronged the imperial court. After the fall of Byzantium, this same tradition of complete other-worldliness transferred itself to the Church of Russia. The Russian Orthodox Church had no pope, no Hildebrand, to impose a theological system of economics on Russian society. It had no scholastic philosophers, no 'medieval clerks' to dictate to kings and rulers what measures they should take to secure social justice. It had nothing corresponding to our seventeenth-century High Churchmen, or to our nineteenth-century Anglo-Catholics, reviving those traditions and reminding men of the ideals of a pre-capitalist age. When capitalism, in the time of Peter the Great, reached Russia, it found a perfectly virgin soil for its operations, and had no such uphill task as it found in the west. In three generations it enslaved a population which could make no appeal to any distinctively Christian social theories. The appeal would have been vain, for the Orthodox Church had no such theories, and had never developed the first beginnings of them. On the contrary, it had become completely identified with the process of exploitation of the Russian people. The contrast between this situation and our own is quite remarkable.

It may be said that the meaning of the phrase 'religious opium' was that by anaesthetising the people, it prevented them from performing those social actions necessary for social progress, combining in unions, rebelling against exploitation, fighting the possessing class in every possible way. 'Scientific opium' could have no such meaning. Yet I think it has, and it may be explained as follows. It is a blindness to the suffering of others. A certain degree of ruthlessness is absolutely inevitable in the period of revolutions when the people are defending themselves against the final attack of the possessing class which sees itself on the verge of expropriation. 'Revolutions,' said Lenin, 'cannot be made without breaking heads.' But just as Lunacharsky (whose role will be better appreciated by later historians) pleaded successfully for the preservation of certain buildings, art treasures, etc. in the heat of the revolution; so it is always necessary for the Christian man (even he who without reservation allies himself with the revolution) to plead for the retention of certain Christian principles in dealing with people. The ruthlessness necessary in a revolutionary period or an age of wars may too easily pass over, especially in a society based on science, and the more so the more it is so based, into a ruthlessness derived from the very statistical character of the scientific method itself. The ruthlessness with which a biologist throws out an anomalous embryo useless for his immediate purpose, the ruthlessness with which an astronomer rejects an aberrant observation, may too easily be applied to human misfits and deviationists in the socialist world order. The witness of the Christian man may then recall the marxist to a sense of the fundamentally unmarxist character of such treatment. It is unmarxist because no philosophy recognises the emergence of levels of high organisation better than dialectical materialism, and the individuals of which the human social collectivity is built up are themselves the most complicated organisms in the living world.[47] Hence Christian love in the form of tolerance is transformed into a recognition of the manifold forms which human thought and being may take. As long as aberrant individuals are not permitted to be a danger to the socialist state, the greatest tolerance should prevail. There is no need for marxists to follow the example of those many unchristian Christians who manned the Inquisition, the witch-hunting tribunals, and the boards of godly divines in Geneva, Westminster and Massachusetts.

We have here a principle of genuine importance. Christian theology has been called 'the grandmother of bolshevism,' since communist planning alone has seen how to incorporate the love of one's fellow-men in the actual structure of economic life. Some have seen another ancestor in the rationalist and philanthropic ethic of ancient Confucianism. But communism is based just as much on the findings of natural science and the method of science itself. The socialist society must therefore guard against taking over from science too much of scientific abstraction, scientific statistical ruthlessness, and scientific detachment from the individual.

Christian Theology the Grandmother of Bolshevism

Important for the decay of religion in our time is the general and increasing domination of the scientific mind, or rather, of a popular version of the state of mind characteristic of the scientific worker. Constantly growing power over external Nature leads to a tacit belief in the possibility of solving the problem of evil by what might almost be called a matter of engineering. The principle of abstraction leads to a weakening of that attention to the individual and the unique which must always be an integral part of the religious outlook. The principle of ethical neutrality leads to a general chaos in the traditional systems of morals, and hence to decay in the religious emotion formerly attached to the performance of certain actions. The emphasis laid by the scientific mentality on the quantitative aspects of Nature runs diametrically counter to the emphasis which religion would like to lay on the other aspects of the universe. And above all, in actively interfering with the external world, in persistently probing its darkest corners, science destroys that feeling of creaturely dependence upon, and intimate relation to, a transcendent and supernal Being, which has certainly been one of the most marked characteristics of the religious spirit. In the modern world, Epicurus and Lucretius have come into their own.

But here we find, paradoxically enough, that communism and the Christian religion are again on the same side. If these effects of the domination of science were to operate alone, we should have a truly soulless society, much as is depicted by Bertrand Russell in *The Scientific Outlook*,[48] and by Aldous Huxley, satirically, in *Brave New World*.[49] This is what we shall certainly get if capitalism can establish itself anew and overcome the forces of fanatical nationalism which threaten to disrupt it. For capitalism has a fundamentally cheap estimate of the value of human life; mine disasters and wars alike are but passing incidents in a society where the only principle recognised is that might is right. Communism and Christianity, on the contrary, estimate life highly. Ultimately the distinction here resolves itself into what kind of human society we wish to aim at, and the choice may be in a sense aesthetic. The logical continuation of the capitalist order would be the tightening and stabilisation of class stratification, which seems to be the essential function of fascism. This could then, in time, be further fixed as biological engineering becomes more powerful. In such a civilisation, the Utopia of the bourgeoisie, where an abundance of docile workers of very limited intelligence was available, the class stratification would be absolute, and the governing class alone would be capable of living anything approaching a full life.[50] Biological engineering would have done what mechanical engineering had failed to do, and flesh and blood would have been adapted to machinery rather than machinery to flesh and blood. Nevertheless the converse process is equally possible, i.e. a continually increasing automatism of machine operations, and hence an increasing liberation of man from the necessity of productive labour. With the increase of leisure would come an enormous increase in the beneficial and pleasurable occupations available for the workers. This is what is meant by the readiness to sacrifice the bourgeois liberty of today for the much greater liberty of the classless State. And these two alternatives are even now offering themselves to us, with capitalism on the one side and Christianity and communism together on the other. It is a pity that Spengler's aphorism is not more widely known : 'Christian theology is the grandmother of bolshevism.'

'Utopias,' wrote Berdyaev, in a passage which Aldous Huxley chose for the motto of *Brave New World*, 'appear to be much more realisable than we used to think. We are finding ourselves face to face with a far more awful question—how can we avoid their actualisation? And perhaps a new period is beginning, a period when intelligent men will be wondering how they can avoid these Utopias, and return to a society non-Utopian, less perfect but more free.' Huxley's book was a brilliant commentary on this.

His theme is twofold, one of its aspects being the power of autocratic dictatorship, and the other, the possibilities of this power, given the resources of a really advanced biological engineering. The book opens with a long description of a human embryo factory, where the eggs emitted by carefully-tended ovaries are brought up in their development by mass-production methods on an endless conveyor belt moving very slowly until at last the infants are 'decanted' one by one into a remarkable world. The methods of education by continual suggestion and all the possibilities of conditional reflexes are brilliantly described, and we see a world where art and religion no longer exist, but in which an absolutely stable form of society has been achieved, first by sorting out the eggs into groups of known inherited characteristics and then setting each group when adult to do the work for which it is fitted; and secondly by allowing unlimited sexual life (of course, sterile). This idea was based on the suggestion of Kyrle[51] that social discontent, which has always been an important driving force in social change, is a manifestation of the Oedipus complexes of the members of society and cannot be removed by economic means. With decrease of sexual tabus, these psychologists suggest, there would be a decrease of frustration and hence of that aggressiveness which finds its sublimation in religion or its outlet in political activity. Thus in the society pictured by Aldous Huxley, erotic play of children is encouraged rather than prevented, universal but superficial sex relations are the rule, and indeed any sign of the beginning of more deep and lasting affection is stamped out as being anti-social.

Perhaps only biologists really appreciated the full force of *Brave New World*. They knew that Huxley included nothing in his book but what might be considered legitimate extrapolations from already existing knowledge and power. Successful experiments are even now being made in the cultivation of embryos of small mammals *in vitro*. One of the most horrible of Huxley's predictions, the production of numerous workers of low-grade intelligence and precisely identical genetic constitution from one egg, is theoretically quite possible. Armadillos, parasitic insects, and even sea-urchins, if treated in the right manner, will 'bud' in this way now, and the difficulties in the way of effecting it with mammalian and therefore human eggs are probably purely technical.

It is just the same in the realm of philosophy. There are already among us tendencies leading in the direction of Huxley's realm of Antichrist. Fascism seeks no justification other than existence and force. Its philosophy is one in which there is no place for science. Science ceases to be the groundwork of philosophy, and becomes nothing but the mythology accompanying a technique. Divorced from religion, ethics and art, as well as from philosophy, it proceeds to do the will of wicked and ungodly rulers upon humanity. 'The scientific society in its pure form,' as Bertrand Russell has said, 'is incompatible with the pursuit of truth, with love, with art, with spontaneous delight, with every ideal that men have hitherto cherished, save only possibly ascetic renunciation. It is not knowledge that is the source of these dangers. Knowledge is good and ignorance is evil—to this principle the lover of the world can admit no exception. Nor is it power in and for itself that is the source of danger. What is dangerous is power wielded for the sake of power, not power wielded for the sake of genuine good.'

This train of thought leads us finally to consider on what ground communism can stand as against Nietszchianism or other doctrines of the 'superman.' These may be, for all we know, perennial, if they derive primarily from specific psychological types, and may appear long after the classless society has been established. Thus if it be claimed that the fulfilment of the personality of one sort of individual necessitates the injury or exploitation of others, on what ground does communist theory refute the claim? The ethical superiority of social equality is in fact at issue. Barbara Wootton[52] well points out that 'every type of economic organisation will turn top-heavy unless it is quite definitely and deliberately weighted in favour of the weak, the unfortunate, and the incompetent.' What justification can there be for this, except the *agapē tou plēsiou* (love of our neighbour) one of the two commandments on which hang all the Law and the Prophets? And this leads us to ask whence came the noble hatred of oppression found in Marx, and whence arises this passion in all the communist confessors and martyrs of the present century? It cannot be a coincidence that marxist morality grew up in the bosom of Christianity after eighteen Christian centuries, as if the phoenix of the Kingdom should arise from the ashes of the Church's failure.

Notes

1. [TRR, pp. 75–91.]
2. He may be called an 'ascetic' in that he has often sacrificed for his intellectual calling those material benefits which Lord Birkenhead referred to as the 'glittering prizes' of the capitalist system.
3. Cf. Bishop A. Robertson, *Regnum Dei* (London, 1901). We shall discuss this subject in more detail below, p. 241.
4. See Pascal, R., *The Social Basis of the German Reformation*; *Martin Luther and his Times* (London, 1933).
5. Hill, A. V., Huxley Memorial Lecture, 1933; abridged version: 'International Status and Obligations of Science,' *Nature*, 1933, **132**, 952. Hill, A. V., and Haldane, J. B. S., *Nature*, 1934, **133**, 65.
6. Benda, J., *La Trahison des Clercs* (Paris, 1927). The word clerk meant originally any man who could read, an attainment chiefly confined in the Middle

Ages to ecclesiastics major and minor, cf. the Book of Common Prayer: 'the priest and clerks.'

7. Cf. W. Cunningham's *Christian Opinion on Usury* (Edinburgh, 1884).

8. Regrating was the practice of buying goods in order to sell them again in the same market at a higher price, and without adding to their value. Forestalling was the purchase of goods on their way to the market, or immediately on their arrival, or before the market had properly opened, in order to get them more cheaply. Engrossing was the medieval counterpart of cornering, the buying up of the whole, or a large part, of the stock of a commodity in order to force up the price.

9. Henry Adams, *Mont St. Michael and Chartres*, Massachusetts Historical Society, p. 276.

10. *De Rer. Nat.*, VI. 39.

11. Chapter viii. 9.

12. See the *Apocryphal New Testament*, ed. M. R. James (Oxford, 1924), p. 36.

13. 'Old men who knew John the Lord's disciple, remember that they heard from him how the Lord taught concerning those times, saying, etc.'

14. Similar accounts occur in the Jewish *Apocalypse of Baruch* and the Coptic *Apocalypse of James*.

15. 'So when the Lord was telling the disciples about the future kingdom of the saints, how glorious and wonderful it would be, Judas was struck by his words and said, "Who shall see these things?" And the Lord said: "These things shall they see who are worthy." (Hippolytus, *On Daniel*, 4.) 'Papias says that when Judas the traitor believed not and asked, "How then shall these growths be accomplished by the Lord?", the Lord said: "They shall see who shall come thereto".' (Irenaeus, *Contra Haer*, 5.)

16. Bukharin, N., *Theory and Practice from the Standpoint of Dialectical Materialism* (London, 1931), p. 5.

17. Cf. for example the essay 'Communism and Morality' by A. L. Morton in *Christianity and the Social Revolution*, 1935, and 'Marxism and Morality' by J. Hunter in *University Forward*, 1941, **6**, 4.

18. Cf. *Moscow Dialogues* by J. Hecker (London, 1933), p. 55, and *Fundamental Problems of Marxism*, by G. Plekhanov (ed. D. Riazanov, London, 1928), pp. 9 ff.

19. *De Rer. Nat.*, II. 1090.

20. There is, of course, the incidental difficulty of continually modifying the letter of the teaching of the great ethical 'mutants' to fit changing techniques and increasing knowledge, without losing their spirit.

21. In this connection C. M. Williams' *Review of the Systems of Ethics founded on the Theory of Evolution* (London, 1893), is still not without value.

22. Cf. Lenin's remarks on religion in *Works*, **11**, pp. 658 ff., and *Lenin on Religion* (London, n.d.).

23. J. S. Huxley, *What Dare I Think?* (London, 1931), p. 187.

24. J. M. Murry, many articles in the *Adelphi*, and especially 1932, **3**, 267.

25. Susan Stebbing, *Ideals and Illusions* (London, 1940), p. 31.

26. Cf. Stewart D. Headlam's *The Service of Humanity* (London, 1882) and *The Meaning of the Mass* (London, 1905).

27. Or the last priest of Zeus in Richard Barnett's story, *The Twilight of the Gods*. First published 1888, now in Thinker's Library Edition No. 81 (London, 1940).

28. Cf. what George Tyrrell said: 'Houtin and Loisy are right; the Christianity of the future will consist of mysticism and love, and possibly the Eucharist in its primitive form as the outward bond,' *Autobiography and Life* (London, 1912), vol. 2, p. 377.

29. See the book of essays, *The Frustration of Science*, by Sir Daniel Hall, J. D. Bernal,

J. G. Crowther, E. Charles, V. H. Mottram, P. Gorer, and B. Woolf (Allen & Unwin, London, 1934).

30. Bernal, J. D., 'National Scientific Research,' *Progress*, 1934, **2**, 364.
31. Budget Estimates.
32. Cf. Joad, C. E. M., *Guide to Modern Thought* (London, 1933); and *Under the Fifth Rib*; *An Autobiography* (London, 1932).
33. See p. 138 [of TRR].
34. The dictum is attributed to Mr. Henry Ford.
35. *New Statesman*, 1934, **8**, 332 (September 15th).
36. Hecker, J., *Moscow Dialogues* (London, 1933), p. 191.
37. On the socialism of the Apostolic Fathers, see the essay of Charles Marson in the collective work by Tom Mann and others, *Vox Clamantium*, ed. Andrew Reid (London, 1894); and also his *God's Co-operative Society* (London, 1914).
38. See especially Otto, R., *The Idea of the Holy* (Oxford, 1923).
39. Rowse, A. L., *Politics and the Younger Generation* (London, 1931), p. 194.
40. Marx, K., *Introduction to a Critique of Hegel's Philosophy of Law*.
41. And also in the great concluding paragraph of John Stuart Mill's *On Liberty* (written between 1854 and 1859).
42. Cf. Kierkegaard's distinction between 'tribulations' (natural troubles which can only be endured) and 'temptations' (troubles due to, and soluble by, acts of will), discussed by W. H. Auden in *New Year Letter* (London, 1941), p. 132.
43. Pascal, R., *Outpost*, 1932, **1**, 70.
44. All sciences have as their aim the transformation of tribulations into temptations, Auden, loc. cit. But the process is asymptotic.
45. A point of view admirably put in Afinogenov's play *Distant Point*.
46. See Milman, H. H., *History of Latin Christianity* (London, 1867); and Stanley A. P., *Lectures on the History of the Eastern Church* (Everyman edition, London).
47. This explains Blake's antipathy to Newton.
48. (London, 1931.)
49. (London, 1932.) We shall analyse this book in what follows.
50. It is of much interest that the similarity between fascism and the ancient caste-system of India is expressly admitted in *Sanatana Dharma*, an advanced textbook of Hindu religion and ethics, published by the Central Hindu College, (Benares, 1923), pp. 240 ff. Both are said to be based on the doctrine of immortality.
51. R. M. Kyrle, *Psyche*, 1931, **11**, 48.
52. *Plan or No Plan* (London, 1934), p. 106.

10

Man and His Situation

(1970)

I am supposed to talk this evening about 'Man and his Situation',
or if you like, 'Man's Place in Nature.' Many a time I have
wished that I had not undertaken to do so, because it is rather like
being asked to talk brightly for an hour about the universe. However, I am prepared to have a go, but I think first that I should
declare, as it were, my private interests, in other words my background, because you are not going to get the views of a Muslim
Sufi, or a Plymouth Brother, or a literary Mahayana Buddhist. To
speak plainly then, I spent half my life or more as a biochemist
especially concerned with embryology, and only after that turned
over to oriental studies to occupy myself, as I do, with the history
of science and technology in the Chinese culture area. I also want
to say at the outset that it is not my intention or desire this
evening to persuade anyone of anything. All I would hope is to
explain how the world process seems to one person, at any rate,
someone who has not been prepared to rule out from his life any
one of the great forms of human experience.

Perhaps the most basic thing about the point of view I want to
describe is the conviction of an evolutionary process, at work
everywhere throughout the galaxy and very notably upon our
earth. It then comes to seem inescapable that there has been an
essential unity of cosmological, organic, biological, and social
evolution. The way it used to present itself to me as a biochemist,
was as a picture of envelopes in space and succession in time.
There are levels of organisation and integration in both. Thus you
have the individual body of man within the social organism, the
organs within the body, the cells within the organ, the nuclei and

other organelles within the individual cells, the enormous protein molecules within these again, the atoms within the molecules, and the elementary physical particles within the atoms. And just as the smaller entities are subsumed within the greater ones, so also there were times when only the smaller existed and the larger had not yet been formed. There was a period before there was any life on earth at all, then there was a time when there were only the simplest forms of life, gradually the metazoa took over, and life embarked upon the whole vast course of organic evolution. Judged by level of organisation and integration man does stand at the top of this, though of course we cannot know what evolution may yet have up its sleeve.

All this cannot be unique to our solar system. Not only in other parts of our own galaxy but in the almost numberless other galaxies which fill the spaces of the heavens, there must be thousands, for all I know millions, of planets in a similar relation to their suns as earth is to ours, and presumably on all of these, conditions for biological evolution may well have been very similar to our own case. The consequences of this I can leave to your imagination, but it has inspired a few themes in the early history of science fiction, for example the Victorian poet who played with the idea that the Christian redemption must have been repeated many times in other solar systems; and you may remember the fascinating book of C. S. Lewis, *Out of the Silent Planet,* which imagined a visitor being present at another temptation of Eve. I have to admit all such possibilities in my world-view. What I feel I know about my own planet, so far as scientific knowledge is possible, is that there has been this continuing evolution, and no forms of human expression, even in the quite different fields of philosophy, religion or aesthetics, which do not take it into account, are any more acceptable.

Arising out of this there comes the conviction of the reality of progress. I have simply never been able to understand how this can be blithely denied. The Victorians may have been stupidly optimistic, but that is no ground for rejecting the basic conception. One has to look at it with eyes familiar with the scattered points one finds on many scientific, especially biological, graphs— scattered they may be, yet a continuous trend there also is which can be depicted by a rising curve, the general course of which over-rides all individual and particular backslidings. One might even say that the idea of progress looked at in this way is essentially statistical, and dependent, as it were, on a calculus of aberrant observations. In spite of all the agonising things which are going on in the world at the present time, in spite of the wars and rumours of wars, I remain convinced that humanity will win through to a society worthy of man at his best, not to some technological tyranny or some reversion to savagery. Those who doubt the reality of progress should learn more of the slave-markets of the ancient world, or the horrors of the religious persecutions, or the conditions of the rowers on the Mediterranean galleys. I know about the Nazi incineration-chambers and the Hiroshima bomb, but today such things profoundly shock the conscience of all humanity while in former ages they would not have done. I have sometimes pictured the fracas which might be expected if an Assyrian king or an eighteenth-century aristocrat were to go into a post-office to buy some stamps—our democratic forbearance would give him an apoplectic fit.

On the mechanism by which this progressive development of mankind has taken place, there is of course much room for difference of opinion. Some historians would do anything rather than accept it, others realise that they have to, but would do anything rather than admit the struggle of social classes as the most important determining factor. As for myself, I have always looked at the matter as a Christian socialist of the Left, and I long ago became convinced that the Christian must take Marxism extremely seriously. A theist of course he is, a believer in the theology of transcendence he may be, but there is no reason why he should not accept the ideas of historical materialism and the class struggle as illuminating the ways in which God has worked during the evolution of society. Here the doctrine of the Kingdom, *Regnum Dei*, is of particular importance. There have been many ways of interpreting this, some more convenient to the ruling classes than others, but my understanding of it has always been that it should be regarded as a realm of justice and comradeship on earth to be brought about by the efforts of man throughout the centuries, not primarily as some mystical body existing already, or some spiritual state to be expected somewhere else in the future. This was the direction in which I was led by my conviction of the essential unity of cosmological, organic and social evolution, where the idea of human progress, with all due reservations, finds its place. That was why a book of essays I produced many years ago, *History is on Our Side*, bore the sub-title 'Essays in Political

Religion and Scientific Faith'. The necessity of faith in anything irrational seemed more and more pointless when everything that we knew of evolution and history indicated a continuous process, or in theological terms, a plan of salvation, which humanity was working out.

Another of my youthful books of essays was called *Time: The Refreshing River* after a phrase in one of the poems of W. H. Auden, who spoke here last week. I had long been in profound sympathy with the philosophers of emergent evolution, such as Lloyd Morgan, Samuel Alexander and now Nikolai Hartmann, and of course later on with the religious form of the same conviction represented by Teilhard de Chardin. That extraordinary Jesuit I never met in China though we both had so much to do with that great country, but only in Paris, after the war, when we found ourselves very close in outlook, vastly different though our French and English lines of development had been. On this point of view the end-result is not in doubt, but what depends on our efforts is how long the suffering has got to go on. That strange Christian phrase, 'the saints under the altar cry, O Lord, how long, how long?'—*Clamabant autem voce magna usquoque Domine qui sanctus es et verax* . . . always rings in my mind, and I think that as beings in time what matters in what we do is how soon the City of God on earth can come. Politics is something that none of us can stay out of, and the more Christian we want to be the less we can stay out of it. Whether it's the wicked and genocidal war in Vietnam, or the oppression of the Africans in South Africa, or the persecution of Orthodox Christians in the Soviet Union, or of Bolivian tin miners in South America, everything depends (it's a terrible recognition) on us, and according to our actions, on us will be the judgement. The judgement of history if you like, as the old Chinese historians would have said; you don't necessarily have to think of it in the rather childlike Christian terms represented in the 'dooms' of frescoes over chancel arches.

May I turn now to the second great component which, as I look back at it, seems to have set the whole framework of my *Weltanschauung* or attitude to life. Even as an undergraduate and as a young research worker I was ineluctably driven to the conviction that life embodies several distinct, and sometimes even mutually hostile, forms or modes of human experience. One could distinguish the philosophical or metaphysical form, the mathematical form, the form of the natural sciences, the historical form, the aesthetic form, and the mystical-religious form, each being irreducible to any of the others; but all being interpretable by each other, albeit in contradictory ways. You could call them the five faces of truth, if that word sufficed to describe their objectives, which it obviously doesn't. This point of view could arise from the ideas of many thinkers, but particularly influential was Collingwood's *Speculum Mentis*. Vaihinger's *The Philosophy of As If* also exerted a great influence, but if there was one book more than any other which moulded my attitude to religion it was Rudolf Otto's *The Idea of the Holy*. From this it became overwhelmingly clear that religion did not reside in any dogmas, doctrines or specific rites, but rather in the numinous sense, a specific form of human experience, not to be broken down into philosophy or aesthetics; applied at first of course by primitive peoples to all kinds of objects unworthy of it, but in the higher religions firmly attached to ethics and symbolised in liturgical practice. One of the struggles I most clearly remember was in Christian liturgiology itself where I was captivated very early by its wonderful symbolism, yet repelled by much of the phraseology, until I came to realise that the words of the holy liturgy were a form of poetry not to be dissected by the scientific scalpel or criticised by the methods of the linguistic philosopher. And it follows, of course, from any world-outlook of this sort, that one must expect to meet with people who are congenitally incapable of appreciating or participating in one or other of these forms of experience. It is no good trying to expatiate on Beethoven's quartets to a friend who has no appreciation of music, nor can mathematical proofs, scientific laws or technological triumphs be appreciated by the literati, yet the highest goal is to be a complete and entire human being, not cut off from any one of these different means of reacting to the universe in which one finds oneself.

This was the sort of reason why, following Robert Boyle, I called another book of essays forty years ago *The Sceptical Biologist*, because I doubted whether the view of the world which one had to adopt in the mechanistic scientific work of the laboratory was the only view that it was possible to take about the world and life within it. And a fourth book I called *The Great Amphibium*, because Sir Thomas Browne had said long before, 'Thus is man that great and true amphibium, whose nature is disposed to live not onely like other creatures in diverse elements but in divided and distinguished worlds'. So the forms of experience, then, are like that many different languages. Some things can only be said perfectly in one of them, many things can't be said at all in the others. And if you fully follow out this way of life you come to recognise that although all of them are 'valid' reactions of man to the universe, no one of them has over-riding authority. That, I think, can hardly be emphasised enough.

One thing I am quite sure about, and that is that if I had been a narrow-minded self-opinionated scientist I could never have entered into real contact with Chinese civilisation when I had the opportunity of doing so. There isn't time to tell fully how that opportunity arose, but I might explain that having been stimulated to learn Chinese by scientific friends from that country who came to take their doctorates in Cambridge in the thirties, I was asked to go to China during the Second World (or anti-fascist) War, and run a mission of scientific and technological liaison with the Chinese. There I met innumerable friends, many of whom were Confucians, Taoists, or Buddhists (as well as Marxists), and I feel quite certain that if I had not been attuned to religion within the framework of my own inherited culture I could never have felt at home, as I did, in temples of all those three persuasions. If one is born within the Christian world, that religion is one's birthright, the most, the only, natural way to respond to the divinity above and within all things, yet not of course a system to be accepted uncritically. Moreover being a dogmatic or fundamentalist Christian would have ruined it just as badly, not merely because one would have been out of sympathy with them all but because one would have been incapable of comprehending what religion can be without a God or gods or any theology. For you must understand that Confucianism has always been a completely this-worldly doctrine, an ethic of living together which never assumed any supernatural authority. Confucian *Thien,* or 'Heaven', would prove through the course of history that the Sage was right, but it was a form of the Order of Nature, without personality or supra-personality. In Taoism one found another form of the worship or veneration of the Order of Nature, that is to say the immanent Tao, the 'Mother of All Things'. Having delighted in the Taoist temples in China, I came long afterwards to realise that this religion had been at the bottom of most of the ancient and medieval scientific advances which the Chinese made, and indeed Fêng Yu-Lan has rightly called it the only system of mysticism which the world has ever seen which was not fundamentally anti-scientific. As for the last of the three doctrines, the *San Chiao*, Buddhism, I suppose we all know that gods are relatively unimportant there. They may be protectors of the faith, they may live in very comfortable surroundings, but they have nothing to do with salvation, which is attainable only by following the noble eight-fold path of the Lord Buddha, whether you happen to be a man or a god. And finally in Marxism you have the paradox that however it inveighs against all forms of religion, the numinous, the sense of the holy, is palpably present in those revolutionary self-sacrifices which it calls upon its adherents to make, and in China called most successfully.

I mentioned before that book called *Time, the Refreshing River*. It came out at the beginning of the last great war, and I did an introductory essay especially for it in the form of a personal stocktaking or self-criticism with an autobiographical content.[1] This is relevant tonight. It recognised ethics as something above and beyond all the forms of experience and it accepted political action as the implementation of ethics. Ethics and politics, I felt, were 'the cement necessary for the unification of the divergent forms'. Thus although the primacy of politics was a powerful marxist element in this thinking, the possibility of uniting the forms of experience only in the individual's life and action was, it seems, an existentialist one. Looking back, therefore, I am inclined to believe that without being directly influenced by any of them my world outlook was distinctly akin in various ways to those of Søren Kierkegaard, Karl Jaspers, Gabriel Marcel, Emanuel Mounier and perhaps even Jean-Paul Sartre. About Kierkegaard, H. J. Blackham has written: 'the only way to avoid confusion, error and misdirection of effort is to hold separate, in their appropriate spheres, the intellectual and the aesthetic, the ethical and the religious; and to give them their unity where it is properly found, in the life of the existing individual under the supremacy of the ethical, not in the abstraction of pure thought under the supremacy of the intellectual'.[2] As Kierkegaard said himself: 'ethics concentrates upon the individual, and ethically it is the task of every individual to become an entire man; just as it is the ethical presupposition that every man is born in such a condition that he can become one'. Perhaps this may have been a little optimistic. But in another place he wrote: 'If thought speaks deprecatingly of the imagination, imagination in its turn speaks deprecatingly of thought; and likewise with feeling. The task is not to exalt the one at the expense of the other, but to give them an equal status, to unify them in simultaneity; the medium in which they are unified is *existence*.' Or again Jaspers declared that Being is split into discontinuities which can be surmounted only in living, and that it is naïve still to look for a general homogeneous structure which can be elucidated by thought.

I don't think I could be at one, however, with all that the existentialists have said about that profound sickness of the modern soul which has been called alienation. It would take a whole course of lectures to do justice to this conception, and in any case I am too old now to be able to say anything much worth while about it. But the feeling of estrangement from the outside world is a terrible thing. Estrangement from the society in which one has to live, estrangement from one's work or profession and its products, estrangement from the values of one's society and even from oneself. I do think that a certain amount of this is due to a failure to adopt the two basic outlooks, the evolutionary and the experiential, which I spoke of at the beginning, but that is far from being the whole story. The world today is enough to estrange anyone. In the eyes of the younger generation, and of many older people too, 'there's something rotten in the State of Denmark'. As one of the graffiti said : 'There's a flaw in reality'. Hence the rise of a cynical despair of all possible societies. But the world-wide evils of war and oppression, of racial hatred and fearful acquiescence, the hunger and poverty of the 'third world', are generating a tremendous revolutionary counter-surge, idealistic in the best sense; and this is found in the socialist countries as much as in the capitalist ones. The difference is that not all the socialist countries are living up to their own ideals, while the liberation and equality of the under-developed peoples have never exactly been capitalist ideals at all. The Sino-Soviet split has been a great blow to all those who hoped that political ideals could transcend racial and cultural differences, yet there are active in the world today powerful forces of inter-racial unity.

In 1844 the philosophy of Hegel, which included both the evolutionary view of the world in an idealist form and the concept of revolution, came under attack both by Kierkgaard and Marx. Both rejected his intellectualism. For Kierkegaard the only meaning of existence was the synthesis accomplished in each individual personality, but for Marx, on the contrary, the inner stresses of the individual consciousness reflected the strains of a class-divided society. On my view the former was not wrong but the latter was still more right.

Many people whom no one could call marxist were saying much the same thing. For example, Thomas Carlyle in *Past and Present* wrote :

'We . . . with our Mammon-Gospel have come to strange con-clusions. We call it a Society; and go about professing openly the totalest separation, isolation. Our life is not a mutual helpfulness; but rather, cloaked under due laws-of-war, named "fair com-petition" and so forth, it is a mutual hostility. We have pro-foundly forgotten everywhere that "Cash-payment" is not the sole relation of human beings . . . Far from it, far deeper than supply and demand, are laws and obligations sacred as man's life itself; these also, if you will continue to work, you must learn to obey . . . He that will not learn them . . . shall not be able to work in Nature's empire. Perpetual mutiny, contention, hatred, iso-lation, execration, shall wait on his footsteps till all men discern that the theory which he attains, however golden it look or be, is not success but want of success.'[3]

Engels reviewed Carlyle's *Past and Present* in the journal that Marx was editing in the year just mentioned. Perhaps it helped to crystallise the idea in Marx's mind that the new industrialism and the whole foreseeable development of capitalism far into the future would have the most proundly dehumanising effects on man. And so he was to write :

'What man has produced, what contains something of man's very nature, becomes, because of the economic system under which he produces, an alien power opposed to himself which enslaves him instead of being controlled by him. Human indi-viduality, human morality itself, becomes at once a commercial object—man estranged from himself and also estranged from other men. Thus the social forms of capitalism become antagon-istic to a true society and to the self-achievement of the individual'.

This takes us straight to what John Lewis has called 'the impoverished soul in the affluent society' and what that great socialist now gone from us, R. H. Tawney, used to call 'the sickness of an acquisitive culture'. There is, no doubt, a way of overcoming the alienation and the estrangement which permeates the world today, but it can only be done by incarnating in the world of human society the values of the Christian gospel; values which have manifested themselves under other names in all the great civilisations for millennia past. Marx did show the way forward in very precise concrete terms, but the spirit which inspired him had been the inspiration of many a sage and prophet in earlier ages.

Today a rapidly increasing number of people subscribe to 'the doctrine that man is the highest being for man; and to the categorical imperative to overthrow all conditions in which man is a humiliated, enslaved, despised and rejected being'. These were Marx's words in the critique of Hegel. In our own lifetime we have seen enormous steps forward in this social evolution, and among them by far the most important probably in the eyes of future historians has been the Chinese revolution, now twenty-one years old. Two decades are almost one generation, and in China today probably 250 million young people have no direct knowledge of what their country was like before 1949. Yet for those of us who vividly remember life in wartime China under the Kuomintang a generation ago seems only like yesterday. Those were the days when in one year (1943) a million people starved to death in two quite separate famines, one in Central and one in South China, and when peasant boys in their thousands were seized as conscripts and marched for hundreds of miles to their death in the North-West. I myself shall never forget the poverty of the Chinese people that I saw during those years, a destitution completely medieval. I can remember too the misery of the young soldiers blinded by trachoma and dying of dysentery and many other diseases, which the Army Medical Corps, to which I was an Adviser, had not the means to overcome.

On the 1st October, 1949, Chairman Mao Tsê-Tung, standing above the Gate of Heavenly Peace in Peking and announcing that 'the Chinese people have stood up', proclaimed the new People's Republic. This was a phrase of special meaning for us because we remember the song of the Levellers in the English revolution of the seventeenth century. 'Diggers All, Stand Up Now!' Mao's words signified nothing more nor less than the final overthrow of an out-of-date social and political system which had become effete, corrupt and inhuman. Traditional Chinese society, already in decline at the beginning of the nineteenth century, had been shaken to its foundations by the impact of aggressive Western capitalism and changed by it into what has been called a semi-feudal, semi-colonial system. In Kuomintang China it was the worst features of the old society that tended to survive, and that party grafted on them what was essentially a fascist system with the single saving grace of relative inefficiency. Despite its strong Western backing, this system, as I know directly from personal experience, had no popular support, and when the country people and the industrial workers, whom Mao had found the way to organise in the Chinese Red Army, first defended themselves against its attacks and then moved to overthrow it completely, it collapsed like a pack of cards.

Thus the way was cleared for the building of a new society. In a single decade the mass of the people attained, broadly speaking, freedom from want and also freedom from worrying about their future. Of course there was a small minority of the discontented, those whose vested interests had been hit, and some of these fled away to Formosa or the Western world, but as time went on acceptance of the Kungchhantang's leadership became ever more willing, for Chairman Mao is, to the vast majority of Chinese, a veritable Moses who has brought them out of the Egyptian bondage of prostrate colonialised society into a land not only promised but palpably real.

Of course there have been setbacks, and difficult lessons to be learnt. During the 'hard years' of natural calamity and the withdrawal of Soviet help (1959–61), and the years of recovery (1962–3), the danger of a retrogression from socialism and social-ist ideas arose, and incipient capitalist tendencies showed them-selves both in town and countryside. It became clear that socialist institutions alone could not guarantee socialism. There was a battle still to be won in the hearts of the people, and each generation would need to be trained in altruistic socialist morality. Hence the socialist education movement launched in the countryside in 1963. In 1967 in one of his speeches, Mao Tsê-Tung spoke as follows: 'In the past we waged struggles in rural areas, in factories, and in the cultural field, and we carried out the socialist education movement, but all this failed to solve the problem because we did not find a form, a method, to arouse the broad masses to expose our dark aspects openly in an all-round way from below.' What a memorable phrase this was, 'our dark aspects'; he meant of course the almost unconscious tendency of any group of people in commanding positions to do better for themselves than the majority, to appropriate goods in short supply, to order people about, to be thick-skinned concerning the needs and hardships of individuals, in fact to commit all the bureaucratic sins. But a way out was found in the cultural revolution, that tremendous educational upheaval out of which a new China is again emerging.

Over here there are many people who have ambiguous feelings about China. There is much interest, widespread suspicion and misunderstanding, and a total lack of any deep comprehension. If I say anything I can claim to speak on the basis of four summers spent there since the Revolution. If I were to be asked to summarise the meaning of the Chinese revolution in two sentences I should say, first, that it was an irrevocable decision of the Chinese people not to follow the way of capitalism through the whole weary path of the 'dark Satanic mills' but to move straight from their age-old bureaucratic society to modern scientific socialism. Secondly I should say that with complete clarity and determination the Chinese people are working towards a truly classless society, knowing this will take a revolution of hearts and minds not easily to be won, and needing, perhaps, perpetual renovation. But *hsin min* ('renewing the people') was an ancient Confucian watchword, and now it is being practised as never before.

A phrase from Gerrard Winstanley often comes into my mind; in one of those civil war pamphlets, he said: 'You jeer at the name Leveller, but I tell you that Jesus Christ is the head Leveller'. Of course you needn't adopt the name Christian to carry out what the Gospel says about the love of one's neighbour, you can vigorously repudiate it, as the vast majority of Chinese people would do today, yet nevertheless you may be putting it into practice. I could use Winstanley's phrase and say: 'You laugh at the Little Red Book, but I tell you it is the inspiration of one fifth, maybe one quarter, of the present population of the world'. You can call it, if you insist, a new religion, and indeed it does draw especially from Christianity and Confucianism, and unquestionably Chairman Mao is a numinous figure, because in China ethics have always been numinous. Only take one of the present Chinese slogans, *chan ssu, tou hsiu* 'renounce self-seeking; repudiate privilege'—is this not putting into practice the *agapē tou plēsiou* of the gospels? A million acts of heroism and mercy in the service of the people are being celebrated today in Chinese culture.

If I often feel inclined to believe that Chinese socialism may have a key which might unlock many doors into the future for the whole world I am not without strong reasons for it. I should like to put before you half a dozen of these. First of all, what is it that is wrong about affluence? There is an alarming paradox confronting us today of disillusionment, cults of senseless violence, corruption in the arts and theatre, and a mad confusion between good sex and evil sadism, an urge to contract out of all society, including the flight into drug-taking, intellectual poverty and alienation in the midst of plenty. The United States, I suppose, has the highest standard of life in the world, and yet it is the unhappiest of countries, from which many are already seeking to flee. To a lesser extent Europe is struck with the same blight. What has gone wrong? After all, that the standard of life should rise, has always been one of the greatest aims of the socialist movement everywhere, and one instinctively supported by all those who feel for their fellow-men. But it seems that abundance, unless controlled by ethics, brings deep evil with it; more washing machines, more television sets, more private cars, more large flats for small families, may mean less pioneering community services, less devotion to duty, less attachment to the pleasures of life that can be enjoyed without expensive equipment. How to overcome 'hire-purchase debauchery' and the selfish passion for the acquisition of things? This is where the Chinese tradition comes in, because for the past 2000 years the Confucian system of ethics, perhaps the greatest the world has ever seen, never depended upon, and indeed rejected, supernatural sanctions. It sprang, in fact, from a doctrine of the nature of man. To act nobly *is* his nature, requiring only the right training. Closely connected with this is the fact, not often sufficiently appreciated in the West, that the idea of original sin was in China heretical—in so far as anything could be called heretical in that culture. In China Pelagius was orthodox, Augustine mistaken. This is a profoundly important point, because the idea of original sin as it has been expounded by many theologians, has for centuries been a positive barrier to the optimistic estimate required for the construction of socialism. Of course it is obvious that we have, built into ourselves, certain traces of our animal ancestry in evolution, which give sufficient colour to the doctrine of original sin to permit of its acceptance when stated in minimal form. But at the present time we are witnessing a recrudescence of the crassest 'biologism' in that movement of thought which I suppose is most typically exemplified in Desmond Morris's *The Naked Ape*. As John Lewis and Bernard Towers have pointed out, this is only original sin in another form, and a form remarkably like the propaganda of the Nazis before the second world war.[4] The Chinese will have none of this. It did not take modern evolution theory to teach the sage of Shantung that man is unique among living beings, forming a new level of integration and organisation, with a social inheritance and a continuing civility totally unknown among any of the lower forms of life.

Let me raise another point. At no time in Chinese history (apart from a few Buddhist schools) was there any strong development of idealist metaphysics. On the contrary the greatest indigenous philosophical schools tended to be materialist, and therefore disinclined to look for reality anywhere but in this present world. Indeed the Neo-Confucians (corresponding in date and systematism with the European Scholastics) worked out a philosophy based on the concepts of matter-energy and a hierarchy of organising principles which was remarkably similar to dialectical materialism—or as it would be better called, dialectical organicism. And again there was no system of transcendental theology, no doctrine of a supreme creator deity. Confucian *Thien* and Taoist *Tao* were divine indeed, but always immanent within the universe, which had never had a beginning and would never end—at least so far as human speech could say, for it was wisdom to recognise the limits of man's knowledge.

Closely connected with this last fact is the remarkable circumstance that what Lancelot Whyte has called the 'European schizophrenia' had no parallel in China. That great chasm of the West between the sacred and the secular, between Pope and Emperor, between the angels and the atoms, was not found at any time in Chinese society. It may have had certain advantages, but it was always desperately open to Manichaean distortions, and the very existence of the Church over against the World meant that it was particularly difficult to visualise the incarnation of the City of God within the actual dwellings and cities of men. Here was another point at which Confucianism mirrored the best elements in Christianity. For the Chinese in all ages, the Kingdom

of God could come on the earth, though of course they would
never have dreamt of using such a phraseology.

The other indigenous doctrine of China, Taoism, also plays a
considerable part in the Chinese ethos of today. To give you any
adequate account of this great system of Nature-mysticism would
be impossible this evening, but I cannot let the occasion pass
without quoting to you a few lines from the *Tao Tê Ching*, the
basic document of the faith, written about the fourth century
BC:

> How did the great rivers and seas get their kingship
>   over the hundred lesser streams?
> Through the merit of being lower than they; that was how
>   they got their kingship.
> Therefore the sage, in order to be above the people,
> Must speak as though he were lower than they,
> In order to guide them
> He must put himself behind them.
> Thus when he is above, the people have no burden,
> When he is ahead, they feel no hurt.
> Thus everything under heaven is glad to be directed by him
> And does not find (his guidance) irksome.

Here we have an extraordinary statement of the principle of
leadership from within, not from above. Isn't this directly
reflected in the system which the Chinese have been introducing
everywhere, that generals should go back and spend a period in
the ranks, while chief engineers should go for a month or two
back to the bench? Such a principle will surely be embodied in
the societies of the future. In this connection we should not forget
that throughout Chinese history, and in spite of a great deal of
bureaucratic mandarin elegance and superciliousness, there was a
classic mystique of the farmer, who came second in the four
ancient ranks, *shih, nung, kung, shang,* the scholars, the farmers,
the artisans, and last of all the merchants. Distinguished scholar-
officials retired to work the ancestral farm. Besides, the scholars
never really disdained manual work; in time of adversity they
had been known to keep wine-shops, and such occupations as the
cutting of seal-stones, the carving of jade and the making of ink
were accorded great respect.

Another great watchword of Taoism was *wu wei*, 'no action
contrary to Nature'. Here we have one root, I am sure, of the

tremendous emphasis on persuasion which has been so dominant a feature of the Chinese revolution during the past twenty years. The injuries and even execution meted out to the worst bullies of the old régime have been, I am convinced, enormously over-estimated by Western propaganda, and an infinite amount of time has been spent on meetings of persuasion, self-criticism and mutual explanation. Of course in such a vast continent and branch of humanity there must have been some dreadful incidents and miscarriages of justice, but statistically that would be inevitable. What we ought to remember here is that all through the Chinese centuries it is impossible to find any analogy for the religious persecutions and religious wars of the West; the phenomenon of the Holy Inquisition (God save the mark) has no parallel in China. Only when religious groups were thought to be in some sort of conspiracy against the State was action taken against them. This explains to some extent a number of recent events. I am not in any way blind to the dangers of totalitarian-ism and dictatorship, but with contemporary China we are in the presence of a truly mass movement of millions of people, inspired by the exhortations to altruism of a truly charismatic and prophetic personality. Of course the Chinese party, the Kungchhantang, is committed officially to atheism, but I can say from first-hand experience that down to 1964 at least the treat-ment of religions was extremely tolerant and enlightened, includ-ing the expenditure of great sums on the upkeep and restoration of all temples of any historical or artistic interest.

Thus by and large if you reflect upon these ancient character-istics of Chinese society, you will, I think, see what I mean when I suggest that the Chinese socialist revolution, far more perhaps than any such revolution which has occurred in countries forming part of Christendom, may have some at least of the healing principles which all societies of the future will need—how to save their souls in the midst of unbelievable affluence, how to bring the peoples and races into unity, how to ensure that man leaves off animal aggression and behaves as the Man he really is. One must hope that these things will come, one must believe that they will, meanwhile one must practise (as in China they try to do) the greatest of the three, the love of one's neighbour, here and now. It has been said by a distinguished Muslim scholar that all systems deriving from Christendom, even the most secular, atheist and anti-Christian, make love the supreme virtue, but that in Marxism this is a parody of the 'charity' of the saints. I disagree here on two counts, first because it can be shown that Marxism has Chinese roots as well as Christian ones (from Neo-Confucian organicism through Leibniz and Hegel), and secondly because I do not believe that there can be parodies of love. The agonising paradox is that of our two commandments 'on which hang all the law and the prophets', the Chinese reject the former (and in general always have done so), but by their just and righteous social order they practise the latter much better than Christians do. What to conclude, I leave to your judgement.

Hitherto I have been talking mainly about things which for me have long been *choses jugées* but which I thought in the light of the title of the lecture allotted to me, might interest you. Now during the rest of the time I should like to turn to a special matter which lies in my own field of work and which therefore very much interests me. We have spoken about social evolution and about progress, and this problem is one in the specific social evolutionary context of the development of the sciences of Nature. Has science and technology been one single thing from the very beginning, or have there been a series of incompatible forms of it in the different civilisations which have emerged?

It is now just about thirty-five years since I first came in contact with Chinese scientific colleagues and learnt something of their language as a relaxation from scientific research. It did not at first occur to me that a tremendous intellectual job was waiting to be done here for I was content to enjoy the introduction into an entirely new world of the spirit, to gain an orientation in a literature as great as that of Europe, and to begin to see everything through distinctively non-Western spectacles. The written language was a delight, and escaping from the alphabet in reading a page or two of it was, I used to remark, as enjoyable as going for a swim on a hot day. Still, as I began to know my Chinese colleagues better the more exactly like myself I found they were, and this awakened grave doubts in my mind—how could they be so intelligent, so subtle and so philosophically penetrating, when actually modern science, of which we were all the devoted practitioners, had originated only in Europe at the time of the Renaissance and the scientific revolution? This was why I began to search eagerly for anything that had been written on the history of science in China. The result was very disappointing; there was nothing of importance in any Western language, except occasional speculations and *obiter dicta,* plus a very few old monographs on particular sciences; while in Chinese there were only similar monographs rather more recent but without awareness of the general problem that was worrying me. So I would have to do the job myself. At first I pictured only a single small volume, or a pair of slim ones, but enterprises of this sort are like neoplasms (benign of course), or embryos waiting to be born, and when they can find a suitable home there is no stopping their growth. Before my collaborators and I had been very long at work it became clear that there was not one question, but two. Not only why modern science originated in Europe alone, but why, during the previous fifteen centuries, China had been much more advanced in science and technology than the cultures of the West. I cannot venture on any answer to these questions tonight because I want to talk about another question. How far has there been real continuity?

My collaborators and I have all along assumed that there is only one unitary science of Nature, approached more or less closely, built up more or less successfully and continuously, by various groups of mankind from time to time. This means that one can expect to trace an absolute continuity between the first beginnings of astronomy and medicine in Ancient Babylonia, through the advancing natural knowledge of medieval China, India and the classical world, to the break-through of late Renaissance Europe when, as has been said, the most effective method of discovery was itself discovered. Many people probably share this point of view, but there is another one which I may associate with the name of Oswald Spengler, the German world-historian of the thirties, whose works, especially *The Decline of the West,* achieved much popularity for a time. According to him, the sciences produced by different civilisations were like separate and irreconcilable works of art, valid only within their own frames of reference, and not subsumable into a single history and a single ever-growing structure. Anyone who has felt the influence of Spengler retains, I think, some respect for the picture he drew of the rise and fall of particular civilisations and cultures, resembling the birth, flourishing and decay of individual biological organisms, in human or animal life-cycles. Certainly I could not refuse all sympathy for a point of view so like that of the Taoists, who always emphasised the cycles of life and death in Nature; yet while one can easily see that art styles, religious ceremonies, or different kinds of music tend to be incommensurable, for mathematics, science and technology the case is altered—Man has always lived in an environment essentially constant, and his knowledge of it, if true, must therefore tend towards a constant structure.

This point would not perhaps need emphasis if certain scholars, in their anxiety to do justice to the differences between the ancient Egyptian or the medieval Chinese, Arabic or Indian world-views and our own, were not inclined to follow lines of thought which might lead to Spenglerian pessimism. Pessimism I say, because of course he did prophesy the decline and fall of our own scientific civilisation. Thus, to take one example, my own collaborator, Nathan Sivin, a brilliant investigator of medieval Chinese astronomy and alchemy, has rightly pointed out that for traditional China 'biology' was not a separated and defined science. One gets its ideas and facts from philosophical writings, books on pharmaceutical natural history, treatises on agriculture and horticulture, monographs on groups of natural objects, miscellaneous memoranda and so on.

'Clearly', he continued, 'to speak of "Chinese biology" is to imply a structure which historically did not exist, and to disregard the structures which did exist. Taking the artificial rubric seriously also implies the natural but specious assumption that Chinese scientists were asking the same questions about the living world as their modern counterparts in the West, and simply happened through some quirk of national character, language, economics, scientific method or social structure, to find different answers. One consequently need never even be curious about what questions the ancient and medieval Chinese scientists believed themselves to be asking. It is my contention that a fruitful comparative history of science will be founded not on the counting of isolated discoveries, insights or skills, but upon the confrontation of integral complexes of ideas with their interrelations and articulations intact. These complexes can be kept integral only if the problems which they were meant to solve are understood. Chinese science must, in other words, be seen as developing out of one state of theoretical understanding into another, rather than as an abortive development towards modern science.'[5]

This is well put; of course one must not see in traditional Chinese

science simply a 'failed prototype' of modern science, but the
formulation here has to be extremely careful. The danger is of
falling into the other extreme, denying the fundamental continuity and universality of all science. This would be to resurrect
the Spenglerian conception of the natural sciences of the various
dead (or even worse, the living) non-European civilisations as
totally separate, immiscible thought patterns, more like distinct
works of art than anything else, a series of different views of the
natural world irreconcilable and unconnected. Such a view might
be used as the cloak of a historical racialism, the sciences of pre-
modern times and the non-European cultures being thought of as
wholly conditioned ethnically, and rigidly confined to their own
spheres, not part of humanity's broad onward march. Moreover it
would leave little room for those actions and reactions that we are
constantly encountering, deep-seated influences which one civilisation had upon another.

Elsewhere again Nathan Sivin has written: 'The question of
why China never spontaneously experienced the equivalent of
our scientific revolution lies of course very close to the core of a
comparative history of science. My point is that it is an utter
waste of time, and distracting as well, to expect any answer until
the Chinese tradition has been adequately comprehended from
the inside.' Fair enough; we must of course learn to see through
the eyes of those who thought in terms of the Yin and Yang, the
Five Elements, the symbolic correlations and the trigrams and
hexagrams of the 'Book of Changes', but here again this formulation suggests a purely internalist ideological explanation for the
failure of modern natural science to arise in Chinese culture. I do
not think that in the last resort we shall be able to appeal
primarily to inhibiting factors inherent in the Chinese thought-
world considered as an isolated Spenglerian cell. One must always
expect that some of these intellectual limiting factors will be ident-
ifiable, but for my part I remain sceptical that there are many
factors of this kind which could not have been overcome if the
social and economic conditions had been favourable for the
development of modern science in China. It may indeed be true
that the modern forms of science which would then have
developed would have been rather different from those which
actually did develop in the West, or in a different order, but of
that one cannot be sure. There was, for example, the lack of
Euclidean geometry and Ptolemaic planetary astronomy in

China, but China had done all the ground-work in the study of magnetic phenomena, an essential precursor of later electrical science; and Chinese culture was permeated by conceptions much more organic, less mechanistic, than that of the West. Moreover Chinese culture alone provided that materialist conception of the elixir of life which, passing to Europe through the Arabs, led to the macrobiotic optimism of Roger Bacon and the iatro-chemical revolution of Paracelsus, hardly less important in the origins of modern science than the work of Galileo and Newton. Whatever the ideological inhibiting factors in the Chinese thought-world may turn out to have been, the certainty always remains that the specific social and economic features of traditional China were connected with them. They were clearly part of that particular pattern, and in these matters one always has to think in terms of a package-deal. In just the same way, of course, it is impossible to separate the scientific achievements of the Ancient Greeks from the fact that they developed in mercantile, maritime, city-state democracy.

A similar problem has of late been taken up by Said Husain Nasr, the Persian scholar who is making valuable contributions to the history of science in Islam. He, for his part, faces the failure of Arabic civilisation to produce modern science. But far from regretting this he makes a positive virtue of it, rejecting that belief I have already outlined in an integral, social-evolutionary development of science. Opening one of his recent books you read as follows :

'The history of science is often regarded today as the progressive accumulation of techniques and the refinement of quantitative methods in the study of Nature. Such a point of view considers the present conception of science to be the only valid one; it therefore judges the sciences of other civilisations in the light of modern science and evaluates them primarily with respect to their "development" with the passage of time. Our aim in this work however, is not to examine the Islamic sciences from the point of view of modern science and of this "evolutionist" conception of history; it is on the contrary to present certain aspects of the Islamic sciences as seen from the Islamic point of view.'[6]

Now Nasr considers that the Sufis and the universal philosophers of medieval Islam sought and found a kind of mystical *gnosis*, or cosmic *sapientia*, in which all the sciences 'knew their place', as it were (like servitors in some great house of old), and ministered to mystical theology as the highest form of human experience. In Islam, then, the philosophy of divinity was indeed the *regina scientiarum* (queen of the sciences). Anyone with my attachment to theology as well as science cannot help sympathising to some extent with this point of view, but it does have two fatal drawbacks, it denies the equality of the forms of human experience, and it divorces Islamic natural science from the grand onward-going movement of the natural science of all humanity. Nasr objects to judging medieval science by its outward 'usefulness' alone. He writes: 'However important its uses may have been in calendrical computation, in irrigation or in architecture, its ultimate aim always was to relate the corporeal world to its basic spiritual principle through the knowledge of those symbols which unite the various orders of reality. It can only be understood, and should only be judged, in terms of its own aims and its own perspectives.'[7] I demur. It was part, I would maintain, of all human scientific enterprise, in which there is neither Greek nor Jew, neither Jain nor Muslim. 'Men of Cappadocia and Bithynia, and the parts of Libya about Cyrene; we have heard them tell in our tongues the marvellous works of God.'

The denial of the equality of the forms of human experience comes out very clearly in another work of Said Husain Nasr (*The Encounter of Man and Nature*). Perhaps rather under-estimating the traditional high valuation placed within Christendom upon Nature—'that other Book' as Sir Thomas Browne said 'which lies expans'd unto the eyes of all', he sees in the scientific revolution a fundamental desacralisation of Nature, and urges that only by reconsecrating it, as it were, in the interests of an essentially religious world-view, will mankind be enabled to save itself from otherwise inevitable doom. If the rise of modern science within the bosom of Christendom alone had any causal connections with Christian thought that would give it a bad mark in his view.

'The main reason why modern science never arose in China or Islam' he says, 'is precisely because of the presence of a metaphysical doctrine and a traditional religious structure which refused to make a profane thing of Nature. . . . Neither in Islam, nor India, nor the Far East, was the substance and the stuff of Nature so depleted of a sacramental and spiritual character, nor was the intellectual dimension of these traditions so enfeebled as to enable a purely secular science of Nature and a secular philosophy to develop outside the matrix of the traditional intellectual orthodoxy. ... The fact that modern science did not develop in Islam is not a sign of decadence (or incapacity) as some have claimed, but of the refusal of Islam to consider any form of knowledge as purely secular and divorced from what it considers the ultimate goal of human existence'.[8]

These are striking words, but are they not tantamount to saying that only in Europe did the clear differentiation of the forms of experience arise? In other words Nasr looks for the synthesis of the forms of experience in the re-creation of a medieval world-view, dominated by religion, not in the existential activity of individual human beings dominated by ethics. That would be going back, and there is no going back. The scientist must work *as if* Nature was 'profane'. As Giorgio di Santillana has said: 'Copernicus and Kepler believed in cosmic vision as much as any Muslim ever did, but when they had to face the "moment of truth" they chose a road which was apparently not that of *sapientia*; they felt they had to state what appeared to be the case, and that on the whole it would be more respectful of divine wisdom to act thus.'[9] And perhaps it is a sign of the weakness of what I must call so reactionary a conception that Nasr is driven to reject the whole of evolutionary fact and theory, both cosmic, biological and sociological.

In meditating on the view of modern physical science as a 'desacralisation of Nature' many ideas and possibilities come into the mind, but one very obvious cause for surprise is that it occurred in Christendom, the home of a religion in which an incarnation had sanctified the material world, while it did not occur in Islam, a culture which had never developed such an incarnation belief. This circumstance might offer a telling argument in favour of the primacy of social and economic factors in the break-through of the scientific revolution. It may be that while ideological, philosophical and theological differences are never to be undervalued, what mattered most of all were the facilitating pressures of the transition from feudalism to mercantile and then industrial capitalism, pressures which did not effectively operate in any culture other than that of Western, Frankish, Europe.

In another place Nasr wonders what Ibn al-Haitham or al-Bīrūnī or al-Khāzinī would have thought about modern science.

He concludes that they would be amazed at the position which exact quantitative knowledge has come to occupy today. They would not understand it because for them all *scientia* was subordinated to *sapientia*. Their quantitative science was only one interpretation of a segment of Nature, not the means of understanding all of it. ' "Progressive" science', he says, 'which in the Islamic world always remained secondary, has now in the West become nearly everything, while the immutable and "nonprogressive" science or wisdom which was then primary, has now been reduced to almost nothing.'[10] It happened that I read these words at a terrible moment in history. If there were any weight in the criticism of the modern scientific world-view from the standpoint of Nasr's perennial Muslim *sapientia* it would surely be that modern science and the technology which it has generated has far outstripped morality in the Western and modern world, and we shudder to think that man may not be able to control it. In fact no human society of the past ever was able to control technology, but they were not faced by the devastating possibilities of today, and the moment I read Nasr's words was just after the Jordanian civil war of last September, that dreadful fratricidal catastrophe within the bosom of Islam itself. *Sapientia* did not prevent it, nor would it seem, from the historical point of view, that wars and cruelties of all kinds have been much less within the realm of Islam than that of Christendom. Something new is therefore needed to make the world safe for mankind, and I believe that it can and will be found.

In later discussions Nathan Sivin made it clear that he was just as committed to a universal comparative history of science as any of the rest of us. That would be the ultimate justification of all our work. 'What I say', he went on, 'is not that the Chinese (or Indian) tradition should be evaluated only in the light of its own world-view, but that it must be understood as fully as possible in the light of this *before* any wide-ranging comparisons are made.' The really informative comparisons, he suggests, are not those between isolated discoveries, but between those whole systems of thought which have served as the matrices of discovery. One might therefore agree that not only particular individual anticipations of modern scientific discoveries are of interest as showing the slow development of human natural knowledge, but also that we need to work out exactly how the world-views and scientific philosophy of medieval China, Islam or India, differed from those of modern science. Each one is clearly of great interest not only in itself but in its relation to the idea-system of modern science. In this way we would not only salute the Chinese recording of sun-spots from the first century BC, or the first correct explanation of the optics of the rainbow by Qutub al-Dīn al-Shīrazī in 1300 AD, as distinct steps on the way to modern science, but also take care to examine the cosmology and philosophy within which they were made, to see exactly how and where it was different from that of modern science. And this not to condemn it for being different, but to see without prejudices what its character really was.

The only danger of the conception of human continuity and solidarity, as I have outlined it, is that it is very easy to take modern science as the last word, and to judge everything in the past solely in the light of it. This has been justly castigated by Joseph Agassi, in his lively monograph on the historiography of science, who satirises the mere re-arranging of 'up-to-date science textbooks in chronological order',[11] and the awarding of black and white marks to the scientific men of the past in accordance with the extent to which their discoveries still form part of the corpus of modern knowledge. Of course this Baconian or inductivist way of writing the history of science never did justice to the 'dark side' of Harvey and Newton, let alone Paracelsus, that realm of Hermetic inspirations and idea-sources which can only be regained by us with great difficulty, yet is so important for the history of thought, as the life-work of Walter Pagel has shown. One can see immediately that this difficulty is even greater in the case of non-European civilisations, since their thought-world has been even more unfamiliar. Not only so, but the corpus of modern knowledge is changing and increasing every day, and we cannot foresee at all what its aspect will be a century from now. Fellows of the Royal Society like to speak of the 'true knowledge of natural phenomena', but no one knows better than they do how provisional this knowledge is. It is neither independent of the accidents of Western European history, nor is it a final court of appeal for the eschatological judgement of the value of past scientific discoveries, either in West or East. But it is the best guide we have.

My collaborators and I have long been accustomed to use the image of the ancient and medieval sciences of all the peoples and cultures as rivers flowing into the ocean of modern science. In the words of the old Chinese saying : 'the Rivers pay court to the Sea'. In the main this is indubitably right. But there is room for a great deal of difference of opinion on how the process has happened and how it will proceed. One might think of the Chinese and Western traditions (as Nathan Sivin has said) travelling substantially the same path towards the science of today, that science against which, on the inductivist view, all ancient systems can be measured. But on the other hand they might have followed, and be following, rather separate paths, the true merging of which lies well in the future. Undoubtedly among the sciences this point of fusion varies. In astronomy and mathematics it took but a short time, in the seventeenth century; in botany and chemistry the process was much slower, not being complete until now, and in medicine it has not happened yet. Modern science is not standing still, and who can say how far either the biology or the physics of the future will have to adopt conceptions much more organicist than the atomic and the mechanist which have so far prevailed? Who knows what further developments of the psychosomatic conception in medicine future advances may necessitate? In all such ways the thought-complex of traditional Chinese science may yet have a much greater part to play in the final state of all science than might be admitted if science today was all that science will ever be. Always we must remember that things are more complex than they seem, and that wisdom was not born with us. To write the history of science we have to take modern science as our yardstick—that is the only thing we can do—but modern science will change, and the end is not yet. Here as it turns out is yet another reason for viewing the whole march of humanity in the study of Nature as one single enterprise.

Thus in the end we come back to the beginning, to the facts of evolutionary progress and to the fact of the different forms of human experience. Of course we know very little about the beginning of the process, or how there came to be galaxies and solar systems, and places like our earth where men, and perhaps other sorts of men, could reasonably live. We do not know the end either, we cannot visualise the cooling or the explosion of the sun, or what will happen in other solar systems. All we know is that we are in the midst of a continuous process, manifesting itself upon a certain planet in ever higher levels of organisation and ever higher values. The best that we know is what we have to be faithful to.

Notes

1. [See above, Essay Eight.]
2. H. J. Blackham, *Six Existentialist Thinkers* (London, 1952), p. 10.
3. As quoted in John Lewis, *The Life and Teaching of Karl Marx* (London, 1965), pp. 54–5.
4. See John Lewis & Bernard Towers, *Naked Ape or Homo Sapiens?* (London, 1969).
5. See J. Needham et al., *Science and Civilisation in China*, vol. 5, pt. 2 (Cambridge, 1974), p. xxii ff.
6. Said Husain Nasr, *Science and Civilisation in Islam* (Cambridge, Mass., 1968), p. 21.
7. *Ibid.*, pp. 39–40.
8. Said Husain Nasr, *The Encounter of Man and Nature* (London, 1968), pp. 97–8.
9. From di Santillana's preface to Nasr, *Science . . . .*, p. xii.
10. Nasr, *Science . . . .*, p. 145.
11. J. Agassi, 'Towards a Historiography of Science,' *History and Theory*, Beiheft, **2** (1963), p. 2.

V

THE CHINESE EXPERIENCE

11

An Eastern Perspective on Western Anti-Science

(1974)*

My first duty is of course to render warmest thanks to this eminent University on behalf of all the honorary doctors who have today been here created. Radiotherapy and medicine, education and civil administration, the law and commerce, biochemistry, embryology and the history of science, have all been honoured on this memorable occasion. I should like to take this opportunity of saying something about the position of science in the world at the present time as it appears to different generations of mankind; and how the great culture of China could be involved in this.

As the Orator has been so good as to tell us, I spent the second world war (1942 to 1946) in China as director of the Sino-British Science Cooperation Office (中英科學合作館), an organisation composed jointly of Chinese and British scientists, engineers, and doctors, which had the task of assuring liaison in these subjects between beleaguered China and the Western Allies. Having already learnt something of Chinese language and culture in Cambridge from friends who had come there to work for their research degrees, especially Dr Lu Gwei-Djen, now my chief collaborator, it fell out very naturally that the history of science, scientific thought, engineering, technology, and medicine in that great civilisation acquired an almost obsessive fascination for me. To cut a long story short, the volumes of *Science and Civilisation in China* are still steadily appearing, though I may or may not live to see the last one through the press. During the last thirty

* Address at an Honorary Degrees Convocation, Hong Kong University, 29th April 1974

years, however, since my first decision to engage in this collaborative effort, two great changes have come about.

First, I had no idea, when I decided to go over from chemical morphogenetics to oriental studies, how topical the subject would turn out to be. It was undertaken as an entirely disinterested enquiry into the history and sociology of science, pure and applied, in east and west. The primary question was, why had modern science originated only in Western Europe soon after the Renaissance; the one that was hiding behind it was, why for fourteen previous centuries had China been more successful than Europe in accumulating scientific knowledge and applying it for human benefit? Alongside these there were the obvious questions: how far did the Chinese really get in the sciences before the modern era of world communications developed, and lastly, could they have contributed something important to the origins of modern science itself? This is not the time or the place for any answers to these questions; suffice it to say that as my collaborators and I worked untiringly on, events occurred in China which led to her unquestionable elevation to great power status, events which induced in people all over the world a veritable passion for information about all the aspects of Chinese culture. This was good incidentally for the Cambridge University Press as an institution in business, but it had not been foreseen when we began our work.

In any case, my forty years of intimacy with Chinese friends showed me beyond all doubt that they were, as Andreas Corsalis wrote in the sixteenth century, *di nostra qualità*. I was profoundly convinced of the baseless arrogance of Westerners in behaving like the fools in Holy Writ, who said that 'we are *the* people, and wisdom was born with us.' Even Arnold Toynbee had fallen for the quite erroneous aphorism that the Greeks and Europeans were distinguished beyond all other peoples by a 'mechanical penchant'. Gradually I came to see why our work was so particularly annoying for conventionally-minded Westerners—it was because the achievements of modern science and technology were what they were most proud of; and to show, as the Syrian Bishop Severus Sebokht said in the seventh century, that 'besides the Greeks, there were others who knew a thing or two', was hitting where it really hurt. I had no wish to injure anyone, but for the misguided certain shocks are salutary and therapeutic. All this probably applied mainly to middle-aged and older people, not so much to the young.

For the second great change that has come over the face of things during these thirty years is a powerful movement away from science and all its works in the generations born since about the time when my Chinese friends first came to Cambridge. One could call it a basic psychological aversion, this anti-scientific movement, stronger no doubt in the highly industrialised countries of the West, but not unknown in the under-developed parts of the world. Youth has become disenchanted with science. For myself, I want to say that I have not lost faith in science as a part of the highest civilisation, and in its development as one single epic story for the whole of mankind. I believe that science has done incalculably more good than harm to human beings. But I recognise that the control of its dangerous discoveries is a political and ethical matter; and this perhaps is where the special genius of the Chinese people could affect the whole world in days to come.

Some time ago at a dinner party I sat next to an elderly woman who had spent her life in plant biochemistry and physiology. She remarked that when she was young, being a laboratory worker was a delightful thing, because one could do what one wanted to do in the happy assurance that it was socially approved; one could enjoy oneself in an occupation that was also thought high-minded. But nowadays if she told a young man or a girl what she did, they would not be at all impressed, and would be likely to comment: 'Ah, something to do with defoliants for use in Vietnam, I suppose'. This was quite a good illustration of what young people feel, namely that the evil application of scientific discoveries has never been more rampant than at the present day. It is common knowledge that a scientist can hardly do anything without attempts by the military to make use of it. The comparative psycho-physiology of dolphins is applied for naval warfare, anthropological studies are appropriated for 'counter-insurgency' purposes, and special-sense physiologists see their findings used for the intellectual cruelty of sensory deprivation techniques. Against all this the young are in full revolt. It is in fact part of the wide movement of student protest which has for some time been sweeping the Western world; and it certainly must have a connection with the fact that in several Western countries student places for the natural sciences are not fully taken up, while for the humanities there are not enough places to go round.

More or less philosophically-minded scholars have not been lacking to formulate this attack on the natural sciences—I am thinking particularly of a book such as Theodore Roszak's *The Making of a Counter-Culture*. He inveighs against 'the myth of objective consciousness', though he cannot deny the pragmatic value of science, that aerodynamics and thermodynamics lead to actual airplane flight, and that pharmacological knowledge leads to the relief or cure of disease. He and the young are against modern science because they feel that it has evil totalitarian and inhuman social consequences. They abhor its 'alienative dichotomy', which separates the observing self from the phenomena in Nature, regarding this as an 'invidious hierarchy', which rates the observer as higher than the object and free to torture it in whatever way will bring intellectual light; and lastly, they feel that science embodies a 'mechanistic imperative', i.e. an urge to put into execution every possible device, whether or not its use is good for human beings or for the world of the living and the lifeless in which they find themselves. Thus there is a call for nothing less than the subversion of the scientific world-view itself, with its egocentric and cerebral mode of consciousness.

Now there are two aspects to all this. First, the complaint is deeply sound that all too often science is taken as the only valid form of human experience; in that case its works are only too likely to be evil. But Roszak probably overrates the number of scientists throughout the world who look at things like this—they certainly cannot be the majority in China, where 'politics [i.e. human values] are in command'. As for me, I learnt long ago from my brother Oratorians, priest and lay, that 'nothing is ever "merely" anything'. Roszak even goes so far as to condemn scientists who make 'occasional private excursions into some surviving remnant of the magical vision', forgetting that only existentially in the individual can the seeming contradictions of science, religion, aesthetics, history, and philosophy be reconciled in a lived life. One can never be sure whether he is speaking for himself or expounding the inarticulate world-view of his hippy drop-outs, but after all it is always open to any of these to end up in a Zen temple or a Trappist abbey—I could have no objection.

But secondly Roszak raises most justifiably the all but intolerable ethical choices which applied science presents and will present to the human societies of our time and in time to come. The young do not want to have to make such choices, and they resent the fact that humanity is challenged by them—better to renounce such knowledge and call a halt to scientific research. Though far from Christian in any traditional sense, they suspect that Faust has sold his soul to the devil once again. It is a commonplace to speak of nuclear power and the devastation of nuclear weapons, but mathematical engineering is following very close behind; and no one is quite sure how to control the activities of computing machines, with their enormous speed of calculation and their fabulous 'memory' stores of information. Here the privacy of the individual is at risk, the right of the child to be taught by a living reasoning teacher, the safety of millions exposed to the danger of an electrical or mechanical mistake in some monitoring computer harnessed to 'defence' decisions.

But it might suit best my own profession to speak of the difficulties already evident in feasible projects of biological engineering, well described for example, in Gerald Leach's book *The Biocrats*. Partly they arise in connection with generation, as in the coming mastery of both contraception and infertility, of population control and foetal medicine. Legal considerations and changes already lag far behind the actual possibilities of artificial insemination, using sperm banks fed from donors outstanding for physical health or intellectual brilliance, and perhaps several generations older than the receiving womb. The current bitter controversies all over the world about abortion are another case in point. Moreover, the new knowledge of the genetic code is likely to furnish us with means for improving human embryos more direct than breeding for quality or breeding out faults. But there is much more to come. In principle, H. G. Wells' *Island of Dr. Moreau* has already arrived, for human cells can, by the aid of certain viruses, be hybridized with those of other mammals· and Aldous Huxley's fictional cultivation of isolated totipotent blastomeres so as to reproduce many identical twins is not at all impossible. Much work is being done on the fertilisation and cultivation of human gametes *in vitro*. Robots of flesh and blood could result from all such knowledge. More urgently needing ethical decisions are the elaborate machines still in short supply, such as kidney-substitutes and 'iron lungs', or the manifold problems that arise in connection with the transplanting of organs, both of man and animals. 'Spare part' surgery has undoubtedly come to stay, but when it involves plastic or metal parts the problems are not so serious as when organs have to be obtained as quickly as possible from the recently dead. After all, we still do not quite know how to define physiological death.

All this forms part of 'man's conquest of Nature' and domination of her, a concept which has recently been given a thorough examination by William Leiss.[1] Though the formulation stems essentially from Francis Bacon, there were earlier manifestations of the idea, and not only in Europe, as Leiss assumed. Lynn White has shown how Christian theology saw man as standing apart from Nature and exercising authority over all creation as of right, hence perhaps the growing pollution of the environment by man's waste-products, hardly recognised as a danger until our own time. But in Chinese thought too, man could 'rob' the powers of Nature and make them work for him; and the title of Sung Ying-Hsing's book *Thien Kung Khai Wu* (The Exploitation of the Works of Nature, 1637) exemplifies a similar thing. The tenth century *Hua Shu* (Book of Natural Transformations) is full of the powers of the Taoist adepts.

Leiss well says that mankind is gravely ill at ease about the future, and the utopias of imaginative writers have mostly become dystopias. I feel this strongly myself, for science fiction would be my principal leisure reading if only I had the nerve for it; unfortunately most of it frightens me out of my wits, seems only too likely to happen, and provides me with anxiety symbols which I do not want. Moreover, as Leiss puts it, the attempted, and successful, conquest of Nature almost inevitably seems to result in frightful new means of the exercise of domination in human affairs. 'The same scientific and technological order which promises to liberate mankind from its universal enemies (hunger, disease, and exhausting labour) also enables ruling élites to increase their ability to control individual behaviour.' From the first electric telegraph to subliminal advertising and propaganda, from the first understanding of central nervous activity to the identification of localised specific pleasure and aversion centres in the mammalian and human brain, this has always proved true. Look only at the possibilities of mind control by psychotropic drugs and brain surgery, as discussed in the books of Steven Rose (*The Conscious Brain*) and Maya Pines (*The Brain Changers*). 'The subjects of earlier tyrannies', says Leiss, 'recognised their slavery in the overt controls which restricted their physical movements, and by the terror which the minions of authority inspired in them, whereas the citizens of the future, manipulated at the very sources of their being, may love their servitude and call it freedom.' One must, he goes on, ask why is there apparently this connection between the 'conquest of Nature' and the 'conquest of man'? Is it inevitable that the scientific and technological instruments utilised in the domination of Nature should produce a qualitative transformation in the mechanisms of social despotism?

Well, it all comes back to ethics and politics; that's where we have to 'put our foot down', and march, or refuse to march. The paradox of the conquest of Nature always turning into the domination of men must be connected at least with the fact that in all historical periods scientific knowledge has been gained by man living in class-stratified societies, and political mastery naturally utilises available knowledge. This situation will not always pertain. As for ethics, Leiss says that as long as Christianity remained a vital social force in Western civilisation the conquest of Nature was held to some extent in an ethical frame. But the present secular context requires a different interpretation, namely one in which mastery over Nature is understood as a stage in human consciousness so advanced that intelligence can regulate its relationship to Nature, minimising the self-destructive aspects of human desires, and maximising the freedom of the human individual within a classless and equalitarian society. Herbert Marcuse has even realised that different cultural traditions in the non-Western world may aid the nations at present under-developed in avoiding the repressive and destructive uses of advanced technologies.

In his brilliant essay 'The Abolition of Man', C. S. Lewis still maintained that the Christian ethic could be the guiding beacon for humanity. As a Christian inhabitant of what's left of Christendom I might like to do the same, but where such ancient traditions of supernaturalism are concerned it is always difficult to disentangle the eternal Gospel from the fears, prohibitions, and prejudices stemming from ages far more ignorant and powerless than our own. Besides, reacting against numinous and liturgical religion Westerners only too frequently throw away ethics as well. It is just here that Chinese culture may have, it seems to me, an invaluable gift to make to the world. In the coming ages its seems likely that the traditional religions will all be the beliefs and practices of minorities, so ought we not to look for a conception of morality, an ethical model, which was never supported by supernatural sanctions? Nearly all the greatest philosophers of China have agreed in seeing human nature as fundamentally good, and regarding justice and righteousness as arising directly out of it, if men and women can have a proper training in youth, and a society which will bring out the best elements already fully potentially within them. The 'humanists' and rationalists of the Western world are saying something similar, of course, but they are always under the great disadvantage of being in revolt against the traditions of their own culture, which has other truths and insights to give to the world. In this respect the Chinese are not; therefore their message is more natural and undistorted, and carries greater weight.

I have no wish, of course, to join in the arguments going on nowadays about the role of Master Khung in Chinese social history, but it is quite clear that although he was totally embedded in the feudal society of his time, not questioning it as many of the Taoists did, his followers through the ages accepted ethics as internally generated, intrinsic and immanent, not imposed by any divine fiat like the tables of the law delivered to Moses on the mountain. And this was true of nearly all the great figures in Chinese philosophy through the ages. One could even go so far as to say that never have the Chinese been more faithful to this doctrine, expressed as it is in terms of selfless service to others, to the people, than they are today. This then is the thought that I should like to propose on the present occasion—if the world is searching for an ethic firmly based on the nature of man, an ethic which could justify resistance to every dehumanising invention of social control, an ethic in the light of which mankind could judge dispassionately what the best course to take will be, in face of the multitudinous options raised by the ever-growing powers given to us by the natural sciences—then let it listen to the sages of Confucianism and Taoism. Of course these men of old will have no exact advice to give us on the choices we shall face in the use of techniques which they would never for a moment have been able to imagine. But what matters is their spirit, their undying faith in the basic goodness of human nature, free from all transcendental elements and capable of leading to the ever more perfect organisation of human society. China has in her time learnt much from the rest of the world; now perhaps it is time for the nations and the continents to learn again from her.

On such a happy occasion as this, significant for the meeting of human cultures, it seems to me indispensable that some words should be spoken in Chinese:

校監，副校監，校長，諸位來賓：

我剛才所講的主要有兩點：第一點是關於現代自然科學的進步給人類帶來了各種道德上的問題；第二點就是我們要從中國文化所包含的偉大的傳統道德精神中取得對這些問題的解答。我的意思即是對〔性本善〕這一道德精神的信仰。〔善行〕乃是基於〔善心〕，而非基於人爲的法律。

讓我借用十七世紀末清初傑出的學者顧炎武與友人〔論學〕書裡的一段話來結束我的演講：

〔恥之於人大矣！不恥惡衣惡食，而恥匹夫匹婦之不被其澤，故曰『萬物皆備於我矣』，反身而誠。嗚呼！士而不先言恥，則爲無本之人。〕

[In my address I have been saying two things. First, that the advances of the natural sciences are more and more bringing humanity face to face with terrible ethical problems. Second, that in the solution of these advantage should be taken of the great ethical traditions of Chinese culture. I mean the belief that human nature is fundamentally good; and that good action comes from the 'inner light', not dictated by laws handed down from some transcendent being. May I end with a quotation from the great scholar Ku Yen-Wu, writing to a friend at the beginning of the Chhing dynasty about the nature of knowledge:

'How important is the sense of right and wrong within human beings! One need not be ashamed of poor clothes or rough food, but one should be ashamed of men and women who have not been endowed with a sense of shame. This is why it is said that all things are complete within ourselves. We have only to change our attitude and be sincere about it. Alas! scholars who do not first consider the shamefulness of wrong-doing are rootless men of no ability.'

[Thus wrote Ku Yen-Wu in the late seventeenth century.]

Note

1. William Leiss, *The Domination of Nature* (New York, 1972).

Further Reading

There is no full-length biography of Joseph Needham. Nor is there a thorough review of the development of his social thought. But one can unhesitatingly recommend what amounts to an autobiography: Henry Holorenshaw (pseud.), 'The Making of an Honorary Taoist,' in M. Teich & R. Young (eds.), *Changing Perspectives in the History of Science* (London, 1973), pp. 1–20. Also useful are Shigeru Nakayama's 'Joseph Needham—Organic Philosopher,' and Derek J. de Solla Price's 'Joseph Needham and the Science of China,' both of which can be found in S. Nakayama & N. Sivin (eds.), *Chinese Science: Explorations of an Ancient Tradition* (Cambridge, Mass., and London, 1973), pp. 23–44, and pp. 9–22, respectively. Even more acute is R. S. Cohen's 'Is the Philosophy of Science Germane to the History of Science? The Work of Meyerson and Needham,' *Actes du dixième congrès international d'histoire des sciences* (Hermann, Paris, 1964), vol. 1.

On the historical and intellectual context within which Needham's ideas developed, there is Gary Werskey, 'Making Socialists of Scientists: Whose Side Is History On?' *Radical Science Journal*, no. 23 (January 1975), pp. 13–50; and also my *Scientists for Socialism* (London, 1976), forthcoming.

Needham's own philosophy of biology was spelt out in the notable *Order and Life* (New Haven, 1936). This work has since been reprinted by M.I.T. Press (Cambridge, Mass., and London, 1968).

The impact on Needham of his years in China both before and after the foundation of the People's Republic is revealed in: Joseph Needham, *Within the Four Seas* (London, 1969); and in the miscellany edited by Joseph and Dorothy Needham, *Science Outpost* (London, 1948). Two other sets of essays can serve as introductions to the China project itself. One of these concentrates on Needham's philosophy of history as it has been applied to ancient and medieval Chinese science. Here I refer to *The Grand Titration* (London, 1969). The other work introduces readers to some of the most notable discoveries Needham and his collaborators have made in the course of their researches: *Clerks and Craftsmen in China and the West* (Cambridge 1970).

Finally, there is of course the great work itself: Joseph Needham *et al.*, *Science and Civilisation in China*, 7 vols. in 15 parts (Cambridge, 1954–).

G.W.

Index

BY M. MOYLE